Making Babies
Infants in Canadian Fiction

Sandra Sabatini

Wilfrid Laurier University Press

This book has been published with the help of a grant from the Canadian Federation for the Humanities and Social Sciences, through the Aid to Scholarly Publications Programme, using funds provided by the Social Sciences and Humanities Research Council of Canada. We acknowledge the financial support of the Government of Canada through the Book Publishing Industry Development Program for our publishing activities. We acknowledge the Government of Ontario through the Ontario Media Development Corporation's Ontario Book Initiative.

National Library of Canada Cataloguing in Publication Data

Sabatini, Sandra
   Making babies : infants in Canadian fiction / Sandra Sabatini.

Includes bibliographical references and index.
ISBN 0-88920-423-3

   1. Canadian fiction (English)—20th century—History and criticism.
2. Infants in literature. I. Title.

PS8191.I53S23 2003   C813'.5093520542   C2003-905607-4

Cover design by P.J. Woodland; interior design by C. Bonas-Taylor. Cover photographs by Sandra Sabatini.

Printed in Canada

This study of infants was inspired and sustained by the five
best babies and is dedicated to them with love.

For Carla, Paul, Bianca, Claire, and James
new wonder in an old world

CONTENTS

ACKNOWLEDGEMENTS

I 'm grateful to Ted McGee and Charlene Diehl-Jones, first readers of this manuscript in all its manifestations at the University of Waterloo. Linda Warley also provided criticism that strengthened the context and arguments put forth.

You need friends to help you complete a project like this, friends who will listen to you, take your children out for dinner, buy you presents, celebrate complete sentences, offer you Kleenex. I had some of these and I am so grateful.

This book would not have been written without Rico Sabatini, a cool spirit who husbanded my resources, provoked my research, soothed my disposition, who turned and always turned toward me, no matter what.

INTRODUCTION

The miracle that saves the world...is...the birth of new men and the new beginning, the action they are capable of by being born. Only the full experience of this capacity can bestow upon human affairs faith and hope, those two essential characteristics of human experience...that found perhaps their most glorious and most succinct expression in the new words with which the Gospels accounted their "glad tiding": "A Child has been born unto us."

— Hannah Arendt, *The Human Condition*

Beside my desk there is a painting of a dark-haired woman in blue and a fair baby clothed in white lying against a white pillow. The woman leans toward the baby who raises plump arms toward her. Neither is smiling, but their shared gaze is intent and direct. Instead of a wall behind the woman, there is the suggestion of wings and behind them, stars. The woman's blue dress disappears against the bedclothes, which in turn disappear against what might be the sky, so that the woman appears to be floating with the baby. The image furnishes an effective analogy for this study of representations of the infant in Canadian fiction over the century. The painting demonstrates the interconnectedness felt by women and their babies who seem pure as they gaze intently. It also implies a sense of divine or angelic influence in the presence of the wings. The painting indicates a strong mother-infant bond that is accompanied by a sense of supernatural or extraordinary power. The edges are somewhat blurred; the lines are softened and invite possibility.

1

In focusing on the infant as the source of faith and hope for the world, Hannah Arendt points out in the epigram to this chapter the extraordinary effects of ordinary babies, a sense that emerges from my painting. Experience with babies, interest in them, and curiosity about what makes their eyebrows contract or their mouths smile when they are only hours old all combine to propel writers' engagement with these small beings. Writing about them seems driven by curiosity and by a profound concern to explore, as Arendt writes, the faith and hope, not to mention the love that babies bestow in the course of human experience. But such writing is also sometimes driven by repugnance. The representation of infants occurs most often as a duality, a tension between desire and rejection. Infants are often appalling because of their baldness, toothlessness, incontinence, crying, and because of the constraints they impose on women's freedom. At the same time, these are some of the same attributes that invite breathless admiration, if not worship, and that motivate people to respond energetically to the demands of the baby, as they understand those demands. Infants provoke intimate involvement because of their innocence, because of their helpless need for care, but also because they provoke a sense of wonder.

Although the infant is a consistent and often powerful image in literature, and although people often engage on some level in everyday life with babies, as a subject of literary study in Canada, or anywhere else, the infant is largely absent. Several studies have focused on maternal or childhood representation in Canadian literature. Di Brandt's *Wild Mother Dancing* provides a contemporary reading of the mother in Canadian literature. Theresa Quigley's book, *The Child Hero in the Canadian Novel*, focuses on children, but not babies. Laurence Ricou's *Everyday Magic: Child Languages in Canadian Literature* explores children in literature, in particular the distinctive features of child language. Elizabeth Goodenough's *Infant Tongues: The Voice of the Child in Literature* explores the nature of child-like expression from a stage of development as early as a child's capacity for baby talk, but both Ricou's and Goodenough's studies occur outside a definition of infancy that focuses on the pre-linguistic infant since, by definition, an infant is, from the Latin, *in fans*, "without speech."[1] Elaine Tuttle Hansen's *Mother without Child: Contemporary Fiction and the Crisis of Motherhood* focuses on situations of child loss, and deals with mothers who have given up children, murdered them, aborted them—women who are prisoners, lesbian mothers, slave mothers, among others.

But where there are mothers and children, there have to be babies. Daphne Marlatt's essay, "Musing with Mothertongue" is an evocative engagement with one's birth into language. She writes that language is "a living body we enter at birth, sustains and contains us...it is both place...and body" (223). The infant's connection to language as sound is "a body of sound," writes Marlatt. She concludes, "Leaving the water of the mother's womb with its one dominant sound, we are born into this other body whose multiple sounds bathe our ears from the moment of our arrival" (223). But Marlatt's musing is with the emergent nature of language in children and the manner in which it shapes adults—not with the baby itself. Infants are represented in literature according to a body of assumptions that thus far has made them all but invisible as a subject of critical inquiry. The role of babies in Canadian fiction has not received the attention it deserves in spite of the considerable shift in the representation of infants, who are unable to walk or talk, yet who nevertheless occupy more space in more texts.

One does not come to Canadian literature with a notion of "baby." Canadian literature has been traditionally connected to, among other things, concepts of northernness, of space, settlement, landscape, and survival in a harsh climate. However, as Barbara Godard writes in her essay, "Structuralism/Post-Structuralism: Language, Reality and Canadian Culture," "To be Canadian, as to be a woman, is to inhabit a Colonial space from which one perceives discourse as a form of power and desire" (46). In contradistinction to Atwood's oversimplified perspective of the infant's role in Canadian literature as a *deus ex machina* "lowered at the end of the book to solve problems for the characters which they obviously can't solve for themselves" (*Survival* 207), babies are figured in more diverse and complex ways that explore, in a paradigm different from Godard's, that very conjunction of power and desire. To be a baby is also to inhabit a dichotomous space where one is both the colonizer, inhabiting, taking over resources, and the colonized, inhabited, invested (or not) with personality and intention, *spoken for*.

In Western society part of what frames understanding of babies, in quite general terms, is familiarity with *the* baby: Jesus. Millions of people believe that the baby born in Bethlehem two millennia ago was the Son of God. This belief has ignited artistic imagination from before Michelangelo or Bach or Tolkein. But babies less immaculately conceived also invite contemplation of the unfathomable. As Arendt suggests, the birth of babies interrupts "the law of mortality" (246). Infants permit people to pause in "the inexorable automatic course of daily life…[to begin] something new" (246). The interruptions of birth serve as "an ever-present reminder that men [*sic*], though they must die, are not born in order to die but in order to begin" (246). The experience of childbirth carries with it the sense of participating in, if not necessarily religious, clearly profound forces to produce what claims us, what interpellates us as subjects of that which will master us through bonds of love. But babies' mastery is not easy, particularly for women who mother them.

In social and historical contexts in the twentieth century in Canada and the Western world, the infant becomes an issue of concern to legislators, who enact laws to protect, and to physicians, who begin with mothers to encourage and enforce pre- and postnatal care. Furthermore, as a subject of study, the infant itself becomes more significant as psychoanalytic and cognitive development researchers begin to focus increased attention on the infant. I want to track the parallel shift in literary representation. Twentieth-century Canadian fiction portrays the infant according to changing beliefs about the baby's importance; there is a marked evolution in both quantity and quality of infant representation. While in the nineteenth century, women writers were a presence in the Canadian writing scene, and while they felt free to write about the trials of pioneer life (including, as Susanna Moodie did, the deaths of her children, and even the depression and suicide of a neighbour), they did not write at length about infants, except to acknowledge their existences or deaths.[2] They did not explore attitudes toward pregnancy or what would have been called confinement, and they certainly did not write explicitly about birth, or breast feeding, or postpartum depression, or unwed motherhood. The reasons for this silence undoubtedly have their basis in the women's sense of the proper or polite subjects of writing in their time, and also their sense of how far into certain subjects they might reasonably go in their art.

This study explores the transformation in perceptions about the infant, as these are evident in Canadian literature, focusing on novels and short stories.[3] The project tracks representations of the infant generally from the perspective of white, mostly English-speaking writers. While these are not the only Canadian writers writing about the baby, nor are Canadians the only ones writing about infants, I chose to focus on this group for several reasons. I chose a Canadian literary perspective because of my interest as a writer and critic in the literature that is closest to me. As Laurence Ricou writes, "I am convinced that Canadian literature offers a wide range of rich and complex texts to support a study which I hope will have implications for understanding a general literary problem/challenge hardly restricted to Canadian writing" (*Everyday Magic* x). In Ricou's case, the challenge has to do with the magic of child language as it is represented in literature. In the case of this study, the challenge has to do with examining infant representation. This is an arbitrary boundary that limits the study even while it enables. Furthermore, because there are no other studies that focus on the infant as it is represented in Canadian fiction specifically, it is important to re-examine what have come to be considered canonical Canadian texts to see how the infant is figured in literature that, for numerous political and ideological reasons, has been the production of a few white writers.

I chose to look at canonical as well as extracanonical texts from the same cultural milieu in order to mark the changes in infant representation therein. I present these texts as examples of the way the infant has been considered with the understanding that the configuration is circumscribed, not only by cultural and generic considerations, but also by the need to choose certain texts with babies over others for extended analysis in order to limit the size of the project. The foremost principle of selection was whether or not the narrative engaged with infants. I wanted representative examples since the scope of the project necessitated economy of choice in order to examine fiction from the first to last decades of the twentieth century. As well, I tried to balance the inquiry in terms of its examination of both male and female writers and both male and female representations of babies. I ended up with a sample of about twenty texts that span regions and degrees of canonization. The sample also demonstrates a variety of infant representations from the humorous to the tragic. I understand that a preliminary study of this type can be only, at best, partial, embarked upon with hope that it will suggest other approaches to texts whose concern is the infant across cultural and national boundaries.

Viewing the Canadian fictional infant along a literary continuum that begins with *Anne of Green Gables* and ends with the writing of Terry Griggs, one discovers a line emerging that demonstrates the measurable difference in the amount of space infants occupy and also, and more importantly, their emergence as agents or subjects in the texts. This through line tracks the development of infant representation as dichotomous and weaving through issues of maternal idealization and rejection, illegitimacy, maternal empowerment, and paternal involvement. The study focuses most on the gendered divergence that occurs after 1960 in writing about the infant; it is informed by feminist writers theorizing about women's biological connection to babies and about men's estrangement from them. The analysis concludes with an examination of Terry Griggs's infants because of her decision to invest the babies with agency and with value that exists apart from relational considerations.

Over time, I will argue, the literary infant moves from a place rather peripheral to the world of the text in the late nineteenth and early twentieth centuries, to a place of centrality. Within that centrality are diverse explorations of infant status and significance that are informed by social and ideological notions of value and by gendered perspectives. For example, in writing about babies born to unwed mothers, the alteration in perception over time is clear. What was, in one mode of consciousness during a specific measure of years, a black mark of illegitimacy, has become something most people can quite easily live with and write about.[4] As well, the early texts reflect a lack of concern with infants, except as heirs or, alternatively, as impediments to survival, until they reach a stage where they achieve mobility and language. Few words are wasted on what babies might be thinking or might be capable of until they mature. However, by the end of the twentieth century, infants begin to occupy a central position in texts where writers are looking to the frontier of infant consciousness to find out more about themselves and to ponder something that seems miraculous. But this sense of wonder is treated differently by men and women writers. Writers begin to explore the effects of infants, an exploration that undermines ideological constructs that constitute women and infants as secondary beings.[5]

Making room for the infant as a subject in Canadian literature involves positioning the caregiver—usually, but not always, the mother—in terms of the infant, a sort of backward approach that displaces the mother's pre-eminent role in a way that is emotionally but not always materially logical. On a personal level, for example, I felt ousted to a secondary position of subjectivity with the birth of my daughter. That's the emotional logic. Put simply, she ruled. Materially, however, this could clearly not have been the case apart from her connection to me. I permitted her conception, gestation, and birth; I fed her and cared for her. In this, I ruled. But while the mere effect of my care was that she grew from being a small person to being a larger one, I, on the other hand, felt beatified. It sounds extreme, perhaps, but it is accurate. While not all women or all authors experience this effect, this is where the potential lies for a miracle—the baby's immanent facility to alter those who care for it. Such alteration is a site that authors visit and revisit.[6]

In the twentieth century, Canadian literary representations of infants in prose fiction portray the infant in increasingly significant ways. In novels written in the first half of the century, babies are not highly significant in themselves and, in most texts, birth or pregnancy are often tangential to the story. Infants are born and mature to sentience, when they can speak and act and so further the plot, within the space of a sentence or a paragraph. This decades-long lack of interest in the infant as subject seems to be part of an overarching view of pregnancy and infancy, an outgrowth of the Victorian view best summarized by the phrase, "children should be seen and not heard." As Christina Hardyment writes concerning the early part of the twentieth century, "babies were not seen as noble, or even fun." She quotes a "society matron" who asserts that "infants up to the age of one year should be neither amusing nor amused" (92). For the most part, until the 1960s, infants in fiction were seldom seen and were even more rarely heard.

In novels written in the early part of the twentieth century, babies occupy a strictly circumscribed range of representations. In an analysis of the writing of L.M. Montgomery and Frederick Philip Grove, chapter 1 argues that babies are objects of desire, but only within limited parameters. Montgomery's "Anne" books sentimentalize the infant. In *Anne's House of Dreams* (1927), Anne, for example, carries for nine months "sweet, unuttered dreams and hopes" (3) and goes quietly to her room to give birth. However, Montgomery's novels also engage with the difficulties that arise for women when they have too many babies and the sorrow women feel at the loss of a baby. In Grove's *Settlers of the Marsh* (1925), the baby is both an object of desire for the male protagonist and an object of fear for his neighbour, Ellen, who avoids marriage in order to avoid babies. The infant is, for Neils, the promise of a future, and for Ellen, the possibility of death, if not in labour, then possibly as a result of exhaustion.

Intrinsic to representations of the infant in mid-twentieth-century Canadian novels is a sense of the social structure within which babies

ought to be born. Chapter 2 explores such proprieties relating to conception and birth, which, if not adhered to, result in dire consequences, usually suffered by the mother who is outcast from society.
Narratives that concern babies explore the fact that pregnancies are
often associated with the shame of illegitimacy, the burden of which
is borne primarily, if not exclusively, by the pregnant woman who has
given into "base" instincts and the persuasive charm of the man. Such
concerns occupy narratives written in the 1940s and '50s. Women
often pay for this weakness with their lives, as do Judith in Sinclair
Ross's *As for Me and My House* (1941), and Hazel in Charles Tory
Bruce's *The Channel Shore* (1954). Interestingly, such conventions of
legitimacy are explored almost exclusively by male writers who may
have a personal understanding of the male need to establish and protect paternity.

When women writers enter into the discourse of "proper" conception, they also conform to patriarchal sanctions against out-of-wedlock
pregnancies. Gabrielle Roy's *The Tin Flute* (1947) is an example of such
conformity since Florentine is rescued from illegitimate pregnancy
when she becomes engaged to a man who will legitimize her baby.
Roy's novel also reveals the difficulties for women in poverty whose
legitimate babies severely exhaust their resources. Yet in spite of the
overt conformity to social expectations of legitimacy, there are currents
within the texts that demonstrate a degree of writerly resistance to the
notion of propriety and suggest that valuing the infant according to the
circumstances of its conception is less than ideal. Moreover, in the other
Roy novels, the mothers are inscribed with a degree of sympathy that
further undermines the stigma of illegitimacy.[7] In other novels written
in the mid-twentieth century in which women produce an abundance
of babies, such prolific reproduction works conventionally, reinforcing
the figure of the mother as self-sacrificial and loving. The volume of
babies seems indicative of the mother's vital engagement with life. This
kind of burgeoning of the life force usually occurs in novels that, for the
most part, explore the more humourous aspects of life in large families.
The infants themselves are not important. They are interchangeable
and the phase of infant dependency, before mobility and language,
does not last long. Gabrielle Roy's *Where Nests the Water Hen* (1951) and
Henry Gordon Green's *A Time to Pass Over: Life with a Pioneer Grandmother* (1962) are examples of this connection of multiple births and
engagement with life as the women are busy trying to meet the eco-

nomic needs of the family while tending to the urgent physical demands of many small children.

Chapter 3 compares the representation of the infant in books by male and female writers in the 1960s and '70s. In writing by men in these decades, the infant remains primarily on the outskirts of the action. Texts such as Ernest Buckler's *The Cruelest Month* (1964), George Bowering's *The Mirror on the Floor* (1967), Juan Butler's *Cabbagetown Diary* (1970), and Matt Cohen's *The Disinherited* (1974) represent the infant in a marginal manner. Cohen's novel is the focus of the first half of the chapter since it offers a representative sense of male detachment from the infant. Robert Kroetsch, on the other hand, fills his book, *What the Crow Said* (1978), with babies. The novel is interesting because, although the babies do not stay babies for long, Kroetsch does create a compelling matriarchy where baby girls come in multiples; the matriarchy works inversely to the world created by Cohen which focuses on establishing a male dynasty. Nevertheless, even with an abundance of babies, the men in the novel still fail to become attached to them.

The chapter also examines infant representation as novels explore the possibilities inherent in reproductive choices available to women in a time when the taint of unwed motherhood begins to fade. In these decades, more women are writing and giving consideration to the subjects of single parenthood, abortion, and the grief and loss intrinsic to miscarriage. The feminist examination of biology's connection to destiny comes to the fore in fiction by women during 1960s and '70s. These women writers articulate women's experience, particularly as it relates to reproduction. This desire to explore and express women's experience finds resonance in the French feminist writer Hélène Cixous, who is more concerned with a politicized stylization of women's writing in her configuration of *écriture feminine*, and urges that women write as those who have been defined in terms of their "struggle against conventional man; and of a universal woman subject who must bring women to their senses and to their meaning in history" (334). It seems that much of the writing in these decades by women is an exploration of what that meaning might be. For a long time, meaning for women has been defined in relation to husbands and children, but in these volatile decades, women are writing against this tradition. What's fascinating is that they create pregnant protagonists to do this. There is a double-voicing evident in these texts as women writers probe the significance of the baby and their own connection to it, and discover that the figure of the infant engenders both longing and rejection. Such feminist explorations occur in Margaret Atwood's *The Edible Woman* (1969) and *Surfacing* (1972), in Audrey Thomas's *Mrs. Blood* (1970), in Margaret Laurence's *A Jest Of God* (1966), and in Marian Engel's *The Honeyman Festival* (1970). These works not only explore the significance of fertility, birth, and babies but they also mark a distinct increase in representations of the infant. There are more babies in the literature than have occurred before, but their agency is limited. During the 1960s and '70s, the baby is represented in terms of the mothers who bear the burdens of pregnancy, childbirth, and the isolation that comes from staying at home with small children.

A paradigmatic shift occurs in recent novels because of the women's movement and the growing social awareness that fathers need and often want to be more involved in their babies' lives. Chapter 4 examines the remarkable revision in male attitudes toward the baby. This revision is most pronounced in writing by men after 1980, when babies become not merely socially valuable and not valuable only as progeny; they are represented as inviting male protagonists into a sustained, highly involved relationship. Narratives that inquire into illegitimacy or the function of babies in relation to the family line still appear, for example, in Nino Ricci's *Lives of the Saints* (1990) or David Adams Richards's *Nights below Station Street* (1988). But there is a further engagement between men and babies in Leon Rooke's *A Good Baby* (1989), in Thomas King's *Medicine River* (1989), in Douglas Coupland's *Life after God* (1994), and in David Arnason's short stories. Men seem to wake up to the fact that babies are important, engaging, and somewhat miraculous. In these decades, men discover babies and write about them as they have not done before.

On the other hand, writing by women during the 1980s and '90s explores some of the fallout from women's ambivalent response to the maternal role and the tedium and isolation of pregnancy and birth. In the 1960s and '70s, women were beginning to establish themselves as vital individuals apart from their role as mothers; part of what women were liberated from was their connection to babies—that is, they fought for the choice not to become mothers. The depictions of infants by women writers in the 1980s and '90s examined in chapter 5 are noteworthy for their complexity and diversity. Women's struggle to assert professional equality and personal freedom, and to assert the importance of being present mothers to babies, is manifest in writing that simultaneously supports and undermines the value of the baby. What I find most compelling about the most recent developments in infant narrative is the possibility for the inscription of infant subjectivity, a possibility that contemporary feminist theory and Canadian fiction published in the last part of the twentieth century are beginning to introduce. The infant as a subject begins to be articulated in the theoretical work of Julia Kristeva and in the fiction of late twentieth-century writers who have begun to turn their attention to the baby itself rather than to its effects.

Two concerns occupy the study of babies in the writing by women of this decade. The first has to do with the desire for babies; the second regards the development of infant subjectivity in the texts. Babies, while absent, are often a site of longing in texts like Barbara Gowdy's *Falling Angels* (1989) and Nancy Huston's *Instruments of Darkness* (1997). Elyse Gasco writes a disturbing narrative of rejection and loss related to infant adoption in *Can You Wave Bye Bye, Baby?* (1999). Terry Griggs inquires into the infant itself, its consciousness and its motivations, expanding possibilities beyond much of what has gone before in her short stories in the collection *Quickening* (1990) and in her novel *The Lusty Man* (1995).[8] All these writers engage to greater or lesser degrees with representations of the baby, usually writing from the mother's or the potential mother's perspective (though Griggs does write from the baby's perspective). Their creation of infancy both structures and is structured by what is known about infants. Such a development seems to reflect social and historical trends that set more value on the infant so that its life and health become issues of public policy.

Writing in the first half of the century indicates a pre-eminent concern with survival so that an infant is both desirable as a means of establishing oneself in a new rough country and extending the family line; but an infant is also undesirable because it perpetuates poverty, increases fatigue, and often causes death. It is simultaneously a figure of redemption, a marker of familial and social value (as it is considered legitimate or illegitimate), and also a threat to survival. In the second half of the twentieth century, the issue of legitimacy is superceded as the infant is reconstituted, in large part because of the feminist movement and the sexual revolution. Furthermore, there are more remarkable differences in the ways that men and women write about babies. For male protagonists, the infant becomes the "miracle that saves the world" (Arendt 247). For women, the infant, as both colonized and colonizer, compels a more complex response.

Psychoanalytic, Cognitive, and Historical Contexts

In order to see how the baby has been articulated as a subject, particularly in the last two decades, we need to become sensitized to its appearance as an agent in the text. Writers in the fields of history, science, sociology, and literature increasingly work against the tendency to see the baby as passive and have begun to recommend a different mode of regarding infants that views them as subjects.

The manner in which infants have been represented across the disciplines, including the social and historical background of infant study, suggests that all that is known about babies is theoretical. Apart from observation of their behaviours, their cognitive and motor development, little can be known for certain. Sociologists and historians discuss how societies have treated babies and how such treatment reflects the value placed upon them. Psychoanalysts and cognitive psychologists approach the baby from opposite ends of life: psychoanalysts theorize backwards, from adult psychoses to possible infant causes; cognitive psychologists theorize forward, constructing frameworks for thinking about infants on the basis of infant behaviour. And literary critics appropriate information from these disciplines and others to examine how babies are represented in literature.

How do babies mean?

The key element in theorizing about babies is the discursive nature of the endeavour. Babies are represented in language. They act, gesture, articulate sound, but from these behaviours one can only make assumptions about what they might be thinking or feeling or what their purpose might be. Observers endow babies with meaning; they interpret babies' actions and reactions through discourse, which has inarguably been shifting over time, particularly over the twentieth century.

Ideologically based assumptions often become clear only in retrospect. How people think about their lived relations with the world, specifically with babies, is allied to their beliefs about what is valuable and necessary. These are beliefs that change over time. Hindsight permits a critical scrutiny only once technology or economics or inspiration have driven people forward. For instance, people have assumed that infants should be breast-fed and have assumed, with equal vehemence, that they should not be breast-fed (Hardyment 94-95). In order to trace changes in ideological assumptions about babies, one must examine the variety of concerns that have occupied adult observers of infants. I offer here a brief summary of developments as they relate specifically to our treatment and understanding of babies, and our interest in them.

Canadian literature engages throughout the century with the figure of the infant, a figure that becomes increasingly important, moving from passivity to activity even as the women who bear it become increasingly active and vocal about the process of reproduction. Representations of infancy are closely linked to representations of the maternal and there is a degree of slippage between these two. I'm examining these infant representations in terms of Julia Kristeva's concept of the semiotic *chora*. Kristeva's insistence on the importance of theorizing women's desire to have children is considered in light of the effects of the baby. Her psychoanalytic construction of the infant and the significance of the maternal in that same construction make up my dual focus on her writing. As well, the work of Adrienne Rich, Mary O'Brien, and Hannah Arendt discloses a feminist view of the infant's importance.

The transformation in perceptions of the infant throughout the century is evident in psychoanalytic study of the baby. The work of Sigmund Freud in the early twentieth century shaped understanding of infantile drives for generations of theorists. In the mid-twentieth century, Jacques Lacan minimized, to a greater extent than Freud, the capacity of the infant to act. Finally, in the latter third of this century, Julia Kristeva offered a view of infant agency that transgressed the boundaries set up by her predecessors in the field, one that glimpses the possibility of a subjectivity that exists apart from language. I came to Kristeva with joy and relief after having studied the theories of Freud and Lacan. Lacan, in particular, carefully sets out an argument for the emergence of subjectivity, the revelation of "otherness" that occurs, he says, at around six months of age.[9] Until the infant looks in a mirror and knows itself as other, it is not an agent in any sense. I read this after having given birth five times and after having been intimately involved with a substantial sample of infants, all of whom seemed to me to be agents from parturition—with opinions and strategies, preferences and charm. Building on Lacan's hermeneutic for child development, Julia Kristeva posits a theory of the semiotic, or pre-oedipal. What makes Kristeva's theory so compelling is the fact that she begins with an assumption of the possibility of infant subjectivity. This is a revolutionary permission, a potential to see infants as capable of signification, to view the pre-linguistic state of human development as vitally important, not simply for the sake of its disruptions and interruptions much later into adult life and art *but for its own sake*. Although hers is just as much an assumption as Freud's or Lacan's concerning infant passivity, it allows for a more open, less mechanistic view of the infant, one that researchers have found to be more accurate about infants—that they act with intentionality. She does this through the dialectic of the semiotic/symbolic. Although she states that these "two modalities are inseparable within the signifying process that constitutes language" ("Revolution in Poetic Language" 92), nevertheless, she associates the semiotic with "functions and energy discharges that connect and orient the body to the mother" (95).

Defining subjectivity is, itself, a complex task. Traditionally, philosophers and theorists have conceived of subjectivity as intrinsic to the self/other hierarchy. Kristeva considers that the subject is "formulated as an operating consciousness" ("From One Identity to Another" 131). Kristeva writes in this essay that "a definite subject is present as soon as there is consciousness of signification" (124).[10] While much of Kristeva's essay is devoted to the speaking subject, she allows that there is signification apart from language, a signification situated in the infant's response to the mother. Kristeva incorporates into her understanding of subjectivity Husserl's consideration that subjectivity is defined at the basic level of "intentionality" conceived as an inner-outer binary relationship. Husserl finds that this relationship between inner and outer modes is "characterized by intentionality, which governs, orders and gives meaning to...the world of our immediately lived experience" (Kockelmans 252-53). According to Husserl,

> To every mind there belongs not only the unity of its multiple *intentional life-process*...with all its inseparable unities of sense directed towards the "object." There is also, inseparable from this life-process, the experiencing *I-subject* as the identical *I-pole* giving a center for specific intentionalities. And as the carrier of all habitualities growing out of this life-process. (126)

That is, objects in the world, referents, are presented to intentional consciousness which ascribes meaning and interprets significance. Husserl's definition of subjectivity relies on intentionality and interpretation of sensory data. In other words, the baby is established as a subject in the text by means both of its ability to act, and to interpret and respond to sense perception.

Kristeva acknowledges that the semiotic as it exists in infant consciousness is not something thoroughly or even easily understandable.

She says of the "semiotic chora" that it is the "distinctive mark, trace, index, precursory sign, proof, engraved or written sign, imprint, trace, figuration" related to the drives that exist apart from language ("Revolution" 93). The chora is a difficult and contradictory concept in Kristeva, as she herself admits when she acknowledges that "the term ultimately encompasses such disparate meanings" (93). The chora underlies signification as neither sign nor signifier, but rather as that which is "analogous only to vocal or kinetic rhythm" (94). The emphasis on both vocal and kinetic rhythms, sound, and motion (both of which the infant is capable of making), rather than the formal symbolic notion of language, makes an inquiry into the chora vital for understanding the infant as a subject. Most importantly as Kristeva sees it,

> the kinetic functional stage of the *semiotic* precedes the establishment of the sign; it is not, therefore, cognitive in the sense of being assumed by a knowing, already constituted subject. The genesis of the *functions* organizing the semiotic process can be accurately elucidated only within a theory of the subject that *does not reduce the subject to one of understanding, but instead opens up within the subject this other scene of pre-symbolic functions.* (95 my emphasis)

Kristeva theorizes about the existence and importance of a pre-linguistic agency existing at the "kinetic functional stage." In her essay "Place Names" she says that "this precocious, presymbolic organization" is virtually impossible to grasp, admitting to "the difficulty, the impossibility that beset such an attempt at gaining access to childhood: the real stakes of a discourse on childhood within Western thought involve a confrontation between thought and what it is not, a wandering at the limits of the unthinkable" (276). Kristeva argues against dating the formation of the subject "from the 'mirror stage'" and encourages emphasizing "the heterogeneity between the libidinal-signifying organization in infancy (let us call it the 'semiotic disposition') and the 'symbolic' functioning of the speaker following language acquisition" ("Place Names" 276). Wrestling with the "limits of the unthinkable" engages theorists in "a confrontation between thought and what it is not" (276), a difficult, if not impossible task.

The baby is a subject but not "a knowing, already constituted subject" ("Revolution" 95). Rather, it is what Kristeva considers a "pre-symbolic" subject. Without language, without a symbolic order of communication, one lacks a means by which to articulate consciousness. But the kinetic functions and vocal rhythms of the infant as it interacts with its caregivers, the engagement behaviours it performs, constitute it as an intentional subject. This lifts the infant from the margins of Freudian and Lacanian theory and provides a theoretical context for considering the infant's subjectivity as axiomatic.

As a theoretical construct that pays attention to babies' profound and esoteric capacity for joy, Kristeva's notion of the semiotic *chora* is critical because it foregrounds the significance of the infant. Furthermore, it strives for a means by which to understand the infant as a subject, an agent acting upon the lives around it. While it may seem as though I want it both ways—the infant as a subject and the infant as semiotic—what I am really arguing for is an extension or regression, if you will, of Kristeva's theory of the disruptive force of the semiotic so that we can examine it where it begins: in infancy. As Judith Butler writes, "the [semiotic] drives have aims prior to their emergence into language" (81). That is, the drives signify; they are significant before one becomes a speaking subject. Those aims have to do with the very erosion of the speaking subject, as Butler claims, "where the subject is understood as a speaking being participating in the Symbolic" (83). Although Butler argues that the semiotic is present in the speaking subject, the fact is that the semiotic constitutes a return for that subject of those rhythms and vocalizations that occurred in infancy, that helped construct the subject as a subject. The semiotic then is dynamic, essential, potent. And there are ways into the semiotic as it exists in pre-linguistic infants whose life—as it is represented in literature—is sensuous and captivating. As Jane Gallop asserts, "the semiotic is the locus of force, revolution and art in Kristeva's work, clearly 'where the action is'" (124). I have found babies, both in real life and in literature, to be at the centre of the "action." I am fascinated by the way writers have "wandered at the limits of the unthinkable," how they have filled up the textual space of infant consciousness, and why they might feel compelled to visit that space.

Kristeva's theories of women's desire for children are also important to consider in a study of infancy since this desire emerges strongly in writing by some Canadian novelists, particularly during the 1960s and '70s. When reproductive choice is available and women persist in their desire for babies, Kristeva asserts, "the time has perhaps come to emphasize the multiplicity of female expressions and preoccupations" ("Women's Time" 193). As Kristeva sees it,

The desire to be a mother, considered alienating and even reactionary by the preceding generation of feminists, has obviously not become a standard for the present generation. But we have seen in the past few years an increasing number of women who not only consider their maternity compatible with their professional life or their feminist involvement...but also find it indispensable to their discovery, not of the plenitude, but of the complexity of the female experience, with all that this complexity comprises in joy and pain. ("Women's Time" 205)

Mary O'Brien asks in *The Politics of Reproduction*, "Where does feminist theory start? I answer: Within the process of human reproduction" (8). Adrienne Rich also writes about the process of reproduction as it polarizes people according to gender and affects women. In "When We Dead Awaken: Writing as Re-Vision," she claims that, "a radical critique of literature, feminist in its impulse, would take the work first of all as a clue to how we live, how we have been led to imagine ourselves, how our language has trapped as well as liberated us, how the very act of naming has been till now a male prerogative, and how we can begin to see and name—and therefore live—afresh" (148). Part of the way that women have been led to imagine themselves is quite strictly in terms of their capacity to bear children, a capacity Rich also addresses in *Of Woman Born*. She says,

Nothing, to be sure, had prepared me for the intensity of the relationship already existing between me and a creature I had carried in my body and now held in my arms and fed from my breasts.... No one mentions the psychic crisis of bearing a first child, the excitation of long-buried feelings about one's own mother, the sense of confused power and powerlessness, of being taken over on the one hand and of touching new physical and psychic potentialities on the other, a heightened sensibility which can be exhilarating, bewildering, and exhausting. No one mentions the strangeness of attraction—which can be as single-minded and overwhelming as the early days of a love affair—to a being so tiny, so dependent, so folded-in to itself—who is, and yet is not, part of oneself. (17)

Rich addresses the fundamental dichotomy of maternity—the provocation in some women of the sense of confused power and powerlessness in their connection to a dependent creature who involves women in a relationship of unique intensity. A feminist theorizing of the infant's significance must address the significance of reproduction, and the "multiplicity of female expressions and preoccupations," as Kris-

teva writes, attempting to reconcile feminist aims of equality and freedom, which seem at first to demand a distancing from the role of
mother, with women's persistent desire for babies in the experience of
motherhood.

My sense that the infant is more active, more of an agent than the
theories of Freud or Lacan have allowed, is supported by the recent
work of infant cognitive psychologists like Dr. Daniel Stern, and
Anneliese Korner. These researchers formulate from observation a
complex and richly nuanced view of infancy and provide a scientifi-
cally grounded context for considering the emerging complexity in
fictional babies over the century. Whether science has influenced art
or art science, the story became much more interesting throughout
the twentieth century. T. Berry Brazelton writes in the foreword to the
1978 edition of Jane Flannery Jackson's *Infant Culture*, "infants [have]
far more affective, cognitive, and communicative abilities than naïve
observers usually presume" (ix). Daniel Stern asserts that "over the
past three decades, there has been a revolution in the scientific observation of babies; in fact, we have more systematic observations on the
first two years of life than on any period in the entire life span" (1-2).
Stern combines an imaginative approach to articulate that consciousness with medical knowledge about "what your child sees, feels, and
experiences" (front cover). Stern explains that his "insights are drawn
from three sources: facts about infants based on extensive research,
speculations based on those facts, and [his] own imagination" (1). Parents, writes Stern, make "their best guess" about a baby's experience.
He claims that none "of us can spend time with a baby without ascrib-
ing to him or her certain thoughts, feelings, or wants at a particular
moment. In a baby's presence we are forced to invent the baby's
inner world" (5). This is a significant admission because it summarizes
the uncertain nature of infant study. Much of what people, even
experts, know about babies, they know by hypothesis. Current infant
studies experts examine every gesture of response to determine boredom, engagement, and cognition. Stern, for example, describes how
the fictional baby, Joey, whose impressions he invents, has visual preferences that include "intensity and contrast" and that without these,
Joey becomes bored (18). He says that a "baby's nervous system is
prepared to evaluate immediately the intensity of a light, a sound, a
touch—of anything accessible to one of his senses." According to
Stern, Joey "is able to calculate distances and quadrants of space" (18)

and is able to watch a patch of sunlight until he "gets bored by the play of appearances he sees in the sun patch. Its infinite approach stops being new and suspenseful. His attention suddenly dies away.... He turns his head away from the sunlit wall" (22). The observable behaviour is Joey's first looking at a wall and then turning away from it, yet Stern, out of his clinical and personal experiences, crafts an entire drama of engagement, suspense, and finally, boredom out of this turning of the head. Stern appeals to the parents' instinct to "invent a child's experience" (6). In doing so, Stern creates a vocabulary for the invention of infant consciousness that has its authority in contemporary medical science.

Recent literary depictions of babies mirror Stern in their revelation of a complex and intricate cognition on the part of the infant that is "totally at variance with the traditional picture" (Jackson and Jackson xi). Scientific studies of infant agency support the claim that infants have subjectivity that accords with Kristeva's notion of intentionality. Infants are able to influence the world around them as agents. Richard Q. Bell studies infant motor activity and its effect on parents. He finds that the infant itself "initiates bouts of interaction" (3) initially by means of crying and fussing which bring the caregiver "into the vicinity" (4). The infant is able to discriminate human forms from inanimate forms, and particularly to distinguish its mother from all others. Bell states that "these infant behaviours indicate to the mother that she has been selected for an intense one-to-one relationship" (6), and that the infant promotes this relationship itself. Bell allies himself here with the notion of intentionality, which, as will become evident in psychoanalytic studies of the infant, is one of the defining elements of human subjectivity.[11]

According to Bell, the relationship that the infant establishes with its caregiver is not exclusively designed to meet the primary need for sustenance. Bell finds through observance of the infant's "contribution to noncaregiving interactions" that infants "launch a social interaction" for its own sake (7). Smiling and vocalizing initiate a relationship with the caregiver, often the mother, and sustain a social interaction. According to Bell "often, a sitting infant gurgles and smiles when a mother passes on her way to do a household chore, thus inveigling her into interaction" (9). The infant solicits the mother's attention, brings her near, and maintains proximity. Infants one week old, once believed to be incapable of intention, have the capacity to communicate. While Bell's interpretation of infant behaviour is also in the form of narrative and hypothesis, it opens possibilities for complex infant interaction and rejects oversimplification. As Anneliese F. Korner writes in her essay "The Effect of the Infant's State, Level of Arousal, Sex, and Ontogenetic Stage on the Caregiver," researchers have become "increasingly aware that the young infant is a great deal more capable of organized responses than has been assumed, and that he [sic] is not nearly the passive-receptive organism he has been described as for so long" (105). Theories about infant development show that babies are capable, through a "vocabulary of signs and signals" (217), of wooing their mothers, creating in them the sense that they are part of a reciprocal discourse. Such discoveries are vital to a sense of the infant as subject, a sense that emerges in fictional representations of infants over the past hundred years.[12] These reflect a growing curiosity about the nature of the infant as subject and the configuration of adults as "other" in relation to the infant.

I incorporate the observations and conclusions of infant development researchers as they relate to fictional infants in order to investigate the nature and possibilities of infant subjectivity and to make evident the remarkable developments in infant representation throughout the twentieth century in Canadian fiction. I have found, in what seems to be a directly causal relationship, that one of the outcomes of the feminist revisioning of the infant is a more vital, engaged father—or male caregiver—infant bond. Numerous studies in the late 1970s and beyond focus on the importance of the father's role in infant development. Among these are Dr. Michael Lamb, Dr. Jerrold Lee Shapiro, Michael J. Diamond, and Martin Greenberg. Increasingly, men have become more involved as caregivers to infants and the results in fictional representation are compelling.

Historically, three forces demonstrate the evolving perceptions of babies in the twentieth century. First, there is a distinct movement away from the economic measure of a child's worth based on the income it could potentially generate toward a more subjectively based sentimental measure of value. This process of sentimentalizing children is connected with emerging social concerns about the poor, about what constitutes a good family (or a good community), about education, and about publicly funded hospitals, among other things (Sutherland 16).

Second, at the beginning of the twentieth century, infant mortality is addressed by medical institutions in Canada, bringing about the medicalization of pregnancy and birth. Childbirth, which had been a private act, became the public concern of doctors and government. As Neil Sutherland writes in *Children in English Canadian Society*, "Of all the reform efforts for children that grew and flourished between the 1880s and the 1920s, the public health movement had the most immediate, the least ambiguous, and the most precisely measurable positive effects on the lives of Canadian children" (39). By 1910, considerable advances had been made in the reduction of infant mortality simply by controlling the quality of milk infants were given (Sutherland 60; Hardyment 99; Arnup 17). While the rewarding measures taken to save infants' lives were laudatory, the next phase of intervention was perhaps less so. There is no arguing the fact that medical assistance in pregnancy, labour, and delivery has saved the lives of mothers and babies for decades. Nevertheless, the movement from private to public domain in childbirth caused an enormous alteration in personal control. The annexation of pregnancy and birth by the medical community, as overseen by the government, was done for the good of society. The aims were to reduce both infant and maternal mortality—it could not at the time have been perceived as a bad idea, or as disempowering to women.

Finally, as though a dam had broken, the twentieth century produced a flood of advice on how to care for babies. Hardyment writes that "medical, scientific and political developments combined at the turn of the century to turn a floodlight of interest and anticipation on the small creatures hitherto left to tumble up together in their nurseries" (98). Infants became the objects of intense scrutiny as "more and more people than ever before put pen to paper on the subject of raising babies" (99). Both the handbooks on baby care and the markets that encouraged their development increased as parents turned more and more to authorities outside the home for information on how to raise babies. Furthermore, the twentieth century saw countless psychological and physiological studies of infant development, some of which had profound effects on popular culture.

In her book *Pricing the Priceless Child: The Changing Social Value of Children*, Viviana Zelizer describes how there has been a "profound transformation in the economic and sentimental value of children" (3). Zelizer uses the term "sacralization" for objects that have been invested

with sentimental or religious meaning. She suggests that in the twentieth century the progression from the economic measure of value to a
sentimental measure of value of children was part of a cultural process
of "sacralization" of children's lives. Such an imparting of sanctity
removed children from "the cash nexus," a change, argues Zelizer,
clearly "shaped by profound changes in the economic, occupational,
and family structures" (11). Legislators in the United States were beginning to be concerned with protecting children's lives. While Zelizer
argues that the arrival of another child was "welcomed as the arrival of
a future labourer and as security for parents later in life" (5), it is also
true that carrying and delivering babies exhausted the women who
needed strength to work alongside their husbands. However, if children survived infancy, they could then be employed and help to support their families. Children were supposed to be useful; their usefulness defined value and babies had not yet achieved usefulness. Hence,
it was possible in 1910 New York to purchase a baby for about twenty-
five cents (Zelizer 174). Zelizer writes about the "baby farms" used by
women around the turn of the century for unwanted babies, the children of women who were "single, widowed, or deserted" (173). For
thirty-five dollars a woman could leave her infant in the care of a baby
"farmer" who would then place it in a "good" home. However, as
Zeliger states, "the prospect of adoption for the infant...was seldom
fulfilled" (173). Instead, baby farming was considered to be a euphe-
mism for baby killing (176). 13

Infant life, then, was held cheaply, but a change was slowly occurring. As early as the 1880s, pediatrics was established as a medical spe-
cialty. Furthermore, public concern with high infant and child mortality rates began to make itself felt at the level of policy. In the United
States during the 1890s, deaths of children under age five accounted for
an average of 40 percent of all deaths. The United States established a
Children's Bureau in 1912 that held "National Baby Weeks" and "Better
Babies" contests in order "to highlight infants' health needs" (Zelizer
29). By 1924, infant mortality decreased by 24 percent (Zelizer 29). In
Canada, at the beginning of the twentieth century, "one in five babies
regularly lost its life before its second birthday" (Comacchio 3).14
Sutherland states that "probably one out of every five to seven Canadian babies died in the first year or two of life." In fact, baby deaths
were so common that Sutherland concludes, "public records of the time
provide figures no more precise than these for the nation as a whole or

even any of its towns, cities, or provinces" indicating the country's lack of "public anxiety about the matter" (57). Katherine Arnup claims that while "there is evidence to suggest that a degree of concern over infant mortality had existed within the European scientific community since at least the middle of the nineteenth century, few concerted efforts were being made to overcome the problem" (16) until the beginning of the twentieth century. What changed at the end of the nineteenth century was that, according to Arnup, there was a general decline in the death rate as a result of "rapid developments in the fields of bacteriology and immunology, spurred on by the demonstration of germ theory by Louis Pasteur in 1876" (20). Suddenly possibilities were opened up by such scientific advances for exploring prevention of infant death, at least when it was caused by gastrointestinal infection through contaminated milk.

By 1906, some records began to be kept concerning infant mortality. Sutherland mentions "the first national survey on the state of infant mortality in the country" conducted by Miss Eliza Ritchie of Halifax, "convener of the National Council of the Women's Committee on Public Health" (58). In the late nineteenth and early twentieth centuries, concern for infants emerged in these loosely kept statistics on infant mortality, and Women's Institute talks on infant health and home pasteurization of milk (Sutherland 58). Indeed, regard for infant welfare is a phenomenon that begins, according to Sutherland, in several countries around the turn of the century and is manifested in conferences about infant mortality in Paris, London, Berlin, and in Canada (59). While Sutherland credits the need for "potential inductees" for war as the impetus for concern about infant and child mortality, infant care nevertheless, became a matter of public policy in the twentieth century. Statistics on infant and child mortality were made available to the public press and created a sense that infants needed care and protection, that such care and protection must be extended by the medical community and by the government.[15] As Veronica Strong-Boag argues, there was a postwar attempt to "reshape early childhood in Canada" because "childcare experts found the relationship between mother and child deficient" (160). Experts, she says, "enumerated the results of such maternal inexpertise in mortality, disease, and dysfunction among Canadian children" (161). The government was set to intervene in such a problematic relationship by mandating "medical supervision" since "experts...placed the responsibility for failure later on in life upon the parent, particularly the mother" (Strong-Boag 163). Canadian mothers and infants required, then, the assistance of educated experts to guide them.

Such ideologically based inroads in the appropriation of infant care capitalized on what Linda Pollock has shown in her book, *Forgotten Children: Parent-Child Relations from 1500 to 1900*, are normal feelings of affection and care. Pollock addresses historical resistance to the reductive notion that all children were valued according to the income they could generate and instead argues that people have always felt emotionally attached to their children. She believes that "past parents were very much aware of their children and concerned with the latter's welfare and education" (260). Pollock writes against Zelizer's thesis that children have only recently begun to be valued as people in themselves rather than as economic commodities.[16] Her study is based on historical documentation in the form of parent diaries, autobiography, and children's diaries. From such anecdotal evidence, she concludes that people have always felt a sentimental attachment to their children. While I agree with the truth of this, it seems to me that Zelizer's contention concerns the national sense of urgency about the value of small children and the government's responsibility to legislate safeguards for them, rather than individual affection for one's own children. As Pollock acknowledges, her sources were obviously literate, which suggests that they were also solvent. Parents who could read and write and support their children were less likely to feel the burden of extreme poverty exacerbated by the needs of several children.

While Zelizer's view is obviously different from Pollock's, it is not irreconcilable. Even if individual families had always placed a degree of value on young children and infants, a marked difference occurs, according to Zelizer, when children began to be valued as "emotionally priceless assets" (32) so that their death "became not only a painful domestic misfortune but a sign of collective failure" (32). Zelizer's study indicates the remarkable development from private concern about infants and children to public concern. The child's "price" as a sacred being becomes a matter for social institutions to create. Parental care began to be enhanced and enforced by both advertising and state programs in order to avoid the "collective failure" of infant mortality. The public impetus toward professional care of infant and mother could not be refused.[17]

Sutherland, Comacchio, and Zelizer, among others, have documented the emerging perception in the 1920s in Canada, the United

States, and Europe that babies were special and needed special care. Sutherland particularly notes that collective concern for infants seems to have been a phenomenon occurring almost simultaneously in North America and Europe.[18] Sutherland refers to this as a "public health movement" (57), where people were mobilized to act in concert on behalf of infants, primarily to reduce infant mortality. Once the problem of tainted milk was resolved through education and monitoring, interest in infant care "quickly expanded into other areas of prevention" (59).

Various experts, medical and otherwise, began to publish advice on bringing up the baby and on caring for pregnant women. As Comacchio finds, pressures were therefore put on women "to be perfect mothers, to look after themselves before, during, and after pregnancy" (106). Such care was demanded by physicians who were in the difficult position of characterizing pregnancy as a normal physiological state while at the same insisting that "maternity demanded a scientific approach" (106). The doctors themselves held "the key to both physical health and peace of mind" (106). A decent mother, then, owed it to herself, her family, and her country "to secure the birth of a healthy baby" (106). Therefore, pregnancy began to be regulated "meticulously" (117). Comacchio argues that the medicalization of pregnancy and the concern to lower infant mortality rates were not only the result of a sentimental view of infancy, but also, in the years between great wars, the result of the nation's need for a healthy and vital populace. Allison Prentice and her colleagues write that this campaign "was fuelled by the findings of a number of studies on maternal and infant mortality by Dr. Helen MacMurchy, perhaps the best-known publicist of the infant welfare movement of Canada" (247).

This need for care is particularly evident not only in the medical community's insistence upon it but also in its permeation of popular culture.[19] Advertisements begin in the 1920s to be aimed at an audience of mothers looking for special products for their babies. Such advertisements include one for Wear-Ever Aluminum utensils specifically marketed for babies with "rosy cheeks, sparkling eyes, good dispositions, steady gains in weight." Wear-Ever utensils supposedly contributed to the baby's excellent constitution by providing "safe, efficient, and hygienic" cookware (Comacchio 188). In this ad, the infant is placed in the foreground and looks straight ahead with a degree of pleading in his or her eyes. The mother is in the background, wearing a housedress and an apron while cooking at the stove. Rhetorically, the visual layout itself speaks to the baby's pre-eminence in every decision, including which utensil to use.[20]

Such rhetoric had a powerful effect on members of a civic-minded community. It became incumbent upon families, and particularly upon women, to measure up—to allow their pregnancies and deliveries to progress under the care of medical doctors who were almost exclusively male. Comacchio says that "childbearing was said to be fraught with danger," particularly for women who failed to seek out or follow medical advice (106). This presentation of pregnancy "must have fed on and heightened the expectant mother's natural anxieties" (106). Pregnancy and babies, then, became objects of medical treatment, subject to control: "Women were to trust doctors implicitly and to follow their instructions explicitly" (106). This management of women was extended to include women who were neither pregnant nor married in an effort to educate them about the best way to prepare for their biological destiny. The purpose of such management is manifest in Comacchio's excerpt from *Maclean's* by Dr. Woods Hutchinson. Commachio cites his catalogue of "the alleged defects of the young woman of the period":

> First, that she is physically incompetent for the tasks and strains of maternity; second, that she is selfish in that she prefers her own comfort and good looks and success in life to either the number or the health of her children; third that she has become so ambitious for independence and public recognition that she is neglecting the duties of her home. Fourth, that the management of her children is remarkably injudicious, that she has no idea of discipline and they are spoiled and pampered and allowed to grow up without any respect for their elders; fifth, that partly by weakness of her own nerves and partly by the unnatural and unwholesome conditions of food, housing, dress and social habits, under which she permits her children to grow up, she is impairing the stamina of the race and undermining the future. (qtd. in Commachio 108-109)

Dr. Hutchinson's prescription is clear: for the sake of the future citizens, women needed to be less self-interested and more disciplined in the care of their children.

The obligation to produce good citizens for the country fell upon pregnant women who, out of civic loyalty, would feel the force of necessity in submitting themselves to the regulation of the medical profession. Comacchio claims that "the advisers of the interwar period refused to depict children in the outmoded manner as 'little adults' but constantly and relentlessly discussed their upbringing in terms of char-

acter building or personality development" (143). Women were responsible to build character into their children. The concept of the baby
evolved to include a sense that it must become a citizen of its country
and so it must be developed into a good one—healthy, obedient,
strong. Children were, as Commachio says, "the inheritors of modern
Canada" (143). The supervisory role taken by government, as demonstrated by the publications of its official Council on Child Welfare (later
known as the Council on Child and Family Welfare), was both insti-
tuted and supported by advice books that delineated the strict parameters of normalcy for babies in terms of growth and behaviour.[21]

The twentieth-century concern with infant welfare was also evident in the emergence of a literature of advice on how to raise babies.
In the early part of the century, such advice urged strict schedules for
feeding and airing. There was one right way that, as Hardyment
asserts, failed to accommodate the differences of individual children.
This view of the baby is evident in advice literature meant to teach parents, mothers in particular, how to keep babies "up to scratch" (Hardyment 161). Babies were measured for physical and mental development. The negative effects of these stringent requirements were
threefold: "the demoralization of parents whose children score below
average…the exaggerated expectations of parents whose children score
above average," and finally, "the apotheosis of the 'normal child'" (161).
The non-existent normal baby would provide the standard for all other
babies. According to Hardyment, "the declared aim of the experts of the
1920s and 1930s had been to produce well-behaved, polite children,
with regular habits, who could easily be disciplined to fit into the
assembly-line culture of the new metropolis" (229).[22]

By the 1950s, a "new model baby" who "was warmly affectionate,
impulsive, dependent, and (preferably) scintillatingly intelligent"
began to appear in advice books which were less concerned with the
schedules, discipline, and self-denial characteristic of wartime advice,
and more concerned with fostering "emotional depth and keen intelligence" (Hardyment 223). This concern marks the new attention being
paid to the manner in which the infant trains its parents to respond to
its needs. Historically, then, not only was increasing attention being
paid to babies, but the kind of attention changed. Focus of concern
shifted from infant health and welfare to consciousness and agency—
and the ways and means of encouraging the "warmly affectionate"
baby. This was the purview of Dr. Benjamin Spock. Spock's advice in

the *Common Sense Book of Baby and Child Care*, "a bestseller only outsold by the Bible" (Hardyment 223), focused on parental instinct and on the miracle of unfolding human development represented in the infant. According to Spock, "there's nothing in the world more fascinating than watching children grow and develop" (18). Such fascination was revolutionary in that it offered the imprimatur of an authorized discourse for parents to engage with babies simply as wonderful and amazing creatures, rather than as future conscripts for war or well-behaved citizens. While it would seem to go without saying that parents would have always enjoyed the babies, the real shift signalled by Spock's advice is the shift to a baby-centred view, the objective of which was sanctioning pleasure. Spock believes that "the best experiences for an infant appear to be those she inherently enjoys—those that are rich with love and caring and security, and those that make sense to her. (How can you tell if something makes sense to an infant? Easy: they smile, they laugh, they coo.)" (20). The critical element of fun emerged in the baby books. Spock's baby-centred view of infant care is countered by his suggestion that parents need not "be afraid to respond to other desires of [the baby] as long as they seem sensible to you and as long as you don't become a slave to her.... The uneasy feeling you have when you hear her cry, the feeling that you want to comfort her, is meant to be part of your nature, too" (72).

This balance of parents' needs with baby's needs is markedly absent in Penelope Leach's *Your Baby and Child*, where she asserts that "there is no such thing as too much attention and comforting" (216). Where Spock admits that it is possible for the baby to become a "slave driver" (73), Leach dismisses the notion that babies can be spoiled, instead offering an infant-centred view that foregrounds the babies' needs in a manner that seems to negate the parents' need for relief from the constant presence of babies. Leach and Spock are significant because both invest the baby with power, with subjectivity, with an ability to act on the parents, to tell them what it needs. Spock urges parents to listen usually; Leach urges parents to listen always. She writes, for example, that if the newborn cries in the crib, one should "put him where he is most comfortable. Slung on your front? Then put him there. Carrying him may not suit you very well right this minute, but it will suit you far better than that incessant hurting noise" (12). Leach is unapologetic in her assertion that the happier parents can make their baby, the more they "will enjoy being with her" (9). Although Spock and Leach have been publishing editions of their baby care books concurrently for the past twenty-three years, Spock's view seems more traditional and marginally less infant-centred than Leach's. But in both cases, the infant has clearly moved from that which parents must shape and train into being a good citizen to that which shapes and trains adults to be compliant parents. If, in the world of baby advice manuals, the baby was once thought of as clay to be moulded, then perception has changed. Manual writers like Spock, Leach, and Stern now advise that infant demands, as they are expressed in an array of vocalizations and behaviours that include crying and smiling, ought to be met quickly. This perception seems to reverse roles, allowing the infant to mould the parent.

Currently, there is an overwhelming range of advice books on baby care. Titles vary from *Pregnancy for Dummies* (1998), which includes advice for mothers about manicures and hair colour, to the more impressive tome, *The Canadian Medical Association Complete Book of Mother and Baby Care* (1998). The broad spectrum of titles includes those offering advice from mother to mother, examinations of other cultural methods of baby care, and theories about maintaining constant physical contact with the baby. Most of these books focus on the parents' actions toward the baby. Among these is Stern's *Diary of a Baby*, first written in 1990 and re-released in 1998. Stern's book goes further than any of the previous baby handbooks do by making an attempt to articulate interior infant consciousness. In short, he attributes agency and inner consciousness and even voice to the infant and he does so with the authority he invokes as a medical doctor. Although his narrative is grounded in scientific knowledge, it is, nevertheless, a narrative, in this case a creative entry into an infant's mind.

Neither Stern nor Leach questions the purpose of having babies. Spock, however, wonders whether people haven't "lost [their] faith in the meaning of life and [their] confidence to understand [their] world and [their] society" (Spock 8). He suggests that "raising a child is more and more puzzling for many parents because we've lost a lot of our old-fashioned convictions about what kind of morals, ambitions, and character we want them to have" (5). Spock raises here an interesting question that has compelled theorists and writers to explore the acts of the baby in life and in art. What is the purpose of procreating? Why *have* babies? If, for at least some of Western history, the answer has been related to the Bible's edict to "go forth and multiply," one wonders, then, about the sig-

nificance and validity of infants in a world whose population has
reached six billion. Why do we, at least in the minority of wealthy nations
who have access to medical care, contraceptives, and education, keep on
doing this? The answers are too numerous and personal to list but some
of the obvious ones have to do with extending the family line, extending
our own genes and therefore our own lives into future generations, and
finally, and most importantly, establishing connections of love that give
our present life meaning and pleasure. These connections, writes Linda
Pollock, "provide interest and variety in life" (209).

These desires for meaning and value, and for connections that
evoke and reinforce one's sense of significance, are manifested in imaginative representations of the infant. It makes sense that value is engendered by voluntary appreciation. Therefore, depictions of babies that
underscore their competency to act suggest that babies initiate interaction because they want to, because the people they are interacting with
are valuable. In representations of infant subjectivity, measures of
value, then, become reciprocal in interesting ways.

In her book, *For the Time Being*, Annie Dillard approaches the maternity ward of a hospital with reverence:

> There might well be a rough angel guarding this ward, or a
> dragon, or an upwelling current that dashes boats on rocks. There
> might well be an old stone cairn in the hall by the elevators, or a
> well, or a ruined shrine wall where people still hear bells. Should
> we not remove our shoes, drink potions, take baths? For this is
> surely the wildest deep-sea vent on earth: This is where the people
> come out. (36)

Dillard touches a nerve. No matter that throughout history billions
of babies have been born. The fact remains that their presence in the
world is awe-inspiring. The way infants are represented in literary texts
reveals a sense that in ordinary life, infants change people and that this
change is amazing; like the blinding light on the road to Damascus,
they alter lives dramatically and irrevocably. The writer's relationship
to babies as they are represented in literary works compels study
because it both conforms to and resists assumptions. Babies "come out"
and things change forever.

CHAPTER 1

Early Twentieth-Century Infants

R eading the infant's place in Canadian fiction in the twentieth
century involves examining its movement from the margins of
textual representation to a more central site. This is the first and
most obvious development. The twentieth century marked a dramatic
change in social concern for infants, specifically for the causes of infant
mortality. What's germane to this study is the remarkable shift in view.
Philippe Ariès, in his comprehensive study, *Centuries of Childhood*,
which tracks the discovery of childhood in literature and art from the
medieval period forward, claims that the invisibility of infancy was the
"inevitable consequence of the demography of the period" (39). So
many infants died that it was barely worth keeping a record of their
short lives in literature or in art. Because of social and medical developments that permitted babies to live past infancy, writers begin to
"see" infants as literary figures and to make them visible to readers.
Second, there emerges a tension in the representations created by the
fact that babies are often simultaneously wanted and unwanted. There
is something about a baby that invites rapt admiration and often
equally intense antipathy. As representations change over the course of
a hundred years, as the infant takes up more space in novels and short
stories, this divided response remains constant. Finally, while the tension is revealed within an appearance/reality binary, the opposition is
not stable. In narratives in the early part of the century, babies are connected to the sphere of women's work and domesticity. Within that
sphere, babies are conceptualized in terms at once ideal and brutally

real. Moreover, the representation of infants is inflected by gender. Men and women write differently about babies, privileging some aspects of them and diminishing others.

In early twentieth-century writing, when babies are written into the text they are often idealistically constructed as that which fulfills the lives of those who have them. In ideal terms, babies often symbolize the consummation of happy married love. And whether it is innocence or beauty that stimulates "rapt admiration," it is often considered to be illusory, the result of unrealistic or uninformed engagement. To think about babies as sweet, or innocent, or beautiful is to align oneself with a sentimental, unrealistic notion of babies. Alternatively, infants are also constructed as impediments to women's happiness and to their very survival.[1] This second view involves a deconstruction of the myth of the sweet baby by the construction of a counter-myth based on the real hazards and trials that babies bring with them into the world. The fact is that neither of these essential views tells the whole story—both are simultaneously true.

In *Survival*, Margaret Atwood characterizes "good" and "bad" babies. A good one "signals spiritual rebirth" (207). Bad babies come in groups, "like the endless series of infants that keep appearing like little piglets born to nonentity mothers" (207). Clearly, the comparison is tenuous since the only difference between "good" and "bad" babies for Atwood has to do with volume. The difference is between one baby—"a good one"—and many babies—"appearing like little piglets." Where babies occur singly, they are celebrated and accommodated. They can perhaps even be sweet and innocent. However, where they occur in multiples, they are obstacles to survival for the women who bear the burden in their bodies and in their homes. These two kinds of babies are both present in the novels of the early part of the twentieth century.

This chapter examines infant representation in L.M. Montgomery's *Anne* novels and in Frederick Philip Grove's *Settlers of the Marsh*. The works of Montgomery and Grove are significant because of their enduring appeal and their position in the canon of Canadian literature.[2] In an examination of the representation of infants throughout the century, these two authors emerge prominently from their time. They offer a sustained engagement with babies that is unique for the early part of the century. Nellie McClung's short story "Men and Money" in *All We Like Sheep* deals negligibly with a baby who grows up quickly and then dies as a man in service to his country. Similarly, the baby in

Howard O'Hagan's *Tay John* also grows out of infancy in a relatively short space. In *Wild Geese*, Martha Ostenso writes against the social taboo of illegitimacy, investigating the manner in which the illegitimate baby in one generation victimizes its mother whereas in her daughter's generation, the illegitimate baby liberates its mother from the tyranny of her father. But in the *Anne* books and in Grove's *Settlers*, the infant recurs as a significant component of the story. The narratives of both authors gesture toward the idealistic; babies are desirable, invested with sweetness, purity, and hopes for a good future. This idealistic depiction of infants is often overt in the text, but the counternarrative suggests that babies cause more trouble than they are worth. They are sometimes despised and loathed by their mothers; they are often distinctly undesirable impediments to survival and self-fulfillment.

My choice to include the *Anne* books in this discussion is also based on their immense popularity, both at the time of publication and today. In the early part of the twentieth century, they were among the most widely read books.[3] Montgomery was and is internationally famous, was a Fellow of the Royal Society of Arts in England, and was listed among Canada's great writers (Rubio 4).[4] Although critics have tended to relegate Montgomery's books to the genres of children's literature, romance, or sentimental fiction, she herself intended them for "a general audience" (Rubio 1). Montgomery's representation is vital to this study because although she appears to inscribe contemporary social values, there exists a resistant subtext that undercuts the ideally romantic construction of the baby. Montgomery, in short, permits a more complex reading of the baby's presence in the lives of the women it affects. In *Anne of Green Gables* (1908), *Anne's House of Dreams* (1922), and *Anne of Ingleside* (1939), Montgomery deploys a series of contradictions that reveal ambivalence toward pregnancy and babies. The dichotomy between baby as object of desire and object of animus is unexpectedly stark in these novels which are traditionally viewed as celebrations of marriage and family. Her portrayal of babies is characterized by a double voicing that is evident in writing by women about babies throughout the twentieth century.

Montgomery is at work in the national literature, engaged in the process of description and inscription in her writing about babies. Montgomery endorses the conventional response to infants, writing that Anne's baby, Bertha Marilla, was a "plump, roly-poly baby, with silky damp curls...long eyelashes...pretty little ears." Furthermore,

Anne asserts that "she is a miracle" (*Anne of Ingleside* 62-63). But Montgomery also undermines this stereotypical of view of infants when she
writes in both *Anne of Green Gables* and *Anne of Ingleside* about women
who have too many babies. Her compliance with traditional representation seems to grow out of the necessity to conform to the ideology
dominant in her time: that a woman belonged in the home, either the
home of her father or the home of her husband. In order to appeal to
her audience, Montgomery would have to acknowledge in the text
that, as Mary Rubio says, "the only acceptable closure of a story about
a young woman was the sound of wedding bells. Thus, Montgomery
had to portray marriage as site of the ultimate female happiness" (5),
and further, that babies contribute in "miraculous" and "sweet" ways to
that ultimate happiness. However, as Rubio asserts, Montgomery "was
a clever and devious writer who found strategies for writing on two
levels at the same time" (5). As a feminist writer, Montgomery explores
the tension women feel between personal freedom and motherhood.
She inscribes a revisioning of conventional views of the infant as "precious" and always only desirable. On the contrary, Montgomery does
not back away from the extreme difficulty imposed by babies upon the
women who bear them, a historically accurate view that departs from
the ideal. Jane Lewis says of such difficulty that frequent pregnancies
in the early twentieth century "taxed women's health severely" (8). In
"Mothering in a Newfoundland Community," Cecilia Benoit describes
how "these women's reproductive and productive lives consisted of
endless series of tasks during each day, each year, their lifetime" (183).
Adrienne Rich finds that in Britain in 1915, "the average woman had
from five to eleven children with several miscarriages, most of them
with no prenatal care and inadequate diet" (*Of Woman Born* 33). Rich
describes "the anxiety and physical depletion of incessant childbearing" that compelled many women to take "drugs to bring on abortion,
which were usually ineffective" (33). The difficulties for women who
bore so many children are evident in "the ill-health, mental strain, and
exhaustion of which [they] write" (Rich 33).

Montgomery rejects the baby's colonization of women. Aligning
herself with writers like Charlotte Perkins Gilman and Virginia Woolf,
she writes against women's subservience to the domestic sphere with
its limitations imposed by marriage and community, and its insistence
that women, unless they are barren, have babies. The text offers some
resistance to the notion of babies as sublime gifts.

Instead, Montgomery reveals her understanding of what R.P. Cuzzort claims concerning the sacred. Cuzzort explains that what "is considered sacred in a society is given its awesome and sacred qualities by
virtue of its capacity to represent values, sentiments, power, or beliefs
which are shared in common" (29). While Montgomery overtly sub-
scribes to the notion of babies as sacred, a notion explicitly supported
by the text which depicts babies as "precious things with curls and
chubby knees" (*Anne of Ingleside* 16), she also subverts that notion
through a subtext that is surprisingly similar to the more realistic *Settlers of the Marsh*. The surprise lies in the fact that Montgomery's work
has been "variously called romance writing, regional idyll, and sentimental novel" (Rubio 1), while Grove's work is far removed from such
classification. Nevertheless, in the discourse of desire and rejection, the
two depictions of infants are often similar.

Grove is also engaged in a demythologizing work. In his immigrant
narrative, Grove uses what Stanley McMullen called a "promised land
motif" (28). That is, "Grove was articulating an essential myth of North
American culture" (28). That myth constructs the New World as "a land
of Promise" (29). One essential fulfillment of that promise was directly
related to babies in the sense that they embody the promise of future
success. Thus Grove's protagonist, Niels Lindstedt, idealizes a future
that includes a wife and children. Yet in *Settlers of the Marsh*, Grove
writes candidly and even sympathetically about the exhaustion caused
by too many babies born to farm women.

Realist novels about pioneering families such as Frederick Philip
Grove's *Settlers of the Marsh* explore tension between desire for progeny
(perhaps more a marker of a man's desire for a dynasty), and a
woman's desire for personal, rather than familial, survival. Grove's specific reference to the impact of multiple births on the woman's world is
pronounced and grim. Whereas Montgomery avoids mention of
women's sexuality, focusing instead on Anne's overly romantic perspective, Grove explores the burdens placed upon women by the dominance of men.

In the past, critics of Grove's *Settlers* have focused on the novel's
psychological depth, upon Grove's characterization of Niels Lindstedt,
and upon the novel's situation in the realist tradition. For example,
Desmond Pacey and John Moss have written in their guides to Canadian literature about the psychological realism of Grove's novels.[5]
Grove witnessed the beginning of the feminist movement at the end of

the century in Germany. As Irene Gammel finds, Grove was familiar
with "women's growing demands for new rights, and after immigrat-
ing to Canada he was faced with Manitoba's strong women's movement, which gained for women the right to vote in provincial elections
in 1916, when Grove was teaching in the province" (213). Grove's
awareness of the plight of women is evident in his novels. More
recently, Gammel has examined the strategies of rebellion evident in
the daughters of Grove's characters, including Ellen Amundsen. Ellen's
rebellion is evident in her candidly articulated refusal to have children,
though it is not a position that she sustains at the novel's end. Nevertheless, it is compelling for the purposes of this study that feminist writers are beginning to review Grove's representation of Ellen, a woman
who refuses "not so much sexual intimacy," but rather "the patriarchal
notion of sexualized power that ruled her mother's life" (Gammel 227).
The rejection of such "sexualized power" that results in repeated pregnancies, miscarriages, and births reveals a corollary rejection of the
baby itself and the woes and difficulties that come with it. Thus representation of the infant is informed by a sense of the complications he or
she creates. Both Montgomery and Grove explore the binary opposition that constitutes the baby as ideal at the level of appearance, but
much more complex in reality. However, critics, while focusing on feminist concerns with power and patriarchy, have tended to overlook this
constitution of the baby.

When *Anne of Green Gables* was first published in 1908, the cover
was designed to appeal to adults. It showed a portrait of a sophisticated
"Anne" with a "Gibson-girl hairstyle" (Rubio 2). Montgomery was creating a complex social world, not merely a straightforward story for
children. Critics have finally begun to reassess Montgomery's place in
the canon of Canadian fiction, looking past what Rubio calls the "sentimental gardens" of her writing and seeing the "plentiful harvest of thistles" (1).[6] Rubio refers here to Montgomery's ability to write in a way
that supported the dominant discourse, undergirded as it was by the
"doctrine of separate spheres," while at the same time articulating a
counternarrative that speaks to the "grave dangers to a talented
woman's autonomy, happiness, and self-fulfilment" (5). Although this
counternarrative, usually coming through the voice of unpleasant,
marginal characters, is veiled, it offers a compelling depiction of infants
as obstacles, along with marriage, to women's "autonomy" and "happiness." Gabriella Åhmansson asserts that in *Anne's House of Dreams*

"there are two types of narrative, one realistic and one romantic, travelling side by side throughout the book" (152). Babies occupy space
both within the romantic narrative as well as in a subtle, though much
uglier subnarrative that explores the harsher realities when women
have too many babies.

Anne's indentured slavery to the Thomas clan begins when she is
barely three months old, being raised "by hand" by Mrs. Thomas. At the
age of eight, Anne has the care of the four children younger than she.
When Mr. Thomas is killed, Anne moves in with Mrs. Hammond to care
for her children "in a clearing among the stumps" (49). The text
describes the stunted life endured by this mother to many babies.
Mrs. Hammond's fecundity, having produced twins "three times in succession" (49), leads Anne to conclude that she likes "babies in modera-
tion" (49), rather than in the abundance supplied by Mrs. Hammond.
When the husband (the family's sole support) dies, the mother gives
Anne up and breaks up the family, distributing her children among rel-
atives. Poverty ultimately compels Mrs. Hammond to give up her children and move by herself to America, thus reclaiming some independence. Mrs. Thomas and Mrs. Hammond are burdened by the cares of a
large family of small children. This is the subtextual emergence of the
sense that babies are not always sweet or even welcome. Their arrival is
not always cause for rejoicing. On the contrary, like Atwood's series of
"piglets," these babies burden the women who bear them.

The women's burdens, in Anne's view, prevent them from treating
her as nicely as she feels they must have wanted to (50). Anne tells Marilla that it "must be very trying to have a drunken husband, you see;
and it must be very trying to have twins three times in succession, don't
you think? But I feel sure they meant to be good to me" (50). Part of
Anne's insistence results from her belief that she is worthy of kindness,
that only the difficulties of a "drunken husband" and too many children inhibited the kindness of these women. In short, reading in the
interstices suggests that they were, in fact, cruel to Anne, passing what
they could of their own burdens onto a child for whom they had no
care. Anne appears embarrassed and "flushed scarlet" at Marilla's question. She defends the women, asserting that she "know[s] they meant
to be just as good and kind as possible" (50) when clearly, they have not
acted on such an intention. It is interesting to note that although Anne
has cared for many small babies, the bitterness and exhaustion that
characterizes the mothers of these children do not taint her. Perhaps

there is something innate in Anne, in her optimism or her tremendous capacity to imagine a better reality than the one she experiences, that makes her better able to cope with babies than their own mothers can. In any case, Marilla perceives all that Anne has elided concerning her own hard experience and feels pity for Anne's "life of drudgery and poverty and neglect; for Marilla was shrewd enough to read between the lines of Anne's history and divine the truth" (50). Clearly, a life with too many babies is one of "drudgery and poverty and neglect," which makes both the mothers and the babies miserable. Anne's embarrassed justification to Marilla of the women's treatment speaks volumes about Anne's forbearance and, more compellingly, about the meanness engendered in women who have too many babies. Here, in spades, are the difficulties that assault a woman's well-being and independence. These requirements limit women's perception of the infant, skewing it so that babies lack any "starry eyed" perfection and are seen only in terms of the work they represent. The real burdens infants occasion overshadow, indeed seem more "real," than the infants' charms.

Added to this list of Montgomery's encumbered women is Mrs. Blewett, "a small, shrewish-faced woman without an ounce of superfluous flesh on her bones" known for her family "of pert, quarrelsome children" (54). She is interested in taking Anne on to help her with her youngest, a baby who is "awful fractious" and whom she is "worn out attending to" (56). Mrs. Blewett's baby is always only irritable and demanding, in many ways a mirror image of its mother. Matthew Cuthbert says of her, "I wouldn't give a dog I liked to that Blewett woman" (58). Not only is Mrs. Blewett among the ranks of beleaguered mothers, but also Mrs. Lynde, the woman who prides herself on speaking her mind no matter what brutal utterance emerges from it, is herself the mother of ten children (80). Interestingly, Montgomery consistently characterizes these burdened mothers in negative terms.[7] Mrs. Hammond lives among "stumps," Mrs. Blewett is "shrewish-faced," and Mrs. Lynde "can manage [her] own concerns and those of other folks into the bargain" (1). They are generally unpleasant characters. Marilla, on the contrary, is a spinster whom Montgomery endows with both humour and compassion.

Since Montgomery makes no reference to the intrusive sexual demands of the fathers, the babies themselves bear blame for the mothers' weariness. Their abundant presence causes these mothers—Mrs. Thomas, Mrs. Hammond, Mrs. Blewett, and Mrs. Lynde—to be cruel and shrewish, not to mention poor. This is the counternarrative Montgomery establishes in opposition to the more idealistic view of the saintliness of both motherhood and infants that she will explore in more detail when Anne herself becomes a mother.

These infants are figures of Anne's recollection of her life before Green Gables and are therefore somewhat insubstantial. However, as she matures, marries Gilbert, and sets up house, the baby becomes more salient. Anne's first pregnancy contrasts with the unfortunate Mrs. Proctor's births. Mrs. Proctor, pregnant with her eighth child, is characterized as one of the weary women, in the company of Mrs. Blewett and Mrs. Hammond, whose lives are burdened with too many babies. Once again, the text navigates the tension engendered by the infant between being wanted and unwanted, a tension that manifests itself in terms of the real versus the ideal.

The real truth of infant mortality intrudes on Anne's nice life with merciless force. Anne's baby is longed for (148). When it dies, it leaves "heartbreak behind it" (149). While one would imagine that Anne's early life caring for countless poor infants might have made her sensible of the dreariness of hard work and of loss, nevertheless, Anne remains naïve until her own baby dies. Most importantly, it is the loss of the baby, more than any of the other losses Anne has experienced (including the loss of both parents and of Matthew) that propels Anne into a maturity that comes with certain knowledge of the uglier and less ideal aspects of life. In fact, the death of the baby puts limits on Anne's imagination and behaviour. Far from expanding the boundaries of commonly accepted female conduct, in the later novels Anne "willingly accepts social restrictions" placed upon her in her role as the doctor's wife, and "is totally absorbed in a dense social network of family and rural community" (Gillian Thomas 37). This absorption extends to the way Anne experiences pregnancy, childbirth, and motherhood. Anne's conformity to the traditional role of wife and mother is found among the darker themes Montgomery explores in *Anne's House of Dreams* and *Anne of Ingleside*.[8] Indeed, as Åhmunsson puts it, "up till the death of her first born baby, Anne behaves like a young girl" (157).

In part because she is a young girl and in part because of the time period, Anne considers her pregnancy in *Anne's House of Dreams* in oblique references to her hopes and dreams. These are foreshadowed by that epitome of motherhood, Diana Barry White. When Anne observes Diana cuddle small Cordelia "with the inimitable gesture of motherhood," her heart is "filled with sweet, unuttered dreams and hopes, a thrill that was half pure pleasure and half a strange, ethereal pain" (3). Babies engender, then, an exquisite "thrill" that is equally divided between pleasure and "strange...pain." The thought of mothering a baby, of having that special capacity for "inimitable gestures" called forth is thrilling to Anne. The language that describes the baby and its connection to its mother is euphemistic and thick with adjectives of sweetness and pleasure that cannot be uttered. Anne, on the brink of marriage, feels stabbed with pain and pleasure at the thought of having a baby. It's important to note that Montgomery refers to the pain as "ethereal," or rarefied, spiritual rather than physical. This is not a pain related to the pangs of childbirth; rather it is connected to the notion of dreams fulfilled, again, an idealistic yearning for the infant as the culmination of happy marriage. Furthermore, Anne's anticipation of the baby's arrival is obliquely represented as "new, poignantly-sweet dreams that were beginning to span life with their rainbows" (79). Anne's pregnancy is related in a discourse of dreams and desires that are like filaments extending into an imaginary future of motherhood. She dreams opaquely about the baby she will have and suggests to Gilbert that he might ask for "*one* thing more" than a home and a "dear, little, red-haired wife" (113).

Montgomery interweaves the desire for babies with the rejection of them through the image of clothing. For example, multiple pregnancies have rendered Mrs. Proctor weak and spiritless, at the mercy of neighbours who help her out. Cornelia Bryant sews a baby's dress for Mrs. Proctor who is "expecting her eighth baby any day now, and not a stitch has she ready for it. The other seven have wore out all she made for the first, and she's never had time or strength or spirit to make any more" (*Anne's House* 56-57). Mrs. Proctor is one of Atwood's "nonentity mothers" who give birth to an endless stream of babies that leave her without "time or strength or spirit." In this environment, one more baby is an unwanted burden. As for Mr. Proctor, Miss Bryant says "He drinks and neglects his family. Isn't that like a man?" (56). Montgomery elaborates a motif of the useless, drunkard husband and numerous babies, both with the power to destroy women.

The anger women feel toward men is evident in Montgomery's text. Miss Bryant's anger reveals itself in pity, in the delicate care she takes while sewing Mrs. Proctor's baby's dress. Miss Bryant goes further, stating that no one wants "the poor mite" so she is adding hand embroidery to its dress (57), decorating the infant's clothing so that its poverty and unpopularity will not be evident. The fabric is "dainty" (56), the dress itself "was most beautifully made, with tiny frills and tucks," with embroidery and "exquisite stitches" (56). Miss Bryant labours over the gown, investing it with time and care so that the baby will have "one real pretty dress, just as if it *was* wanted" (57). Montgomery juxtaposes the care that the dress receives with the lack of care bestowed upon the infant itself. Whatever the reality, the infant will appear well cared for. However charitable, the gesture will not deceive anyone, least of all Mrs. Proctor, concerning the infant's value. Nice clothing will not mitigate the real burden that this eighth baby adds.

Anne's own baby also receives a "dress of exquisite workmanship— delicate embroidery, wonderful tucking, sheer loveliness" (133), made by Leslie Moore. Moreover, we are told that "Miss Cornelia had, for the time being, given up sewing for *unwanted, unwelcome* eighth babies, and fallen to sewing for a very much wanted first one, whose welcome would leave nothing to be desired" (133, my emphasis). The details of Anne's baby's layette—"marvellous garments" made of "good material and honest stitches"—both the gifts and the clothes that Anne stitches herself (133), contrast sharply with Mrs. Proctor's supply of clothing, donated by the charity of neighbours since for that unfortunate baby she has "not a stitch." Montgomery uses the baby's layette to contrast the vast difference in the community's evaluation between Mrs. Proctor's eighth baby and Anne's first—one "unwanted and unwelcome" and one "whose welcome would leave nothing to be desired." Anne's baby is one of Atwood's "good" ones, valuable because it is one and not one of eight, represented in ideal terms, not as a burden but as a blessing. The binary opposition between real and ideal is evident in these two babies.

However, the birth of Anne's baby involves an intermingling of the real and the ideal. The baby lives for only a day. The labour itself is long and difficult. Susan Baker, Anne's housekeeper, spends the day "in the kitchen with cotton wool in her ears and her apron over her head" (146), suggesting that Anne suffers loudly. The gravity in the faces of the doctor and nurse communicate the seriousness of the situation. Gilbert's difficulty with the birth is also articulated in the text. Gilbert comes down to the kitchen, "his face gray and haggard from his night's agony" (147). Anne's labour is a "baptism of pain" (147) that Marilla characterizes as "passing through the shadow" (149), implicitly, the shadow of death of the twenty-third Psalm. In the early part of the century in Canada, this reference to death in childbirth was no turn of phrase, but a real threat.[9] Painful labour and possible maternal and/or infant mortality are the realistic risks of the birth and the baby, sharply contrasted to ephemeral "hopes and dreams."

The real pain of giving birth to the baby exposes the ephemeral hopes and dreams, but no less so does the real joy that the baby causes. After the baby is born, we are told that Anne "tasted of happiness so rare and exquisite that she wondered if the angels in heaven did not envy her" (147-48). Anne herself tells Marilla, "I thought I was happy before. Now I know that I just dreamed a pleasant dream of happiness. This is the *reality*" (148, my emphasis). Anne feels the happy reality of the baby no less sharply than the pain of bringing her into the world. She is "aglow with the holy passion of motherhood" (147). Thus the infant itself synthesizes the ideal and the real; the baby is the prime cause of both exquisite pain and exquisite happiness.

Anne's first baby is for her a site of immense desire and even greater disappointment. Its loss is something Anne feels she will never recover from, a loss for which there will be no restoration in spite of Captain Jim's assurances to the contrary (154): "There was something in the smile that had never been in Anne's smile before and would never be absent from it again" (153). The "something" present is the knowledge of hard loss, a knowledge that shapes Anne's life. Furthermore, Anne herself tells Captain Jim that she is "done with dreams" (154). Gilbert insists that Susan should stay on to help Anne "until the old spring comes back into your step, and those little hollows on your cheeks fill out" (166). The ravages of pregnancy, childbirth, and grief are evident on Anne's physiognomy. This loss is tragically ironic when considered in light of the "gains" of Mrs. Proctor, worn out not from losing babies but from getting them.

In spite of the clearly delineated joy and pain concomitant with the birth of Anne's first child, the narrative returns to euphemisms when Anne has her second baby. The language recalls a fairy tale:

One morning, when a windy golden sunrise was billowing over the gulf in waves of light, a certain weary stork flew over the bar of Four Winds Harbour on his way from the Land of Evening Stars. Under his wing was tucked a sleepy, starry-eyed, little creature. The stork was tired, and he looked wistfully about him.... The big, white light-house on the red sandstone cliff had its good points; but no stork possessed of any gumption would leave a new, velvet baby there.... Then the stork brightened up. He had caught sight of the very place—a little white house nestled against a big, whispering fir-wood...a house which just looked as if it were meant for babies. (244)

We read that when "the stork" pays another visit to the house of dreams, he leaves behind "a certain young gentleman" who has arrived without much luggage, "but he evidently means to stay" (245). The stork comes from the "Land of Evening Stars" and carries with him "a sleepy, starry-eyed, little creature" (244). Half an hour after the stork "alighted on the ridge-pole" (244), Anne's baby is born. Anne's son appears miraculously, without disturbing anyone. Her second delivery is ideal; all of the pain and anxiety that would have been associated with the birth of her second child are elided in the text. While this may be the result of Anne's deliberate choice to turn away from mourning, the fact remains that the language is childish and childlike. The narrative returns to an unrealistic rendering of the birth and the baby, to the familiarity and consolation of the ideal. It is a comforting portrayal that would reassure readers of a happy outcome. The baby is large—ten pounds—and loud (245). He has "dear, darling toes," remarkable hands, and "the nicest little ears" (246). The new baby is perfect and Anne marvels at its construction. The baby's perfection and the fairy-tale rendering of its arrival underscore the notion of the infant as an incredible, fantastic entity.

The miraculous nature of the baby is further emphasized in the text's articulate comparison to the birth of Christ. The narrator tells how "Anne's convalescence was rapid and happy. Folks came and worshipped the baby, as people have bowed before the kingship of the new-born since long before the Wise Men of the East knelt in homage to the Royal Babe the Bethlehem manger" (246-47). Adoring adults surround the baby. Montgomery casts Anne's friend, Leslie, in the role of "beautiful, golden-crowned Madonna" (247), while Anne rests in bed.

The blessing bestowed by infants on mothers is evident in the overt text. In a revisioning of the *Anne* books that foregrounds infant representation, it is important to consider the baby's power to enrich, indeed, to bless. The infant as blessing is a power that Julia Kristeva has poetically described. In "Stabat Mater," Kristeva explores her own personal beatification in motherhood in a text with parallel columns. One side of the page is given to a poetic unfolding of her individual engagement with motherhood; the other is occupied with Kristeva's theoreti-

cal discussion of the cult of the Virgin Mary. The image of the
Madonna, Kristeva asserts, has become "one of the most powerful
imaginary constructs known in the history of civilizations" (163). Kristeva traces the development of the cult of the Virgin throughout history
and literature, marking the margins of the text with images of labour
and delivery. Kristeva claims that the "fulfilment, under the name of
Mary, of a totality made of woman and God is finally accomplished
through the avoidance of death" (168), in other words, through Mary's
Assumption into heaven. While it was celebrated in Byzantium "as
early as the fourth century.... For the Vatican, the Assumption became
dogma only after 1950" (169). Kristeva's questions in both the historical
and personal texts have to do with death. Referring to the Vatican's
institution of the Assumption, she asks, "what death anguish was it [the
Assumption] intended to soothe after the conclusion of the deadliest of
wars?" And she asks, having just given birth, "Death, then, how could
I yield to it?" (169). Kristeva suggests through these narratives that in
women's connection to birth and to babies, there is a sense of transformation and empowerment. In the hardest work possible, the work of
giving birth to babies, women feel power. Kristeva believes that birth
suspends mortality for a time, connecting women with their babies in a
way that affirms life. Similarly, even while much of Montgomery's
writing offers a critique of a culture in which women seem doomed to
exhaustion because of too many babies, it also affirms the baby's importance in empowering women, in transcending, if only momentarily, the
power of death.

While it may seem strange that Leslie should be cast in the role of
Madonna to Anne's baby, there are several possible reasons for this.
Her blonde hair may suggest nothing so much as the golden halo that
usually accompanies paintings of the Madonna. Moreover, it is possible
that Montgomery invests her as an adoptive or surrogate mother to the
new baby. Genevieve Wiggins finds that Leslie Moore is a "foil to
Anne." While she is "embittered and frustrated," Anne is "happy and
fulfilled" (59). However, with her new freedom and "the new conditions of her life" (247), Leslie is newly positioned to receive the baby's
blessing. Montgomery, possibly to mitigate Leslie's loneliness, puts her
in the position of the Madonna who is beatified by the gift of the baby.

The birth of the baby, as Arendt suggests, interrupts "the law of
mortality" (246). This sense of being aligned with some sublime force,
recurrent in texts about babies, pulls against the textual undercurrent

that persistently represents babies as a debilitating force in women's lives, undermining their strength, confining their bodies, obliterating their individual identities. The moment of birth seems suspended in its own particular inviolability. Anne's baby invites worship. He is a figure of redemption, giving Anne back something that she lost when the first baby died, healing the "heartache" she has had ever since (245). Furthermore, he is honoured "as people have bowed before the kingship of the new-born since long before the Wise Men of the East knelt in homage to the Royal Babe the Bethlehem manger" (246-47). The language is idealistic and sacred, but it also points to a truth that literature returns to again and again: the transforming power of the infant. That power is possible because Anne is in good health. She has good support for her maternal work and is having a second, not an eighth child. Recall that Mrs. Proctor's baby is "unwanted and unwelcome" (133). There are no references to the Christ child or to the Madonna in regard to Mrs. Proctor's experience, or for that matter, in regard to Mrs. Blewett's "fractious" baby (*Anne of Green Gables* 56). Instead, the texts appear to contrast the realistic and necessarily dreary aspects of babies born in multiples against Anne's sweetly idealistic anticipation and enjoyment of her babies. Montgomery represents babies in a voice that is doubled, where binary oppositions of real and ideal prove unstable. Indeed, there is an interplay of opposites where the baby as an object of joy is, in fact, real. The real opposition in Montgomery's representation of the infant occurs between "good" or singular, and "bad" and multiple. Anne's baby affirms her identity and success as a wife and mother, whereas Mrs. Proctor's obliterates her limited resources and her individual identity.

This obliteration of identity is something that Ellen fears in Grove's *Settlers of the Marsh*. Ellen has watched her mother work herself to actual death for the farm and for her father, and has also been witness to her mother's repeated pregnancies and miscarriages. There is in Ellen that same anger that motivates Miss Bryant—anger over the lack of control they feel as the victim of men's sexual desire and their own bodies' ability to become pregnant. As the neighbour woman, Mrs. Campbell says, "when a woman has got to work like a man, children are just a plague" (107). Grove's narrative explores the bleak lives of the settlers, focusing particularly on the difficulties of the women who have too many babies. This novel articulates some of the allusions to social conditions in L.M. Montgomery's novels. The physical presence of babies is marginal in the text. There are references to Bobby's babies, but this reference also includes mention of the degree to which such fertility has aged Bobby's wife (203). The infant is an object of fear for Ellen, something she spends the entire novel avoiding. It is also a site of abject fear for Ellen's mother and of severe inconvenience for the settler women who induce miscarriage, to the detriment of their health, so that they can keep up with the relentless farm work.

Her mother's suffering has shaped Ellen's opinions about marriage. In confronting the issues of sexuality, pregnancy, and birth, Ellen finds that she is incapable of acting against what she knows, that all three result in weariness and death. Ellen baldly informs Niels, her suitor, of her reasons for refusing to marry. Paramount is her mother's dying wish that she never marry: "Ellen, whatever you do, never let a man come near you. You are strong and big, thank God. Make your own life, Ellen, and let nobody make it for you" (112). Mrs. Amundsen's life has been made for her. She makes no decisions for herself; she has no personal autonomy to set her course in the future or in the present. Her husband forces her to emigrate from Sweden, forces her to leave two of her children with her parents, and finally, forces himself on her, regardless of her pain and fatigue, regardless of yet another imminent pregnancy. Ellen vividly recalls overhearing her mother's feeble protests at night against her father's "vile, jesting, jocular urgency...the words he used to that skeleton and ghost of a woman" (112). Mrs. Amundsen copes with her pregnancies the way Mrs. Campbell suggested: by means of self-induced abortion. Mrs. Campbell tells her, "When I'm just about as far gone as you are now, then I go and lift heavy things; or I take the plow and walk behind it for a day. In less than a week's time the child comes; and it's dead" (108). This, she suggests, is what "lots of women around here do" (108). Mrs. Amundsen follows her advice as it becomes necessary and prostrates herself with weakness. Mr. Amundsen then takes "a little box into the bush to bury" (111) and then rapes his wife, all the while saying of the babies, "God has been good to us...he took them" (112).[10] His brutality is manifest. The babies are nothing to him. What matters is the appeasing of his sexual appetite.

Ellen, having overheard her father's repeated assaults and witnessed in her mother's body the wreckage of too many babies, refuses to give up her power to a man who might do the same to her; she determines to make her own life. In order not to have babies, she chooses to live without a husband. Irene Gammel argues that "the mother's legacy turns into a true discourse of power in her daughter's life," but it is a power that compels Ellen to reject "the role of wife-cum-child-bearer" (226). Ellen reverses her position only after Niels has married Mrs. Vogel, murdered her, and been released from prison after ten years. Grove's description of the pathetic Mrs. Amundsen, continually inducing miscarriage and destroying her own life, is vividly realistic. Ellen's vow to avoid her mother's fate makes sense in light of the brutal exchanges that she witnesses between her mother and father. Her mother's babies are unwanted, rejected in the most final manner. This is hard reality for Ellen and one that takes her years to overcome.

She acknowledges to Niels at the novel's end that her determination not to marry or have children remained firm "so long as [she] lived under the shadow of [her] mother's life." After all the tragedy of the novel—Ellen's loss of her mother and Niels's crime and punishment—there is a sudden, inexplicable change. Having lived with her choice and grown dissatisfied with it, Ellen says, "I knew then as I know now that it is my destiny and my greatest need to have children, children.... And I knew then as I know now that there is no man living on earth from whom I could accept them if not you" (217). What is to account for Ellen's radical change of heart? She repeats the word "children" as though she is astonished by her own admission. Ellen entertains the amazing possibility of having not just one child, but more than one. The plural is important since it complicates Atwood's notion of bad babies that appear in multiples: the babies are bad because there are so many of them and because their arrival necessitates an assault on the mother's personal resources. Nevertheless, Ellen wants "children." Her change in attitude in the context of this "realistic" novel seems highly romantic. Her sense that having children fulfills for her a personal destiny is constructed in idealistic terms. She must have children and she must have them from Niels. Her proximity to Niels, along with the possibility of a future life together, shared experience, and even love seem to motivate her to reassess her position in spite of the dreadful years of witnessing her mother's suffering. What is significant is the fact that Ellen chooses her destiny, whereas her mother did not. She makes a decision to have a life with Niels and to take on what that life will offer in the nature of hard work, companionship, sex, and babies.

If Ellen's view of babies is shaped by the harsh realities of her mother's life, Niels's view is informed by his immigrant desire to fulfill a vision of life in the New World. He immigrates to Canada hoping to establish a farm and a family. The reader is told how, "he had seen in his visions a wife and children" (39-40). Niels understands that his tenure is uncertain in the country of his adoption, but "if he had children, they would be rooted here.... He might become rooted himself, through them" (45). Children would provide him with a sense of belonging that he does not have on his own. But they must come from a worthy woman. There is tension in the novel between pure, matrimonial love that inspires Niels's settler vision—a love that produces wholesome domestic happiness, the natural extension of which is a baby—and the lust inspired by Mrs. Vogel that permits a dream of marriage but no children. While Ellen inspires in him tenderness and a zeal for hard work, Mrs. Vogel makes him feel "as if he were thrown back into chaos" (90). He is overcome by her sensuality, led like a sheep to slaughter, away from his vision of establishing his family in Canada and toward Mrs. Vogel's life of debauchery. Once he realizes the kind of match he has made, he understands that he cannot have children who "would be a perpetuation of the sin of the moment.... He did not want children out of this woman!" (138). Niels daydreams about "the vision again of that room where he sat with a woman, his wife. But no pitter-patter of little children's feet sounded down from above; nor were they sitting on opposite sides of a table in front of the fireplace" (56). The children are not actual, physical beings, but exist only in Niels's dream where they are represented synecdochically and simplistically as "pitter-patter." While Niels's vision is idealistic, Grove does not write sentimentally about the baby. There is no sense, as there is in Montgomery, of the fairy-tale sweetness of babies who are brought by the stork. Instead, babies are connected to Niels's vision of the future and to Ellen's understanding of her mother's past. It is in these two contradictory views of the baby that the tension is established between longing and rejection, between the ideal and the real. It is a tension that will be resolved in a surprisingly romantic fashion.

Niels's vision of family life is connected to his notion of purity. The infant is to be a marker of morality. It is a reward for a morally lived life, something he cannot accept as true since he committed the sin of fornication with Mrs. Vogel and then trapped himself into marriage. When he has served time in prison for killing her, Niels returns to the marsh and to Ellen whose newfound child-bearing destiny rekindles "a vision" that "arises between them, shared by both" (217). This is not compromise. Ellen acknowledges what must be an extremely visceral need, a need that is not primarily for Niels. When she announces her destiny, she states clearly that it is her "greatest need to have children," and secondarily, that the children must come from Niels (217). Grove here offers a blend of realism and romance in Ellen's serendipitous about-face. Ellen, who harbours no illusions about babies, wants suddenly and certainly to have them; Niels will be able to fulfill his dream of fathering children.

Grove's narrative probes the severe realities of pioneer life, but ends in a stunning fulfillment of both Niels's and Ellen's destinies that reconciles the infant as a site of loathing and of longing. Both Montgomery and Grove explore the infant's connection to death, a connection grounded in historical fact, considering maternal and infant mortality rates. Babies often died or caused their mothers to die. While babies were necessary for the survival of the family to the next generation, they were also impediments to women's individual survival, exhausting and expensive.

But women also long for babies. Ultimately, it is her sense of "greatest destiny," her longing for babies, that compels Ellen to overcome her mother's deathbed injunction against marriage and connect herself to Niels. Leslie Moore also wants a baby and struggles with violent jealousy when Anne gets pregnant. Anne herself configures the infant contradictorily. On one hand, she acknowledges the extreme difficulties for women who have too many babies; on the other hand, Anne's life is infused with the joy of her own infants, even while she speaks of them in terms at once idealistically sentimental and oblique. Babies spend much of the first half of the twentieth century in the margins of stories like Grove's and Montgomery's. They are both present and absent—present in the sense of being a threat, an obstacle, and more often a site of rejection than desire. Babies are absent in the sense that they do not take up much space in the stories. Where they do occur, babies are often constructed in the texts within a binary distinction between the real—that which inspires rejection—and the ideal—that which inspires longing. This proves to be an often flimsy distinction for women. The instability of the binary is made evident upon challenging the notion that beauty or joy as they exist in the figure of the baby necessarily form an idealistic view and that the suffering and exhaustion caused by the baby are the only actual truth. A nuanced reading of the figure of the baby compels one to lift it from the margins and from the oppositions by which it is represented to come to a fuller understanding of its significance.

CHAPTER 2

Two Men and a Lady: (Il)legitimacy in Infant Representation 1940-60

Early twentieth-century babies, as Montgomery and Grove wrote about them, were sites of tension between desire and rejection, and to a degree, between romantic ideal and hard reality. Illegitimacy does not present itself as an issue in these early texts, but that changes in the writing of the middle decades of the twentieth century. Infants have often served as social markers for their parents, markers of both personal identity and social status. Anne's babies give her the fulfillment of her dreams even while Mrs. Proctor's exhaust her; the desire for babies ignites Niels's quest for stability in Canada even while the repeated pregnancies of Mrs. Amundsen erode her health. In fiction of the 1940s and '50s, the focus shifts with writers' emerging candour about social issues like illegitimacy. With that candour comes a transformation in the representation of infants who, although they are still sites of tremendous longing and equally compelling rejection, are now inscribed as citizens who must also meet standards of acceptance. While Montgomery and Grove, among others, wrote about babies as objects of desire or as burdens, the infants themselves are all born within marriage.[1] Babies are markers of status, a status influenced by their legitimate or illegitimate conception and also influenced by the degree to which their parents can afford to have them.

Writers begin to explore in more depth the question of illegitimacy, some inscribing the standards of a society intent on preserving the name of the father, some resisting the stigmatization that occurs when a woman has a baby without being married. Coming out of the Great

Depression and during World War II, baby advice experts had begun encouraging women to raise good citizens who would contribute to the country's well-being.[2] The proper prerequisite for this good citizen included being the offspring of married parents. But there is a sense of a slow ideological modification emerging in these decades that will come to fruition in the next thirty years.

Several novels explore the shame associated with unwed pregnancy. In their sensitive exploration of the burden caused by an illegitimate baby to its mother, writers begin the process of changing social ideas about legitimacy. The novels usually express an implicit or explicit need to rehabilitate both mother and child, to bring them back into the fold of properly behaving members of the community. There are limited possibilities for redemption. Usually the pregnant woman must either die or be married and, even if she marries, chances are she might still have to die. Sexual transgression resulting in pregnancy in the novels is met with stern repercussions. The infant survives because its mother finds an honourable way back to social acceptance through marriage, or because married people adopt it. The authors are often less concerned with the state of infancy or the character of the infant, and more concerned with what the baby, or the pregnancy, represents. Babies begin in these decades to move from the margins of text to a more central position that is shaped by propriety to be sure, but the movement is critical in understanding the growing significance of the infant in literature. It's compelling, furthermore, that even as writers acknowledge the social restrictions of legitimacy, in some cases, the authors' intricate portrayal of the levels of stigma associated with illegitimacy works against the dominant ideology, and nurtures sympathy for both the woman and the baby she will bear.

Writers are engaged in both what Terry Eagleton calls "the process of legitimation" (5) and the process of destabilization. Sinclair Ross's *As for Me and My House* (1941), Charles Tory Bruce's *The Channel Shore* (1954) and Gabrielle Roy's *The Tin Flute* (1947) explore issues surrounding the birth of babies. The texts examine the problem of babies born out of wedlock and the concomitant connection with moral weakness and lust. In this, they subscribe to a dominant ideology of propriety—the parameters of proper conception. Illegitimacy is the concern of men who, as Mary O'Brien claims, are alienated from the process of reproduction (36), "separated from biological continuity" (36) and who "annul the alienation of their seed" by appropriating the child, by giving him or her a name (O'Brien 37). This notion of legitimacy being men's concern is also explored by Adrienne Rich who defines a baby as illegitimate when it is born "without the father's name" (*Of Woman Born* 42). She argues that illegitimacy is among the deviant or criminal behaviour that threatens "male interests" (24) in the "social institutions and prescriptions for behavior created by men" (24). While Ross's text and Buckler's tacitly conform to an ideology that condemns the woman, if not the baby, both Bruce and Roy begin to destabilize assumptions about propriety in subtle ways that manifest and inspire sympathy for the devastating effects of transgression on individual women's lives and that foreground the baby's importance in and of itself. These writers begin opening up perception to the infant's value apart from mainstream social convention, a process that several women writers in the coming years will build upon.

The texts explore the stigmatization of illegitimacy, as characters consider how to protect the child from the knowledge of its improper birth. Illegitimacy has consequences both for the woman and for the infant to the extent that one must examine mother and baby together in order to understand how the authors simultaneously inscribe and yet also resist propriety. What begins to happen in these novels is a strange legitimizing—in the social/political sense in which Eagleton uses the term—of what has been considered illegitimacy. The question of society's acceptance of the illegitimate baby, assuming the baby survives, is intrinsic to the social response to the mother. However, even considering the two, infant and mother together, these texts simultaneously reinforce and subvert what Eagleton has called the "naturalization" of ideological value as it relates to legitimacy (5). If ideology is bound up with the interests of perpetuating a certain view of life and propriety—or for that matter, challenging that view—then the question to answer is what role the infant plays in either case. Furthermore, there is sharp contrast between Ross and Bruce, both male writers for whom the infant exists at the perimeter of experience, and Gabrielle Roy, who conveys women's intimate experience of pregnancy, childbirth, and babies. As Mary O'Brien argues and Di Brandt affirms, "the moment of childbirth...is a crucial moment in the making of human history, since it is the moment when our continuity as a species, from one generation to another...is most clearly affirmed through the basic fact of women's reproductive experience" (Brandt 12-13). It is in the writing of Gabrielle Roy that the focus on the importance of childbirth is evident, the baby's value unequivocal for the moments after its birth regardless of the social and economic context of its arrival.

Within the context of wartime good citizenship, and his rigid Scots-Presbyterian background, Sinclair Ross wrote *As for Me and My House*. Ross's text is critical to an analysis of infant representation because it is one of the few examples of writing by men in these decades where the infant plays a significant role. Moreover, it makes exemplary use of the dominant ideology of the day that requires punishment in literary texts for the sins of adultery and illegitimacy. Furthermore, for decades since its publication, Sinclair Ross's prairie novel has been canonized as a Canadian "classic." David Stouck, whose study compiles fifty years of Ross criticism, describes how the book "was hailed as an important work of fiction and Ross was seen as a young author with great promise" (5). An early *Globe and Mail* review states that "in social significance no less than because of the uncompromisingly sincere craftsmanship, the novel attains a certain importance to Canada.... He is interpreting contemporary Canadian life earnestly and skillfully" (qtd. in Stouck 19). Ross's interpretation of contemporary life places great importance on the infant as a figure that has the potential to save marriages and draw the alienated principal characters—the Bentleys—together. Other critics, including Robert Kroetsch and John Moss, have examined the novel in terms of its salient oppositional motifs, specifically house/horse, stasis/motion, garden/desert, and his art/her piano playing, among others. But what remains consistent in the novel is the need to create, attenuated by the overarching longing for a baby to fulfill this need.[3] Ken Mitchell says in 1981 that "through Sinclair Ross's writing we are empowered to see past social manners, to penetrate hypocrisy and obfuscation, to perceive directly the rhythm of life in process" (76). Ross's ability to see through hypocrisy and obfuscation has been called into question by the most recent critical scrutiny of his work and his life, so that Mitchell's assertion is ironic in retrospect. In current critical analyses of Ross's text, there is a layering of illegitimacies that complicate the role of the infant.[4] The novel deals with the straightforward adultery and consequent baby that Philip fathers, but it also carries with it a homoerotic subtext in light of what has come to be known about Sinclair Ross himself.

Perceptions about Ross's text have undergone major revision since the release of Keath Fraser's biographical memoir in 1997, *As for Me and My Body*. Fraser says that it took Ross four years of friendship before he

would admit that his novel, *As for Me and My House* is, in fact, homoerotic (41).[5] Fraser's view is that because of the novel's central hypocrisy,
the failure to acknowledge the homoerotic imagery and "make it matter
with respect to the plot," Philip's character is "misread," the novel itself
forced into "a dramatically unsatisfying resolution, a kind of syrupy
dénouement" (*As for Me and My Body* 53). It is in the "syrupy dénouement" that the baby makes its appearance and in the context of Ross's
intentional or unintentional reference to a homoerotic subtext, that the
baby becomes significant in ways more textured and more tangled.[6]

The novel is haunted by the absent baby. There is no sense, in spite
of their poverty, that a baby would be an added burden as it is for
Mrs. Amundsen in *Settlers of the Marsh*. On the contrary, the baby is the
locus of the couple's hopes, Philip's for success by proxy and Mrs. Bentley's for their marriage. Having grown up with the stigma of illegitimacy, Philip has been shaped by years of bitterness and self-loathing
and he spends much of the novel searching for a way to alleviate that
loathing. Philip wants a baby to redeem his past hardships for which he
holds his mother responsible, coming to feel "that for all the ridicule
and shame he was exposed to, it was his mother to blame.... The early
years had left an imprint that was not to be erased by sentiment or reason" (40). Mrs. Bentley has obviously tried both sentiment and reason
to assuage some of the imprint left on Philip by growing up listening to
the "drunken customers... who laughed suggestively about his mother
and his birth" (40). In some ways, the notion of illegitimacy here could
be seen as a red herring, distracting readers for years from the sexual
subtext that Ross himself concealed almost to the end of his life. Nevertheless, it corresponds to moral strictures of the time and contributes
to the overwhelming sense of frustration and failure that both the Bentleys feel.

Valerie Raoul argues in "Straight or Bent: Textual/Sexual T(ri)angles"
in *As for Me and My House* that "in spite of their irreconcilable differences, the Bentleys do not renounce the desire to found a 'house,' a lineage" (17). Indeed, they build it up as their only hope. But Philip hopes
for a son in order to see a reflection of himself. He already sees Steve as
an "unwanted, derided little outcast, exactly what he used to be himself" (70). Keath Fraser finds that the "double image of Philip becomes
increasingly narcissistic as the novel unfolds. Lacking self love he seems
obsessed with finding it" (48) whether through Steve or through his and
Judith's baby.

Mrs. Bentley characterizes Philip's relationship with Steve in terms that reflect her unease with its symbiosis. She states that Steve is "ominously good-looking" (54), that she "seemed to feel [herself] vaguely threatened" (56) in his presence, and that Philip's hands on Steve's shoulders are "so firm and possessive" (70) and provoke her response of nervous laughter. Philip's purpose for the boy is evident to Mrs. Bentley who says, "Philip brought him out of the bedroom dressed up in his new clothes. He had on one of Philip's ties. His head was up; there was a little glint in his eyes.... [Philip] starts in to dream and plan for the boy it's his own life over again. Steve is to carry on where he left off. Steve is to do the things he tried to do and failed" (69-70). Philip dresses Steve in his own tie, that male symbol of maturity and propriety. In Steve he sees someone who is marginalized, as he was, and who has a chance of succeeding where he himself has not. The suggestion that the child is a reflection or extension of the parent comes into play more significantly after the loss of Steve and arrival of Judith's baby.

The baby appears at the end of the novel as a plot device. As Atwood has argued, this is something in the nature of "the Baby Ex Machina" that solves "all the problems for the characters which they obviously can't solve for themselves" (*Survival* 207). But Atwood insists that the baby ex machina will not afford any real or lasting solution. However, initially, the Bentleys' baby appears to be a source of strange redemption for Philip, as well as for Mrs. Bentley. Throughout the novel, Mrs. Bentley has iterated her desire for a child, specifically a son. She looks at her "dull bare walls" and wishes: "huddling there I wished for a son again, a son that I might give back a little of what I've taken from him, that I might at least believe I haven't altogether wasted him, only postponed to another generation his fulfillment. A foolish, sentimental wish that I ought to have outgrown years ago" (7-8). Mrs. Bentley has her shoulders up against her ears, cowering against both the present and future and against their inescapable lack. She wants to redeem Philip's present and past by offering him "fulfillment," even fulfillment "postponed to another generation." This longing is one she recognizes as sentimental. She gave birth to a "baby, stillborn" (45) the year after their marriage and has not produced another in the subsequent years. One has to consider what sorrow is accommodated by that single comma between "baby" and "stillborn." Mrs. Bentley wants a baby in order to expunge the misery of her husband's life, to give them

both some sense of future possibility, some hope that their lives are legitimate and meaningful.

It is, perversely, through illegitimate means that the Bentleys achieve this sense of legitimacy. Philip Bentley's response to the hypocrisy and emptiness of his life is to have an illegitimate child with Judith West who is "slim and frail," with a "white face," and "a childlike, wistful look" (74-75). Judith's frailty is significant since she also proves to be both physically and morally weak. The narrator states, "Judith is going to have a baby" (192) and offers a comment to her husband on the "kind of girl" Judith is, the kind "that unless she cared a great deal for someone—" (192). The open-ended sentence offers some slight mitigation in the face of a censorious community of Judith's sexual activity.[7] Knowing what she does about her husband's infidelity, Mrs. Bentley's refusal to complete the thought can be a sly reference to the object of Judith's care, or it could be considered a refusal to judge Judith harshly. The narrator expresses certainty that Judith could not have transgressed unless she had been moved to do so by profound "caring" for the person. In any case, in accordance with an ideological concern to preserve social strictures against immorality—women's immorality, not men's—Judith pays for her transgression with her life. This is consistent with other novels of the time that explore the issue of illegitimacy or sexual trangression.[8] Interestingly, Ross himself felt "he'd taken the easy way out" by killing Judith off (Fraser 53). Fraser recalls that Ross told him he "wished to rewrite the ending by keeping Judith West alive and her baby from the Bentleys" (53).

Ross's text does not explicitly undermine the notion that illegitimacy should be punished. However, his depiction of Mrs. Bentley, wrestling with her own repugnance toward Judith and then demanding Judith's baby to raise, certainly suggests Judith's punishment is excessively cruel. It may be true that, as Valerie Raoul asserts, Mrs. Bentley wants to satisfy a deep yearning of her own, that having given birth to a stillborn, and subscribing "to the belief that being a 'real woman' necessarily entails motherhood" (Raoul 17), she longs to be a mother. "Indeed," as Raoul asserts, "Mrs. Bentley has to restrain herself from mothering her husband, needing so badly to mother something" (17). Nevertheless, the prospect of accepting Judith's baby fills Mrs. Bentley with "bitterness." She writes, "I felt my blood go thin, and my lips set hard and cruel" (204). The word choice is compelling since it is clear that Mrs. Bentley will incorporate all means, including hard and cruel ones, to persuade her husband that he must convince Judith of the necessity of giving up her baby. She insists that Philip must make Judith agree never to see the baby, never to see them, again, insisting, "I want it to be my baby—my son. I won't let her remind me that it isn't" (204). Mrs. Bentley wants the question of ownership and possession settled, but not for the baby's good, although she does urge Philip to use this argument when she encourages him to tell Judith that they will give the child "opportunity and a name" (204).[9] Mrs. Bentley has leverage. She knows about Philip's past and the effect it has had on him and she knows how to use it against him. She presses her point further, almost torturing both Philip and Judith with the certain knowledge that the child will suffer lifelong repercussions if Judith does not agree. She insists, "Tell her how he will suffer if she keeps him, grow up and eventually hate her" (204). Mrs. Bentley ruthlessly exploits Philip's own life experience against him in her determination to get the baby and save whatever life she can have with her husband.

Regardless of her anxiety, her wish that "the baby were here, and we were away with it" (210-11), and the degree of guilt that she feels at taking the baby from its mother (a mother who will "haunt" them for a long time, "with that queer, white face of hers" [211]), Mrs. Bentley's determination is frightening. If Ross implicitly undermines the text's explicit condemnation of Judith, it's by the heavy irony he uses when describing the Bentleys' "charity" in taking in an illegitimate infant. Judith, who has always been a ghostly figure in the text, no sooner provides the Bentleys with a baby, than she politely dies without a whisper of blame toward the man who made her pregnant.[10] When Judith's mother brings the baby to Mrs. Bentley, she says, "that her family had never before been brought to shame" and that Mr. and Mrs. Bentley "are good people...real Christians" (211). Setting aside, for the moment, the homoerotic subtext of the novel, the overt text itself reinforces the dominant ideology. Bringing her family to shame costs Judith her life. However, Ross's side-by-side use of the words "shame" to describe Judith, and "good people," "real Christians" to describe the Bentleys, borders on sarcasm. Mrs. Bentley is feral, ferocious in her determination to take that baby and raise it and save her marriage. The discrepancy in the Bentley household between their reputation as "good Christians" and their life within the four walls of the house, a life characterized by animosity and turgid silences, undermines the force of Judith's punishment by calling into question the righteousness of those who punish. Furthermore, when Judith dies the narrator's relief is pal-pable. She admits that Judith's death is "what I've secretly been hoping for all along. I'm glad she's gone—glad—for her sake as much as ours. What was there ahead of her now anyway?" (212). The desire both for the infant and for some kind of revenge not on the husband but on the transgressing "other woman," renders Mrs. Bentley bloodthirsty and appalling.

Nevertheless, she accomplishes her desire. Her possession of the baby provides a connection to her husband that the narrator has never been able to forge herself. She admits to him what she "had always known," that she had "wanted the baby so that in time his son would be my son too" (214). With this admission, Mrs. Bentley can no longer face her husband. She has admitted her need of him, a need that over-rides both his unfaithfulness and his disquieting attraction to boys. The baby will supposedly bind her to him and will, perforce, bind Philip to her. The baby gives her power to change their relationship. Mrs. Bent-ley is immediately comfortable holding and caring for the baby because of his helplessness and his need of her. She says, "I have an easy, relaxed feeling that the rest now makes no difference" (211-12). What is most disturbing about her relationship to the baby is that its utter help-lessness, indeed its very ugliness, evoke feelings of confidence in her, that "easy, relaxed feeling" that enables her to care for it. Mrs. Bentley is repeatedly stymied in her efforts to care for her husband. Presum-ably, the baby offers her a fresh opportunity to do a better job.

Like all babies, this one is small. Mrs. Bentley writes that he is "mostly lungs and diapers" but that they "like him" (217). The synec-dochical description of the baby as "lungs and diapers" contributes to a sense that he makes noisy demands for attention and physical care and that he has not occupied a space at the centre of their lives, but is merely likable. What Mrs. Bentley sees when she looks closely is that Philip "is starting to look like [the baby]," that they both have a "stillness, a fresh-ness, *a vacancy of beginning*" (216, my emphasis). In this "vacancy of beginning," Philip begins to resemble the baby, rather than vice versa. This is the clean slate articulated. As such, the baby is constituted as a site of potential worth rather than present worth. Keath Fraser writes of the baby's role that the "complex relationship of Philip and son is intended to mirror his past, I think, to reflect his abiding feelings of loss as a bastard himself, to see in his stillborn son and dead preacher father, not to mention a consolation of sorts for losing Steve, his adopted son, and possibly even to show off the infant as a sort of heterosexual trophy. The pattern-making is pronounced" (*As for Me and My Body* 63).

For Philip, the baby is a much more complex figure of dubious redemption. His new son carries not only the burden of Philip's own past, but also the burden of hope for the future. However, the narrator's choice to name the baby after her morose husband, combined with her desire to be confused sometimes about which Philip is which (216), does not establish hope that the future will be better, baby or not. Keath Fraser finds the last line of the story—Mrs. Bentley's assertion that she wants "it that way," that she wants to confuse the two Philips—most disturbing. He refers to Philip's concern that she will be confused as "self-satisfied." For Fraser, the ending is "facile, self-regarding, or even incestuous," and alludes to the disturbing "incestuous" suggestion implicit at the novel's end when one considers Philip's attraction to boys (*As for Me and My Body* 62). But in light of Ross's own admissions about the homosexual gestures in the text, Fraser's statement that the conclusion of the novel is "incestuous" is troublesome. Mrs. Bentley has not been the character to convey confusing sexual messages. It's unlikely that her desire for confusion relates in a sexual way to the baby, especially since her marriage seems singularly lacking in physical contact, intimate or otherwise. It makes sense to me that Philip's relationship with the baby should be facile and self-regarding since this is how Philip's character has revealed itself throughout the text. But I think the suggestion of incest overstates the case.

Valerie Raoul acknowledges the Bentleys' need of a son who will "bear Philip's name and be confused with him" in order that "the winding and tenuous Bentley line" will continue (18). Thus, the Bentleys establish a lineage creating "a semblance of the patriarchal oedipal triangle" (Raoul 18). Timothy Cramer believes that Philip's relationship with his son will fall "from idealistic to realistic" and that "Philip will once again find himself withdrawing" (59). Mrs. Bentley supports that notion of a fall from ideal to real since she's witnessed Philip idealize his relationship with Steve. This, to me, suggests that he may be doing the same thing with the baby. Regarding Steve, Mrs. Bentley states that once Philip's "pity and imagination" run out, their adopted son will be "left just an ordinary, uninspiring boy" (71). Similarly, Philip "just stands and looks and looks at [the baby], and puts his cheek down close to the little hands" (216). The fascinated eye contact and proximity offer an intimation of that same idealism. There is no doubt that the Bent-

leys' baby, all "lungs and diapers," is an ordinary one and will, perhaps, prove equally uninspiring.

In any case, the baby as it appears in the text is granted legitimacy so that it can in turn grant cohesion and meaning to the Bentleys' lives. Current critical examinations of this Canadian novel have compelled a reassessment of the troublesome relationship of the Bentleys. Re-examination of Philip's character and the significance of the baby indicate that both are legitimized by the false front of the Bentleys' marriage.

Like Judith, Hazel in Charles Bruce's *The Channel Shore* also pays for her child's illegitimacy with her life. Bruce's novel has received little critical attention, a fact that critics who do write about it do not fail to note. A.T. Seaman says, "*The Channel Shore* remains largely untested by literary criticism" (159). J.A. Wainwright remarks that "the fiction of Charles Bruce is not mentioned in the *Literary History of Canada*...nor have contemporary critics, with the exception of John Moss, paid much attention to Bruce's prose writings" (238). However, as Janice Kulyk Keefer acknowledges, "*The Channel Shore* gives us a way of knowing our world, a perspective which helps us to question and test the truth of inherited or imposed schemas" (9). Moss writes that the issue of illegitimacy "provides the basic plot structure, the moral conditions to be resolved" (*Patterns of Isolation* 189). While critics like Moss and Kulyk Keefer have focused on the distinctive qualities of Maritime fiction, and more specifically, on the nature of community as it unfolds on the Shore, as a figure central to the novel's unfolding, the infant has been neglected. Yet Hazel's illegitimate baby is the focus of the novel's concern with the community and its mores.

Hazel gets herself "talked about" (9) because she is spending more time than is considered proper with a young man named Anse. Hazel is a girl with dreams. She imagines being a singer, "But it wasn't practical. Music had no place on the Shore except in church concerts" (10). Life on the Channel Shore is steeped in tradition and practicality. The only escape from a future of marriage and babies was to go into "household service" or learn stenography or teach school. This is not a future that Hazel can face with equanimity. Hazel is curious about her body. She is curious about what life might have to offer, particularly about the threshold between innocence and experience, which she knows carries with it some mysterious importance, "almost like birth and death." The significance of this transition from girl to woman is "implied in every attitude of the women and girls she knew: the care for reputation, the

fuss over weddings, the tight-lipped shock at transgression" (13). Hazel
seems to know intuitively that this care for reputation is a socially constructed care, far removed from sensual experience or desire.

Hazel is distracted by the possibility of transgression and the potential freedom from tradition that might accompany misbehaviour. Her
interest in Anse is as much a function of her curiosity as it is a result of
her rebellion. Hazel becomes pregnant because of her sexual curiosity
and rebellion, and because of her ambition to do something with her
life that reaches beyond the strict limitations of tradition. Instead of
being put off by the "tight-lipped shock at transgression," Hazel finds
transgression seductive. Thus, part of what forms her nature will result
in the destruction of her reputation and the destruction of her life. Most
importantly, Hazel's sexual curiosity will result in a baby who will
eventually have to come to terms with his illegitimacy.

Hazel compares the sensation of waiting for Anse to the cold
spring water of Graham's Lake: "What she felt in her marrow now, a
thousand times intensified, was the dark excitement, the chill of the
lake, its cold insistent meaningless message along the nerves of the
lower body, the breast, the mind" (14). On the Channel Shore, while
illicit sexual awakening is characterized as exciting and intense, it is
also rhetorically constructed in terms of a *dark, chill, cold, meaningless*
assault on the "*lower* body, the breast, the mind." Bruce's use of the
word "meaningless" suggests that Hazel's sensuality offers her an
escape from a life fraught with meaning, with strictures about present
conduct and about her future role as a wife and mother. It's interesting
also that intensity of passion and excitement are chilling, not warming.
As for Anse, he seeks out Hazel because of her "spark of life or daring
or discontent that livened to meet him" (15). Her daring and discontent will cause Hazel to eagerly flout the sanctions of her community
and pay the price with her life. However, her daring and discontent
make her among the most engaging characters of this decade. Hazel is
alive to the possibilities of life, responsive and engaged. In this sense,
Bruce has created an extremely sympathetic character of depth and
dimension.

Hazel's fear of pregnancy grows in "her mind and flesh":

> Hazel tried to find relief from this sense of being watched and con-
> sidered, and from the fear that was overtaking her.
>   She was not sure when this sense of fear and foreboding had
> become definite. At the time of Anse's disappearance, there had

been nothing but the vaguest sort of doubt.... Gradually it had
grown, was growing, in her mind and flesh.
    She felt the flush of it now. (62)

Instead of growing a baby within, Hazel grows "fear and foreboding."
With that fear comes the sensation of heat, the "flush" that, strangely,
did not accompany her sexual awakening with Anse. She imagines
going to the doctor to have her fear confirmed, to hear him say, "'we'll
have to talk to your mother'" (62). She remains silent, exhausting herself with the haying, until she wakes up one morning knowing "she
could not bear, alone, the burden of her fear" (64). Bruce reiterates the
fact of Hazel's fear, as though it is impossible to overstate the case. Her
fear becomes unbearable. Facing her father, Hazel is disconsolate. She
realizes that "there was nothing here to end aloneness.... For this
instant her mind swam in the depths of a blind sea, lost and without
hope, and there was nothing she could say" (66). She is without excuse
before the moral uprightness of her father and all that he represents in
terms of traditional life on the Channel Shore. Her separation from that
life leaves her alone, in "a blind sea, lost and without hope" (66). If
Hazel were able to continue in her attitude of curiosity and engagement with life, she might be able to make a life with the baby, regardless of the stigma of illegitimacy. But the fact is that she is complicit in
the community value system. She understands herself to be in the
wrong and she knows all too well what kind of response the news of
her baby will engender among her people. Although curious, Hazel is
not involved fundamentally in any conflict of value. Therefore, she is
lost. Having already been characterized as "no good" and "wild" (8),
Anse is long gone and Hazel is speechless in the enormity of her isolation from her family and her community. Her father invites her to
unburden herself and though her fear "vanishes," she must, nevertheless, bear the burden of her transgression both literally and figuratively.
Hazel is banished from the Shore to live and work in Toronto, to cope,
as best she might, with the pregnancy, the lies about a dead husband,
and the curiosity of strangers.
    Anse's mother, Josie Gordon, after the death of her own young
daughter, reminds Grant Marshall that there is still "a girl alive...a child
maybe" (165), people still within reach of being saved. Josie's concern,
as Grant perceives it, speaks to the difference between death and
shame. Josie's daughter, Anna, has been tragically killed. Over time,
Grant knows, "Josie would reach that sort of peace," an acceptance of

death that comes over time (165), that although Anna is dead, "there is
no shame" (165) attached to that fact, no deliberate action through
which her family has been made to suffer. However, the shame of
unwed pregnancy would never dissipate. We are told, "Shame was
another thing. To Josie, shame was another thing. This now [Grant]
understood. A time would come when the sound of Anna's name
would be a small and distant bell, a sweet faint ringing in the mind. But
what of Hazel McKee?" (165).

Anna's name would always be marked by "sweetness." It would
resonate through the years like a "small and distant bell." But Hazel's
name would, without redemption, be a source of shame in the memories of her family and community. The disgrace of her son's act and the
shame borne by Hazel McKee would never die in Josie's mind, either.
Since her son will not put things right, she asks her foster-son to do it
for her. The gesture seems indicative of the possibility, if not the necessity, of forgiveness. The baby and the mother must be saved and
brought back into community. The narrator says, "Now the heart of it
was clear, a thing of flesh and blood, as much a part of life as the people who faced it: There's a girl alive…a girl alive…a child" (166). Grant
is motivated to action because he understands the heart of the matter—
the girl and the child who must be saved. As Kulyk Keefer sees it, "by
restoring Hazel to the community and by legitimizing Alan, Grant
secures for Hazel's parents their necessary role and rights as grandpar-
ents" (57). Grant's action is not simply a function of duty, but rather,
when he is "told by the keenly suffering Josie of Hazel's pregnancy and
consequent disgrace, [he] is conscious of a fundamental altering of his
perceptions" (Kulyk Keefer 61). Hazel's story becomes for him one of
flesh and blood, personal and integral. His attachment to her baby
takes on similar qualities. But for Kulyk Keefer, Hazel's pregnancy is
parenthetical. The baby is itself the magnet that polarizes the community so that the good members conspire to protect him from the taint of
his own origins. In any case, Grant redeems Hazel McKee's name,
removing it from its perpetual association with shame. Hazel becomes
for Grant "a thing of flesh and blood" rather than the main character in
a story of "hard disgrace" (166). He cannot ignore her need.

Grant wants to help Hazel and he wants also to be helped. What he
and Hazel learn from each other is that "not a damn thing matters but
what people can do for each other when they're up against it" (208).
Grant's statement insists that the focus be shifted from propriety to

human kindness and understanding. As Kulyk Keefer declares, the focus turns on "the deepening and widening of community loyalty and love" (55). These become centred on the infant, Alan. Now married, Hazel wants to return to the Shore "in a kind of bitter honour to the country she fled from" (210). Having borne the shame of fornication and illegitimate pregnancy, Hazel has been brought back into the fold of community through the only permissible means: marriage. In her short life with Grant, it occurs to her that she may not survive the pregnancy. No explanation is offered about why a healthy young woman should die from being pregnant; however, Hazel, who, Grant believes, must have "sensed" something, solicits Grant's promise, placing his hand on her "swollen belly," that if anything happens, Grant will raise Hazel's baby as his own (211).[11]

The shame of his illegitimate beginnings haunts the child, Alan, until he learns the truth about his parentage from his maternal grandmother. This haunting takes the form of indecipherable taunts from the boys at school and references made by the wretched Vangie Murphy who refers to Hazel as the woman whose "belly" was "filled by Anse Gordon" (227). As Philip Bentley's baby was configured synecdochically as "lungs and diapers," so also is Alan composed metonymically as Hazel's "swollen belly." The baby is constituted by his parts or by what conceals him. He is not a whole entity and when he appears, he does so only briefly. Alan himself remains a baby for only a sentence in the text. The narrator tells how Alan was "helpless in the cradle; black-haired and mischievous in the playpen" (211). The reference is brief, but his existence is vital to the plot's unfolding. Josie Gordon summarizes: "something wrong was done, years ago. Grant Marshall made it right" (229). The baby offers Grant a chance to redeem his own life from the shame of rejecting Anna. Grant's marriage to Hazel alleviates the burden of her shame. The plot is driven forward by the tension between shame and redemption and the infant serves as the device that propels these forces.

Bruce's novel comes out of a time when women were just beginning to move out of the parental home and live on their own (Prentice et al. 319). As well, premarital sex "continued to be socially unacceptable for 'respectable' young women" (320). The social taboos against unmarried sex and against illegitimacy were firmly in place, and the novel would seem to support such values. But Hazel, Alan, and even Anse are met with a degree of sympathy in the narrative that mitigates

the condemnation and draws attention to the suffering and loneliness
of a young girl. Vangie Murphy, the most odious character in the book,
a woman with "something in the smile and the husky ingratiating
voice" that sets "up a current of revulsion" (227) in people she encounters, is the only adult to offer innuendo about Alan. Her harsh judgement ignites the instinct of the people around her to safeguard Alan
and support him. Bruce's project is innovative according to Kulyk
Keefer, an "impassioned attempt to transform, redeem and, for coming
generations validate the concept of community" (61). The sympathetic
depiction of Hazel ameliorates the tendency to judge her, and permits
a sense that the infant's value is not contingent on the circumstances of
its conception or birth, that it should, no matter what, be protected and
nurtured by the community.

Gabrielle Roy also mitigates the contingent value of babies who are
both legitimate and illegitimate, giving voice to the particular hardships
and joys inherent in both circumstances. Roy's *The Tin Flute* is an intricate rendering of the problems of city life; it is also important to a study
of infant representations for a variety of reasons, including its focus on
the burdens of poverty and illegitimacy as they have an impact upon
women. According to Patrick Coleman, Roy's first novel "arose out of
her indignation of the condition endured by the poor people of Montreal. Her unflinching portrayal of their suffering and broken hopes set
a new standard for realistic fiction in Canada" (13). *The Tin Flute* is also
significant because of its prominence as a widely read Canadian novel
that has "attracted an enthusiastic and wide-ranging international
readership" (Clemente 149) and garnered for Roy the Médaille "Feu qui
dure," the Médaille Richelieu in Québec, the Governor General's
award in Canada, the Prix Femina in Paris, and selection as a Literary
Guild book of the month. As well, it was subsequently translated into
at least fourteen other languages (Clemente 149). There can be no
doubt as to the book's immediate and enduring popularity, but, as
Agnes Whitfield claims, "traditional critical approaches have, themselves, obscured feminist elements in Gabrielle Roy's writing" (20). Roy
explores the shame that accompanies both unwed pregnancy and
poverty. In both contexts, babies are a curse. However, Roy's compassion for women in difficult straits extends to her figuring of the infants
they bear. Thus, even as hindrances to survival, babies simultaneously
traverse a delicate line between the considerable difficulties they present in these contexts and the untenable sense of hope that they never-

theless inspire. Roy articulates the tremendous obstacles both for Florentine, who is pregnant and not married, and for her mother, Rose-Anna, who is pregnant with her twelfth child and poor, yet she does so without demonizing the infant or marginalizing it.

Babies in these narratives foreground the lives and difficulties of the women who bear them; relatively little attention is paid to infants themselves in these texts. While it may seem strange to draw here on the thoughts of an African American theorist and writer, there are provocative similarities evident between the invisibility of blacks in literature and infants in literature. In "Black Matters," Toni Morrison claims that her "assumptions as a reader were that black people signified little or nothing in the imagination of white American writers" reflecting "the marginal impact that blacks had on the lives of the characters in the work as well as in the creative imagination of the author" (15). That blacks were present in American literature, in whatever peripheral capacity, made Morrison want to "identify those moments when American literature was complicit in the fabrication of racism, but equally important...to see when literature exploded and undermined it" (16). Similarly, my desire is not only to identify the infant in writing as a figure that complies with social impositions of value contingent on legitimacy, but also to identify the beginnings of the manner in which writers "explode" such contingencies of value. There are plenty of babies in Roy's writing, but her focus is essentially on their effects, rather than on the babies themselves. This indirect focus indicates that infants act not as agents in the lives of the people around them, but rather as devices. However, Roy's voice is significant because of her authentication of intimate female experience. She has insight that seems to me to be lacking in the previous two male representations, insights that go even further in the move to explode contingent value.

Barbara Godard has argued that "any activity which seeks to place the female in a position of equality with respect to males in society and literature" ("Mapmaking" 20) is by definition a feminist activity. Roy creates a fictional world that reveals in stark detail the inequality in the lives of men and women, a feminist revelation in its impulse since it demands acknowledgement of injustice and inequality. Central to this inequality is the figure of the baby, a figure of tremendous constraint for women who live in poverty, even while it has the potential to inspire hope. The men who sire the babies in the text are at liberty to walk away, as in the case of Jean, or to live alongside the mothers but without taking responsibility for the babies. Azarius is a case in point. Even while the text unfolds a theme of devoted motherhood in the character of Rose-Anna, it also baldly exposes inequality and the exigencies to which such inequality drives women. Gendered divisions of responsibility for parenting are described by Adrienne Rich, who says that "to 'father' a child suggests above all to beget, to provide the sperm which fertilizes the ovum. To 'mother' a child implies a continuing presence, lasting at least nine months, more often for years" (*Of Woman* xiv). Roy calls attention to men's lack of involvement in childbirth and the care of infant, a lack that Di Brandt describes as, "reproductive consciousness...[which] would mean responsible parenting (literally and figuratively) by both sexes, which could lead to a partnership in caretaking wholly unlike the history of domination and submission that has characterized gender relations under patriarchy" (17). These unequal gender relations as they concern infants occupy a good part of Roy's focus in the novel.

Patrick Coleman's thesis is that Roy's writing in *The Tin Flute* is characterized by a determination to change the "idealistic, sentimental terms" in which women had previously been portrayed in fiction (18). This change ignited new Canadian writers. For example, Margaret Laurence recalls: "When I read *The Tin Flute* for the first time, I began to understand what a woman writer can do, in portraying woman characters" (qtd. in Coleman 18). Marian Engel also comments that the publication of *The Tin Flute* "signalled a turning point in women's fiction from the work of 'lady novelists' to that of 'serious women writers'" (qtd. in Brady 187). Engel explains: "It was Gabrielle Roy who first brought that life my mother's generation called 'sordid' to women's writing in Canada. *The Tin Flute* was a body-blow to the genteel tradition" (qtd. in Brady 187).

The representation of the "sordid" begins with Roy's most unsentimental and complex character, Florentine Lacasse. In an exploration of the issue of illegitimacy, Florentine plays an obviously important role since she is the woman who will "fall" and who will, without some kind of rescue, give birth to an illegitimate baby. Roy crafts her character so that Florentine's innocence and emerging sensuality make for a dangerous combination. By no means straightforward, Florentine has a "childish face" and a "quivery mouth." Yet her eyes are framed by the "high arch of her plucked and penciled eyebrows" and her hands are "as fragile as those of a child" (2-3). Such description suggests that Florentine is a strange admixture of the naïve and the worldly, childish enough not to realize the risks she invites with the arch of her drawn-on eyebrows. She is conscious of herself as a creature on display and she wants to make a certain kind of impression. As Ellen Babby says, Florentine is always curious about "the spectacle she presents to Jean" (16). Indeed, the novel opens with her "watching" for him, wondering "Where was the young man who gave her so many admiring glances yesterday?" (1). Florentine, though barely out of childhood, has already developed a sense of herself as she appears to the world of men who would admire her and affirm for her in their gaze a vision she has of herself.

Roy carefully establishes Florentine's innocence in order to render her as a sympathetic character caught off guard, rather than as a calculating and sensual woman. Thus Roy is able to raise the issue of illegitimacy and alleviate some of the blame attached to Florentine. The sexual encounter almost reads like a rape. We are told:

> But he would not let her go, and over her shoulder he stared at the old leather sofa.
> She fell on her back, her knees twisted, and one foot waving in the air. Before she closed her eyes, she saw the Madonna and all the saints looking down on her. For a moment she tried to pull herself up again toward all those mourning, pleading faces. Jean might still be induced to let her go. Then she slid down all the way in the hollow where she slept every night beside her little sister Yvonne. (144)

Florentine "slides down," but her ambivalence is evident. Her submission is more like resignation and has little to do with pleasure. According to Patrick Coleman, "it is difficult to say to what extent, if at all, Florentine consents to Jean's advances" (64). Paula Gilbert Lewis goes further, calling the encounter a "seduction-rape" in which "Florentine remains a pitiful figure" (71). The issue of consent is always important, but it is compounded in this context because of social and religious strictures about premarital sex. Roy is able to inspire and maintain sympathy for Florentine's illegitimate pregnancy because of the ambiguity of the seduction and because of the contradictions of Florentine's character. Moreover, Gabrielle Roy is a French-Canadian writer writing in a predominantly Roman Catholic environment and Florentine's family home is decorated with pictures of the Madonna and the saints who regard the goings-on with "mournful" faces that make Florentine want to "pull herself up." Roy invokes the image of what Adrienne Rich has called "the eternally suffering and suppliant mother" (*Of Woman* 162) who compels "the identification of womanhood with suffering" (163). Rich says of this image that the "allocations of power in patriarchy demand not merely a suffering Mother, but one divested of sexuality: the Virgin Mary, *virgo intacta*, perfectly chaste" (180). Florentine, used by Jean, appears as a woman divested of sexuality; she is passive and supine, and certainly emerges as a suffering mother. Roy uses the image of the Madonna to create resonance in the text, not only to engender sympathy for Florentine, but for all women who suffer under "power in patriarchy."

Roy focuses on the combined burdens of illegitimacy and poverty in her description of Florentine. The growth of the baby within fills Florentine with fear and with an overwhelming sense of loneliness. As Coleman argues, Florentine has "no model of personal independence to which, as a young woman, she would appeal" (66). She cannot look to her mother for a model of independence, nor to the women she works with. Jean's seduction, such as it is, "creates a new situation for which Florentine both is and is not responsible, a situation through which she becomes a separate individual" (Coleman 66). The fear that she might be pregnant has "stalked her for days, for a long time, perhaps ever since that Sunday in March" (172). Like Hazel, she has no way of quieting her fear, no plan of action. The sight of "ranks of smooth-skinned apples, of blue-veined onions...this festival of colours, this wealth of earthly smells," fills her with despair since it represents an engagement in a life in which she "could never again take pleasure." The emerging flowers, open air markets, "the living effluvia of hothouses," the burgeoning life of spring all around Florentine tell her "that life was easy on some people and hard on others, and that there was no way of escaping this pitiless law" (173). To be poor, unmarried, and pregnant is to be beyond the pale. Here Roy's critique of urban Montreal and the poverty of its inhabitants comes to the fore. Into such an environment, a baby is unwelcome. Florentine's response to the effects of the season implies that she blames "life" for her pregnancy, that she has, through means not her own, fallen victim to a "pitiless law" that has resulted in her present fear and unhappiness. Florentine considers that "this horrible state, this loneliness was an offshoot of poverty." She understands that the bitterness of such thoughts is "so frightful, so ugly," that it has the capacity to "poison" her "whole spirit" (173).

Roy is scathing in her exposure of male/female inequality when it comes to reproductive responsibility. She is pointed in her condemnation of men who escape the responsibility of their actions. This is evident in the fact that Florentine's bitterness about poverty is not as potent as her resentment toward Jean who, as a man, is able to break off an affair with "no backward looks, no regrets" (173). Jean has, from the novel's beginning, been in a position of power. The only interest Florentine holds for Jean, and that only fleeting, is the pathos of her situation, of her desire for him and of her pathetic efforts to interest him by looking as nice as she possibly can. He enjoys briefly the view of himself that Florentine provides, that he is "a dangerous fellow, rather a scamp, but attractive, like all really dangerous people" (12). But his interest in Florentine is based on pity and is soon killed (52). That Jean can leave her so easily is "infinitely more tormenting than the burden of her own fault" (175). Her "fault" is that she had premarital sex and the result, the baby that is to come, lands exclusively on her shoulders. Roy turns the tables on Jean, however, since Florentine eventually feels disgust for Jean, which finally gives her strength. She understands that she has sold herself short, has "given herself to him in exchange for such niggardly alms" (176). Florentine's understanding leads her to hold in contempt "her womanhood" which she believes had compelled her to fall into "the trap that had been laid for her weakness." She is referring to the biological capacity to get pregnant, her "traitorous womanhood" (176). The trap itself, intimacy with Jean, she considers to have been "brutal and coarse" and the "unutterable scorn" she feels is "stronger even than her fear" (176). She is ashamed of having been taken in so easily by Jean's fragment of reluctant affection. She is ashamed of the result of her liaison, the pregnancy, and the coming baby. Her disgust with Jean garners for her what little strength she has.

Emmanuel is Florentine's saviour. That she has need of a saviour in her time and community is without question. Florentine is saved by the gentle Emmanuel whom she makes fall in love with her (233). She gives "him her mouth coldly, resolutely" (240), determined to seal a pact that will legitimize her situation no matter what the cost. Emmanuel's offer of marriage rehabilitates Florentine in the eyes of her family and in her own eyes. She is "saved" (243). She considers herself now, "of course," to be "worthy of their esteem" (246). Marriage allows Florentine to re-enter the mainstream of social and family life. She is no longer marked by the immorality of her actions; her pregnancy will instead become a badge of honour, something in which the matrons of the community she has joined will take an interest. By the novel's end Florentine is able to begin to think about her child "without resentment," although she is not yet prepared to love it. Part of her rehabilitation will be to "dissociate the child from her own fall, from her own blunder," and this she is beginning to accomplish, "little by little" (273). The baby is significant as a marker of social value, while the degree of value is affected by legitimacy. The baby is marked by the discourse that inscribes it as the result of a "blunder" or "fault" on the part of its mother. In time, Florentine will be able to distance herself from her "fall" and accept the baby. However, for the community at large, as soon as Florentine is married, the baby is a "blessing," its birth an event to be celebrated.

The Tin Flute provides insight not only into the representation of the infant as illegitimate, but it also reveals the impact of the baby whose circumstances of birth are legitimate—but whose presence adds a tremendous burden to its mother. Rose-Anna heroically bears this burden for the twelfth time. Patrick Coleman calls Rose-Anna the "most deeply felt of Roy's characters" (77). She is "patient and long-suffering" (77), the "home's moral centre" (80), a woman whose "heart is never hardened," who, in spite of obstacles, "does not withdraw into herself" (85). Coleman insists that Roy has not sentimentalized Rose-Anna, but rather that she is "rooted in everyday reality, constantly coming to grips with practical needs and aware of her limited power to act" (77). Paula Gilbert Lewis writes that Rose-Anna is a "strong and energetic 'femme de peuple,'" and one of Gabrielle Roy's favourite characters (65).

Rose-Anna has been "deformed by so much child bearing" (57). Her lengthy career as a pregnant woman and mother has caused her to bear "in her body with bitterness the scars of so many children and so many worries" (58). She wonders how they will survive, asking, "What will become of us…. When there were only ten of us it was hard enough to get along, but soon we'll be eleven" (57).[12] The impact on this beleaguered family of another mouth to feed will be devastating and Rose-Anna resents the fact that she is the one who bears in her body and in her mind the burden of its arrival while her husband, Azarius, remains, "young and blooming" (58).

Again, Roy does not retreat from implicating men in women's suffering through pregnancy, whether they are married or not. The baby's existence is a given for Florentine and for Rose-Anna, yet both the men in their lives are able to ignore the tremendous burden that they have helped to create. Azarius is usually out of work and inordinately opti-mistic about the family's fortunes, always "making plans" that will not be fulfilled, blindly certain that things are about to improve for them (59). Paula Gilbert Lewis describes how Rose-Anna is "imprisoned within this circle of misery" unable to expect either "financial or emo-tional support from her husband" (66). Her fertility is her enemy, but so is her husband. Roy foregrounds the fact that women get pregnant because of men who, apart from taking pleasure (a pleasure so obliquely referred to as to be virtually non-existent), have no part in the process or the responsibility for pregnancy. Azarius abnegates his responsibility to his family. Jean rejects both Florentine and his respon-sibility for her condition, wrapping himself in a cocoon of self-centred-ness that is as impenetrable as Azarius's optimism. Women are con-nected to babies, isolated in this connection, and forced to deal with the consequences of an act in which they seem, in this text, barely to have a part.

In Roy's treatment of Rose-Anna, the infant is polarized simultane-ously as a burden and as a blessing within the context of marriage. Rose-Anna has intimate knowledge of the suffering connected with childbirth. For Rose-Anna, "spring was in a measure her enemy. What had it meant for her? During all her married life two events were always associated with the spring: she was almost always pregnant, and in that condition she was obliged to look for a new place to live" (61). A new baby is a new obstacle to survival, a new burden to bear. Throughout her pregnancy she has had a "foreboding of death" (255). For the woman in labour, the infant does not represent new life or a clean slate; rather, it is the source of wrenching bodily anguish and fear of death. Rose-Anna prays that she will be spared to die later when her children are grown up (258). She prays also, as she always does "at the last moment…that she might give birth to a male child, one who would suffer less than she. Always in those last, dark, lonely moments, while her body was wracked with pain, she had been terror-stricken at the thought of giving birth to a girl" (257). *In extremis*, Rose-Anna wants to stop the cycle of suffering by giving birth to a male who, implicitly, will cause more pain than he will ever have to suffer. Such pain is connected to a woman's lot in life for Rose-Anna, a lot she would spare her prog-eny. Here Roy explores the discrepancy between male and female babies, those who will grow up to forge a way for themselves, unhin-dered, and the "others" who will bear burdens and restrictions. No mat-

ter what the baby's gender turns out to be, the birth itself is bittersweet
for Rose-Anna. As Coleman sees it, "Rose-Anna experiences the delivery of a new baby as an affirmation of life, but also as the moment when
the child can no longer be shielded from the sorrows of the outside
world" (88). As Lewis says, "Roy's description of the birth of this child
clearly underscores the author's pride and pity for this woman" (65)
who endures through so many obstacles.

Her concern about the baby's gender fades once the infant is born
and Rose-Anna has grown accustomed to the fact that he has no defor-
mities. The act of giving birth, as Sara Ruddick sees it, is a "reciprocal
relationship of woman and infant. This relationship is marked…by the
dissolution of boundaries—a living being inside another, emerging
from another, a body feeding off another body" (210). Birth renders
actual a strange reciprocity where one doubled subject, a subject within
a subject, becomes two singularities. Committing "oneself to protecting
the unprotectable and nurturing the unpredictable" (209) is an act of
tremendous hope, says Ruddick, an act that can cause the mother to
feel ecstatic. Upon the birth of her baby, Rose-Anna feels "a sudden
rush of joy." The manifestation of the infant as a source of hope, intrinsically, tangibly renewing, is lambent. Roy's text articulates something
of Rose-Anna's personal *magnificat*:

> And with a sudden rush of joy, Rose-Anna yearned to hold him.
> When he was washed and wrapped in a quilt, he was brought to
> her. His tight little fists stuck out of the covers, and long blond
> lashes, as fine as down, lay on his satiny cheeks. The fragility of a
> newborn baby had always moved Rose-Anna deeply. She relaxed
> completely at last, one arm cradling the tiny bundle. All pain, all
> sorrow had been drained out of her. After each confinement, she
> felt this same tenderness and courage welling up in her heart, as if
> she had drawn once more on the mysterious, inexhaustible springs
> of her youth. It seemed as if this were not her twelfth, but her first
> and only child. (260)

Her baby is perfect, washed clean, composed of "little fists," which he
will need to face life's hardships, and "long blond lashes, as fine as
down" that lay against "satiny cheeks." The infant is finely composed
of satin and down. That he rejuvenates, encourages, and blesses his
mother exclusively by virtue of his existence is unequivocal. Roy's
word choice is precise. As a mother, Rose-Anna is a vessel, drained of
"all pain, all sorrow" and filled by "courage welling." The adjectives
suggest that her baby is the wellspring of "joy," "tenderness,"

"courage," "mystery," providing Rose-Anna access to the "inexhaustible springs of her youth." The baby's arrival has left her "more light-hearted" (261), more able, in spite of everything to face her difficulties with hope. Clearly, she loves the baby and desires its well-being. Its birth mitigates, to a certain extent, even her resentment of her husband's irresponsibility and she is calm and hopeful about the future.

In writing about the impact of the baby as causing Florentine's horror and Rose-Anna's courage, Roy draws attention to the inequity between men's and women's experience of babies, illegitimate or otherwise. Yet, critics have persistently considered Roy to be a traditionalist and have obscured the "feminist elements in [her] writing" (Whitfield 20), viewing Rose-Anna as a stereotypical suffering mother and Florentine as the stereotypical fallen woman. Yet as Whitfield and others have insisted, "central to Gabrielle Roy's world vision was the conflict between the male and female universe" (Whitfield 25).[13] This conflict is embedded in the response to the infant; Roy both inscribes and resists stereotyping this response. She acknowledges the value of babies even as she presents the distress of the women who bear them.

Her concern for the lack of social support for mothers and their babies is manifest in the text, as well as her concern for men's lack of involvement. Jean can begin a relationship and leave it easily, no matter what the outcome of his affair. Florentine, on the other hand, must deal with the shame she brings on herself, on her family, and on the baby that will be born. The intolerable nature of this burden drives Florentine to the safety of marriage to a likable man whom she manipulates into proposing. Thus, the dominant ideology marking the infant as legitimate or illegitimate, depending on the context of its conception, is not directly subverted in Roy's text. She does, however, in imaginatively and sensitively offering Florentine's innocence and suffering to the reader, invite a sympathetic understanding that perhaps would mitigate judgement in the 1940s. Such mitigation can operate as the first step in an ideological change that contributes to valuing the infant regardless of the circumstances of its origin. Roy also enlightens her readership, through the character of Rose-Anna, concerning babies' capacity to fill their mothers with courage and to evoke a sense of mystery and profound tenderness. Engel characterizes Roy as "a serious female writer" (qtd. in Brady 187) whose intimate representation of these two women provides a unique insight into the baby's significance.

In representations of the infant in the first half of the twentieth century, writers consistently probe the difficulties caused by the combination of babies and poverty. But the representations are not uniform. Several factors make up the fictional construction of the infant so that it is dichotomous. The baby is an object of desire and it is also an object of constraint for women like Mrs. Amundsen and Mrs. Proctor who are victimized by too many babies. For the most part, the infant remains in the margin during the first half of the century, except for being conceived idealistically as a site of hope for men such as Niels who see in babies a stake in the future of his new country. The Bentleys also see the infant as a blank slate, in their case, the promise of a new and more successful beginning beyond Horizon. Moreover, perceptions of the infant are influenced by the burdens of a landscape that must be settled with women's physical labour as much as with men's. Montgomery, Grove, and Roy all offer more or less detailed descriptions of the power of babies to oppress women to the limits of their physical and emotional capacity to endure. In the "Anne" books, *Settlers of the Marsh*, *As for Me and My House*, and *The Tin Flute*, women deal with the severe hardship of too many babies—in Judith's case, only one too many—and too few resources. The women who have too many babies are usually poor and certainly weary, financially and physically exhausted. Added to this is the burden of illegitimacy suffered by Judith, by Hazel, and by Florentine. All three writers (Ross, Bruce, and Roy) write about illegitimacy and all three texts develop in varying degrees the notion that the transgressing woman and the baby must be redeemed and restored to propriety. But even though their narratives seem to reinforce the dominant ideology, these writers also challenge that ideology by creating characters who inspire sympathy and understanding rather than condemnation. Also, apart from the discourse that constitutes the infant as an ideal or negative figure, there is a persistent and generative representation of the infant in writing by women as something that "interrupts the law of mortality" (Arendt 246); it associates women, even women who have given birth eleven times previously, with sublime natural forces that rejuvenate them and fill them with joy. Gabrielle Roy is eloquent on this point. As such, the infant is also for women a locus of power and happiness of a kind that, most compellingly, male writers do not know about.

CHAPTER 3

Speaking of Reproduction:
The 1960s and 1970s

There is a transformation in the manner in which infants are represented in Canadian literature after 1960. During the 1960s and '70s, the baby begins to occupy more space in the literary world. Canadian women writers like Margaret Atwood, Margaret Laurence, Audrey Thomas, and Marian Engel take up the work advanced by Gabrielle Roy, whose distinctive female voice articulates the tension intrinsic in the figure of the baby. While these are all writers who have received a considerable amount of critical attention, little if any of this has focused on the figure of the infant as it develops during these decades. I want to look at this writing in new ways to foreground the significance of the infant.

It's important to see the evolution of this representation in terms of the tremendous social and historical transformation during this time. There is a distinct difference in the writing by male and female writers about the infant in these decades that results from the emergence of feminism. While it would be difficult to demonstrate a directly causal relationship, there is a parallel process of women's increased consciousness, their increased accessibility to widespread means of expression, and increased opportunities for them to speak to their own experience. And while women's writing about babies in the 1960s and '70s shows a profound engagement with the infant as a figure of both constraint and love, writing by men as it relates to babies in these decades remains somewhat stagnant; it is characterized by distance, by a lack of engagement, as though babies have no place in the lives of men. There is no sense of tension established between how babies appear and how they really are since they are so peripheral to the men's lives. Infants are mentioned, but they are not explicitly significant to the characters. Not yet completely welcome in the delivery room, not yet socially encouraged to be active fathers to their babies, men demonstrate in the novels they write a sustained distance in space and time between protagonists and babies. The infant remains in the margins of this fiction.

On the contrary, the representation of infants in writing by women is informed by women's need to appropriate power and assert their voices socially and politically, exploring in a more public fashion than ever the issues that concern them, including pregnancy, childbirth, and concomitant issues of subjectivity. The women's movement and the sexual revolution created an environment more conducive to the artistic exploration of women's response to the infant as feminist writers explored in more intricate ways Kristeva's question, "What does it mean to give birth to a baby?" It's a question whose answer continues to form around that binary opposition of desire and rejection; an opposition that is not by any means clear cut, because one side interpenetrates the other.

In the late 1960s and early 1970s, representations of the infant are intrinsically connected to representations of the maternal and both stories, the baby's and the mother's, were only just beginning to be told. As Di Brandt argues in *Wild Mother Dancing*, the role of the mother had been, prior to this literary moment, largely absent. The "rich canon of Western literature" offered Brandt no examples of mother stories that would help her understand her own experience of pregnancy, when, she writes, "the reality of my maternal body and transformed subjectivity were insisting their unmetaphorical otherness unpolitely into my consciousness" (4). Women who bear babies begin in these decades, as Brandt confirms, to explore the "amazing transformation" that occurs when women become mothers (6). As Brandt describes her own experience: "there I was, and there they were, all the other mothers, women with children that I knew, and whether or not we organized a revolution, our very survival past the ordeal of childbirth, our very being alive and wanting to speak about it, not only to each other but publicly, challenged the old framework to its roots" (6-7). Women writing the experience of sex, pregnancy, birth, and child rearing are "challenging the old framework to its roots." They are claiming a voice and revolutionizing our perception of women's experience to fill a marked absence. Brandt's work in inquiring into the mother's story in Western literature underscores the importance of this challenge. But women's writing about the baby is also vital in the process of articulating women's experience. The baby becomes, then, a means of reclamation. The infant is represented in terms of its gestational connection to the mother, not only as a benign growth but also as a powerful agent in the mother's revision of herself. The baby is inscribed within the mother's body, both in the experience of pregnancy and motherhood; the nuances of such an inscription are ones that women writers want to explore.[1] The way women become mothers (and how they feel about the process) becomes the subject of literary discovery.

This chapter examines writing by men and women in these turbulent decades. Male writers do not yet appear to be awake to the political, social, and personal ramifications of the baby's acts in the textual world. In Matt Cohen's *The Disinherited* (1974), for example, the male protagonists remain aloof from the babies they father, while the babies themselves remain at the periphery of the novel's plot. Although both Richard and Erik are disengaged from the infants and children around them, Erik's encounter at the end of the novel with a pregnant girl seems to indicate that even he sees the baby as offering some slim hope for the future. Cohen's work is singled out from other male writers such as Juan Butler, Robertson Davies, George Bowering, and David Adams Richards, among others, as typical in his articulation of male lack of connection to the infant. Male writers do not participate yet in a discourse that, in the 1980s and beyond, will pay more attention to the infant as a complex textual creation. Robert Kroetsch's *What the Crow Said* is an interesting departure from conventional representations of the infant, but although there are several babies, they remain on the outskirts of the action.

Women writers of this decade articulate their own disparate responses to the figure of the baby. What stands out from this work is the material connection between the discourse of the maternal and the effect of the infant on the mother's life. Audrey Thomas's *Mrs. Blood* (1970), Margaret Atwood's *The Edible Woman* (1969) and *Surfacing* (1972), Margaret Laurence's *A Jest of God* (1966), and finally, Marian Engel's *The Honeyman Festival* (1970) explore a variety of articulations of the mother-infant nexus. The works make evident the ambiguity at the heart of relationships between mothers and their babies. The infant continues to be a site of tension between poles of constraint and love. And the tension becomes more fully expressed by women in these vital decades who are pushing the boundaries of what it is possible to say. Thus, Thomas's *Mrs. Blood* gives expression to the appalling experience of miscarriage. Atwood's Clara reveals her distaste toward her babies. The unnamed narrator of *Surfacing* ponders the loss of her babies through abandonment and abortion. Laurence's Rachel faces the issue of illegitimacy, and finally, Engel's Minn deals with the burdens of several small children in what is essentially single parenthood since her husband is away throughout the story. The infant is at the heart of these narratives of miscarriage, mess, abandonment, abortion, and chaos. Yet, each of the novels gives persistent expression to the hope marked in writing about the infant, to the relationship of love that the infant compels, sometimes unwillingly, with the woman who bears it.[2] The texts are so varied and nuanced that it is important to examine them in some detail.

Expanded opportunities to write, increasing social activism, and a need to give voice to women's experience all had an impact on the fictional representation of infants. This impact was evident particularly in attitudes toward illegitimacy. In the 1940s and '50s, this issue occupies a central position in several texts. However, in the 1960s and '70s, perceptions about illegitimacy and the work of pregnancy and child rearing (as these are represented in literature) are transformed. The change in representation is manifested on several levels, not the least of which is the pragmatics of book publishing. As time has passed, as women have gained a more equal footing with men in Canadian society, as more publishing houses have been established, and as greater numbers of books are being published, babies become increasingly visible in these texts, but it's a visibility that seems to depend on gender.

In the 1960s and '70s, political, historical, and technological developments nurtured a climate conducive to the arts.[3] The availability of financial support provided an environment propitious to the development of new presses and the emergence of new writers, many of whom were women—writers who benefited from an offshoot of Canadian nationalism directed at encouraging artistic development. Matt Cohen, in his essay, "The Rise and Fall of Serious CanLit," says that after the Second World War, there was a major "wave of nationalism, " particularly after the 1967 anniversary of Confederation. It was responsible for the inception of small presses, initially established to publish "political books and novels that weren't sufficiently conventional or international to attract the attention of the more established houses" (279). Cohen goes a step further, pinpointing the season and year of the greatest development in publishing in Canada. He writes, "In the fall of 1970, the rising nationalist sentiments were crystallized in publishing by two events; W.J. Gage sold its educational division to an American firm, and Ryerson Press, Canada's oldest and most respectable publisher, let itself be bought out by the American-owned McGraw-Hill" (279). Such Americanization was unacceptable to an arts community struggling to consolidate a national literature and, through it, a national identity. Cohen writes that the "arts community protested loudly and demanded support from the Canada Council" in order to save Canadian literature. These demands were met by a Liberal government that was, according to Cohen, "in a spending mood" (279). The Canada Council funded "writers' tours, writers-in-residencies, block grants for publishing programmes, new national organizations for publishers and writers" (279). Cohen attributes the growth in the number of students wanting to study Canadian literature to this rise in cultural nationalism, a creative circle the exigencies of which created a larger reading audience, more critical review, and more demand for education.

Furthermore, not only were there more publishing houses—as well as more money—available for writers, but these were also increasingly accessible to women. In her essay, "By and about Women," Shelagh Wilkinson states that "in the late 1960s, several cultural and political events coalesced to provide Canadian women writers with a more hospitable creative environment" (208). One of these events was the women's movement and another was, as Cohen also mentions, the emergence of Canadian literature as a bona fide field of study. The institutionalization of Canadian literature, its growing prominence in university courses and as the subject of serious critical review, has contributed to the growth both of the publishing industry and of the reading audience which supports that industry. Wilkinson discusses the proportionately large number of women writers who emerged during the 1960s and '70s, writing that

> Since 1965, there has been such an explosion in the number of novels and books of poetry by women published in Canada today that it is impossible to derive a sense of the true texture of Canadian literature without looking at the writing by women. Yet this has not always been the case. Before the 1960s, the published literature was dominated by male writers. (204)

Such a burgeoning of women writers had a profound impact on the subject matter and voice of literary texts. While Wilkinson recognizes that women are well-represented in the Canadian literary tradition, she asserts that "women writers were not acknowledged as part of mainstream writing" (206), that "it took special effort on the part of (mainly women) scholars to unearth the early work of women writers and get it reissued" (207).[4] Wilkinson may be insisting here more on the critical attention paid to, and less on the prodigious output of, early women writers. That is, male writers may have dominated a patriarchal canon that ignored literary foremothers. In either case, the argument that women writers received more opportunity and more attention in the 1960s and '70s seems a valid one, if only in light of the multiplying of government subsidy to artists and publishers.

Prominent among the concerns of women writers during this period was exploring one of a woman's most powerful experiences, the experience of childbirth. Wilkinson reminds us that literature concerns itself with "great" issues like death. But, she adds, "birth is as universal as death, and until very recently little has been written about the process, or about the cultural and political relevance of birthing" (210). This can be extended, obviously, to the cultural and political relevance of babies. Women, then, began to do more writing exploring their experience as women, their experience of birth, and their experience of babies.

These were clearly culturally volatile times. The widespread availability of birth control led to a radical change in social mores. The demographic transition from rural to urban placed the burden of responsibility for child care almost exclusively on mothers who, in an urban setting, were often separated from the support of the extended family. As the Royal Commission on the Status of Women reported in 1970, "This is a relatively recent phenomenon in Western civilization" (Canadian Association 18). As well, the traditional view that women should live at home with their parents until they were married was also eroding. In *Canadian Women: A History*, the authors state that "during the late 1950s and 1960s it became more common and acceptable for the young to leave home to live on their own or with people their own age while working or completing their education" (Prentice et al. 319).[5] The tendency of young people to live independently of traditional familial connections marks a considerable divergence from the previous norm of the 1940s and 1950s when "the propaganda of the day pictured women at home and strong families as hedges against another war or as ballast in the cold war" (MacDaniel 106). Such freedom instigated a downward spiral in the birth rate after 1957 which was directly attributable to the "increased knowledge of and access to birth control devices" (Prentice et al. 321). Statistics show a decline in the birth rate from a high in 1959 of 3.9 births per woman on average, to a low of 1.7 percent by the early 1980s (MacDaniel 105). This decline is significant for a variety of reasons, not the least of which is that it reflects a new empowerment for women who could now take control of when and whether they would become pregnant.

Moreover, those who did have babies began to resist the constraints placed upon them by the routines of hospital birth. Having babies in hospitals was a relatively recent phenomenon. In 1941 less than half of all Canadian babies were born in the hospital. By 1951, 80 percent were hospital-born and by 1961, 97 percent of all Canadian babies were born in the hospital. This increase in the medicalization of the birth process paralleled a felt loss of control for women who began to re-examine their own role in the process of delivery in the 1960s and 1970s. Wendy Mitchinson finds that when women "tried to regain some control over the process by demanding a more natural childbirth in the 1950s and 1960s...the profession did make some concessions." For example, the "introduction of a hospital birthing-room was deemed acceptable" in order that women "respond to parenting" and "accept her role in society" (255).

In essential and admirable movements to reduce infant and maternal mortality rates, pre-wartime physicians had come to view pregnancy as a medical condition needing treatment with women, obviously, as ill patients. In his 1944 book, *Childbirth without Fear*, Dr. Grantly Dick-Read asserts that the best help one can give during labour is to "realize the power of words upon the suggestibility of an obstetrical patient" (107). Dick-Read compellingly situates the labouring woman as an "obstetrical patient," even though he is urging women to experience "natural childbirth" by means of relaxation. His is a carefully orchestrated relaxation under the direction of a qualified physician. He appears unaware of the rhetorical irony he expresses here. Although Mary O'Brien isn't speaking specifically about Dick-Read, her 1981 critique points out the fact that

> childbirth has become a responsibility of the "health industry," a
> hospital occasion presided over by obstetrical entrepreneurs, usu-

ally male, in conditions of depersonalized asepsis which transforms woman, in every sense the agent, into a patient. Medical developments have no doubt reduced the life-risking dangers of parturition, but they have done so at the price of concealing and reducing the unifying female sociability attendant on the birth of a new life. (10)

O'Brien is concerned with women's resistance to the (mostly) male dominance of obstetrics and the great degree of control exerted over them, but not all critics find such a resistance. For example, Prentice and colleagues write that in mid-century "for many women the hospital experience was a positive one, providing them with a chance to rest and be looked after." Women, however, also reported the drawback that "doctors increasingly treated the process of giving birth not as a natural event but as a medical one" (248). The authors are concerned with tracking women's loss of control in pregnancy and their struggle to regain it. They do not explore in detail the tremendous gains to women and infants as a result of medicalization of pregnancy in terms of lowering mortality rates. In citing, for example, the increase in births by Caesarian section between 1970 and 1981, the authors acknowledge that the probable cause was connected to "the increased use and efficiency of new fetal monitoring devices, which could show when infants were in distress." However, they state that "feminists were convinced that the causes also included doctors' convenience and their fear of malpractice suits" (395). Configuring pregnancy as an illness or condition in need of medical treatment, and the consequent loss of control, gave rise to a countermovement, the aim of which was to give women more control of their birth experiences.[6]

This movement is evident in the number of natural childbirth books and classes available to women in the 1970s, as well as in the new inclusion of fathers or partners in the labour and delivery experience. As Prentice and colleagues see it, "women's increased autonomy was expressed in demands for less mechanized child bearing" (394). Two separate issues, one relatively new, the use of forceps and total anaesthesia during the 1950s, the other, the practice of denying the father access to the birth of his child, a more traditional interdiction, began to seem less than ideal (394). As well, women began to experiment with "less alienating forms of delivery" and the babies themselves were "'allowed' to be bigger and less fragile" (395), presumably by means of the lifting of severe dietary restrictions on gestating women.

Laws relating to the conception of children were also undergoing rapid change. Until 1969, there was in force a "legal ban on the sale and advertisement of contraceptives" which had been introduced into the Criminal Code in 1892 (Canadian Association 27). Further, physicians who performed sterilization procedures on people for contraceptive purposes risked facing civil or criminal liability. In 1967 abortion was legalized in Canada (Prentice et al. 365), in spite of the fact that the commission was "aware of strong opposition to abortion from those who consider that the foetus is a human life" (Royal Commission 28). Notwithstanding the "eloquent appeals" it heard, the commission made its decision to allow accredited hospitals to "procure a miscarriage" based upon "surveys by the Gallup poll, *Chatelaine* magazine and others." Right or wrong, the commission concluded, there was clearly "a large public demand for legalized abortion" (28).

The demand for legalized abortion was the outcome of a change in the moral climate of the time, again the result of increased freedom and independence. While in the 1950s, premarital sex "continued to be socially unacceptable for 'respectable' young women" (Prentice et al. 320), premarital sex became more widespread in the 1960s; by 1967 the number of infants born out of wedlock "constituted 8.3% of live births" (Royal Commission 28). The Royal Commission on the Status of Women set as one of its resolutions that the government must "make every effort to integrate the unmarried mother who keeps her child into the community, by making sure that she is not discriminated against in housing and employment, that she receive help with child care, and has access to counselling" (29). Thus the commission took upon itself the responsibility of resisting the social stigma attached to unwed pregnancy. This is a considerable departure from a centuries-old representation in Western culture of what constitutes legitimacy and decency, and it is a departure that is reflected in the literature of the time.

The radical struggles for power and voice that occur in women's writing about pregnancy and childbirth are not evident in the way men depict the relationship between male characters and babies. Male writers maintain a distance from the figure of the infant, perhaps as an extension of the distance that fathers, at this socio-historical point in Canadian culture, also feel. In *The Politics of Reproduction*, Mary O'Brien asserts that the disaffection men feel with regard to babies "rests squarely on the alienation of the male seed in the copulative act" (30).

Apart from DNA testing, paternity "is an abstract idea" (30) that fails to enable men to engage with babies. Instead, men have concerned themselves with controlling women in childbirth through medical institutions in order to compensate for their lack of paternal connection. O'Brien lists the "series of real oppositions" brought about by "the alienation of the male seed":

1. The man and the child, who may or may not be his;
2. The woman who labours to bring forth her child and the man who does not labour;
3. The man who is separated from biological continuity, and the woman whose integration with natural process and genetic time is affirmed in reproductive labour;
4. Following from 1, individual man and all other possible potencies, men in general. (36)

Male uncertainty about paternity disaffects men, according to O'Brien. They have little or no investment in the biological production of babies. Social convention pictures the expectant father in the hospital waiting room, smoking and pacing until he is presented with his offspring. As O'Brien claims, the father is "separated from biological continuity" and has no real share in the work of bringing the baby into the world. Men have historically made up for this material alienation by taking over birthing as "obstetrical entrepreneurs" (O'Brien 10) who transform the active reproductive process into a controlled experience that reduces "the unifying female sociability attendant on the birth of a new life" (10). Instead of negotiating a greater involvement, a contributory involvement, in the birth process, men have historically sought to control the process itself.

Two of O'Brien's stipulations concerning male alienation have to do with male uncertainty about the "seed" planted within the woman to produce the infant, but at least one deals directly with the fact that the man does not labour to give birth to the infant and has, until very recently in Western culture, even been physically removed from the presence of the birthing woman, apart from his role as physician. This speaks to a social and psychological, as well as a material sense of alienation from the seed and its products that undermines the male role in infant care and connection. Moreover, in asserting the need for "a feminist philosophy of birth," O'Brien asserts that "reproduction in the biological sense...is necessarily social from any perspective, practical or abstract" (40). It is men's social sense of the "alienation of the seed" that

I attend to as it is manifested in Canadian fiction, particularly focusing on the evolution of men's involvement in the social act of parenting small children.

Michael Lamb's work on fathering is useful to this discussion. Lamb claims that "most theorists...have assumed that the mother-infant relationship is unique and vastly more important than any contemporaneous, or indeed any subsequent, relationships" (2). He states further that "social scientists have contributed, perhaps unwittingly, to the devaluation of the father's role. There is a peculiar tendency to infer sequentially that, because mothers are the primary caretakers, they are more important than fathers" (29). Whether distance is chosen or imposed, men remain removed from infants, a fact that is evident in the fiction of both men and women during these years.[7] This lack of connection between men and babies is evident in literary works against a complex representation of babies.

Matt Cohen's *The Disinherited* is set during a time of emerging sexual freedom. While there are illegitimate babies in the text, they are not problematic, certainly not for the men who father them. The novel is centred on the dying of Richard Thomas; the babies appear at the periphery of the story—at a distance from the male protagonists, they occupy the space of a few paragraphs. O'Brien's notion of the material alienation of the seed is evident on a psychological level in the men, both Richard, who fathered a child extramaritally with Katherine Malone and wants nothing to do with the infant, and his son, Erik. While all the men in the novel encounter babies, Richard, his father Simon, and his sons Erik and Brian, all remain distant from them. John Moss claims in the introduction to the 1974 New Canadian Library edition that the novel "has turned tradition back on itself in an exposé of the literary and social assumptions on which it is based" (xiii). Moss also states that "themes of man's relationship with the land, with time, and with himself are explored with resounding irony" (*Reader's Guide* 49). Moss's synopsis is significant for affirming the novel's inscription of a set of values that excludes the infant as a figure of importance. The novel's men suffer as a result of this estrangement. Moreover, in his study of *The Disinherited*, Moss writes that the novel "signals the closing of an era, the conversion of human resources and necessities to the conditions of a new world" (*Sex and Violence* 198). Robert Lecker acknowledges that Erik "symbolically severs himself...from his family" (107), and not only his family, but also every human connection he so tenuously makes. Both Moss and Lecker agree that the book "eulogizes the dying agrarian tradition" (Mathews 82); however, the men's connection to the infant has been ignored in studies of the text, whether the men are preoccupied with the land or alienated from it. For Richard Thomas and his adopted son Brian, babies are important because they extend the family dynasty. However, Erik, who has opted for urban life in Toronto, is not only alienated from his father's way of life as a farmer, he is also alienated from the infant as a source of meaning. Indeed, without connections to the farm or to family, Erik is a character whose life lacks meaning. While Lawrence Mathews agrees with Lecker and Moss on the issue of alienation, he sees Erik's "alienation from this [agrarian] tradition" as "ultimately…healthy" (83) because it will impel him to embark on a journey of self-discovery. But the discovery is limited by his lack of connection to family and to the infant, whom Erik will ultimately turn to in his longing for acceptance and forgiveness. The novel's tensions lie between generations of grown men and the lives they choose to live, the commitments they make to rural or urban environments, and the women they choose to live with. In light of the social freedom to live and work where one chooses, and the sexual freedom to engage in more or less casual encounters, the men in the text, particularly Erik, have difficulty figuring out what they believe is important.

As with Niels in Grove's *Settlers of the Marsh*, Richard Thomas thinks of babies in terms of the farm he has made. His concern is whom he will leave it to, who will take up the life he is about to leave. He recalls inheriting the farm from his father, Simon, whose death gave him the farm "in some different way than previous" (142), and it also falls to him and to Miranda to find "someone else to give it to when they were finished" (142-43). The need for an heir is what drives the narrative forward as Richard considers what Jon Kertzer calls "the fate of a Canadian dynasty" where "family provides a continuity of kinship that triumphs over the dislocations of time" (98). George Woodcock calls the novel "a rural, dynastic chronicle centred on the death of one member of the family and evoking the past of several generations through the apparently erratic, but really cumulative, operation of memory" (144). A strong sense of succeeding generations and the establishment and erosion of their connection to the land permeate the novel. The narrator tells how, "The farm had first been settled by Richard Thomas's grandfather.… This first Richard Thomas had built the house, married, built three barns, cleared some fields. When he was too old to work, he passed the farm to Simon, who, in turn, married and had children. The first child was male and named Richard, after the grandfather" (53).

The emphasis on succeeding generations of men and their abiding connection to the farm is evident. Richard comes from a line of men who "settle," "build," "marry," "clear," and "work"; they perform these actions in order to tend to the land. Having children to take up their work is another aspect to that tending. It would therefore seem important to them to place high value on babies because of their future promise. Nevertheless, the story also undermines the significance of individual infants, indeed denying the "importance or uniqueness of the individual by subsuming his brief span of years within a large process of regeneration and degeneration" (Kertzer 98). Richard's focus on a dynasty prevents him from valuing infants as singularly important. His legacy from Simon, his "duty" (143), is to participate in "the holy mission of colonizing the earth: generations of men to be beaded out along the land like so many successive waves of trees and vegetation" (143). It is a duty that sits uneasily with Richard who wonders "whether there was any larger purpose" to his life than supplying generations "to feed the land" (143). He compares the generations, obviously made up of individual babies, particularly male babies, to "waves of trees and vegetation." This is perhaps an apt and valuable comparison for someone whose life is devoted to the land, but it does not inspire a sense that the infant itself is important.

A dynasty is something Richard has difficulty establishing. At the time of his father's death, his wife Miranda is not easily made pregnant; her body is "trim and preserved" and begins "to go its own way, without children, as if sterility were permissible on this farm" (143). When Richard hears about his inheritance, he entertains hopes that he and Miranda will be like "Abraham and Sarah in their new possession of this land" and that "they would be able to have children" (143). The alternative leaves them "condemned to purposeless self-preservation" (143). So children are a means of achieving purpose. Although Richard is not interested in babies, he is drawn to Katherine Malone whose "fertility…demanded him" (140). This attraction might be what Mary O'Brien calls "a principle of genetic continuity" (30); that is, a baby makes tangible the cause and effect relationship of copulation and birth, uniting parents in the body of the child (30). However, far from feeling united with Katherine Malone, Richard responds to the knowledge that she has conceived a baby by remaining detached, both from her and from his baby after its birth. Katherine gives birth to "a long thin baby that looked sick already," one that her husband, "fat fertile Peter Malone," would know was not his, "that any child of his would be healthier than this…unattractive child" (154). As the father of the baby that results from an adulterous relationship, and as a man complicit with his community's system of legitimacy, Richard is not in a position to act as a parent. The infant's existence shocks him into leaving abruptly and getting drunk. This is, in the psychological sense, the "alienation of the male seed" to which Mary O'Brien refers, alienation felt by "the man who does not labour" in order to give birth (36). Richard has no uncertainty that he is the father of the child; however, he is alienated from the living result of his own action. Richard does not feel responsible for Katherine's suffering through another pregnancy, nor does he feel anything for the baby. Instead, he goes home after having seen the baby to get drunk. In the waves of vomiting that follow, with "his stomach contracting and cramping, pulling him to the floor, forcing him to shout, pounding the knotted muscles with his fists" (155), Richard feels he must be experiencing what it is "like to have a baby" (155). His focus is on himself and his own suffering, not on what Katherine Malone would have had to endure in pregnancy and childbirth and in the community's gossip about the baby's father. For Richard, the act of producing a baby is similar to alcohol poisoning. Yet Richard's bingeing and vomiting produce nothing, whereas Katherine Malone's labour results in the birth of a baby.

Cohen explores the sense of male alienation most fully with Erik. Richard's son is estranged from all connections: to the land, to the women he has sex with, and to the baby. This is alienation rendered more poignant by his sense that he is missing something vital. When his father offers him land, he says, "'I don't want anything'" (28). The force of his frustration is evident when he throws his wine glass against the wall: "It broke with a sharp crack, showering fragments all over the room" (28). The suggestion that much more than a wine glass is fragmented with Erik's refusal to partake of his father's farm is evident in Erik's sudden departure from the farm and his once-annual visits. Erik lives in Toronto and teaches "the rules" (145) at university. He insists that "things have changed, the whole world is connected together" (145), when in his own life, nothing is further from the truth. He is busy "excising" Valerie from his life (33) and dabbling in an affair with Rose Garnett. He is without ties to his family or to the women he is most intimate with. The one family heirloom—the scorched ring—that he inherits, he leaves with a young seventeen-year-old who is also pregnant. In his liaison with her, he attempts to come to some understanding of what it is that he lacks and how he might connect with it. When he has sex with her, he

> tried to sense the body in her, this life she carried which he had mistaken for death, as if either was equally dangerous, to feel the extra heartbeat of this hidden child, to feel something for this girl who moved beneath him in harmony with Richard's death, finally drawing the tears out of him, opening his throat and his belly but knowing nothing of what she was doing, living out her own fate in this one night they borrowed from each other. (239)

The life within her, "the extra heartbeat" of the baby within, makes its presence known. Erik feels it and knows the baby to be important, vital in some way he cannot articulate or even grasp. George Woodcock believes that Erik appears "to achieve the kind of union with another person that takes him out of himself"; however he nevertheless "projects the loneliness, the unrelenting alienation of modern urban man" (148). The symmetry of the two postfuneral encounters—Richard's with Katherine and Erik's with the girl—reinforces the essential loneliness of the novel's men. Erik has been unable to grieve for the death of his father until his physical connection to the girl unleashes emotions that have until now been contained. Erik struggles to adjoin with the pregnant body, to see the baby within as significant.

As his father comes to an awareness of his own death with Katherine, so also does Erik. In the act of sexual congress, Erik sees the reflection in the window of the girl's teeth, "like a row of gravestones" (239). Again, Cohen enforces a connection between sex and death, between fertility and destruction. In the girl's reflection, in her mouth with its markers of death, Erik sees also the reflection of "his own face, transparent and desperate that there would be something to forgive him, swallow and forgive like a mother who has only imagined her children" (240). Erik's desperation is that of a man whose relationships are fundamentally severed, whose need for forgiveness will never be fulfilled because he has no one in his life whom he can ask forgiveness of. He is, in all senses, disinherited. He performs acts of intimacy and sharing without being able to emerge from his own self-absorption. When he is finished, the girl makes "small noises, her body fluttering, her mouth closed and turned into itself, its own release which was absolutely private and removed from him, this new beginning" (240). Contrary to Hannah Arendt's assertion that the baby is the "miracle that saves the world" by offering people the capacity for new beginnings that "bestow upon human affairs faith and hope" (247), the girl's pregnancy affords no such beginning for Erik. In fact, nothing does. Erik has cut off ties with his father, his brother and mother, the farm, his girlfriend Valerie, whose phone number he cannot remember, and with the woman he renews involvement with when he returns to the farm, Rose Garnett. Cohen speaks here to the isolation of men who share with women the most intimate space while each is isolated, while each "lives out their own fate." One senses in Cohen's Erik a yearning not only for forgiveness but also for an alliance of love with the baby in the face of human solitude.

In contradistinction to Cohen's novel is Robert Kroetsch's *What the Crow Said*. His novel is important to consider for its remarkable departure from the standard male text about babies. Kroetsch plays with the parameters of reality. He creates a maternal narrative that explores in an entirely different way from Cohen's the generational relationship as it is created through childbirth. Agreeing with Mary O'Brien, Di Brandt says the "moment of childbirth…is a crucial moment in the making of human history, since it is the moment when our continuity as a species, from one generation to the next…is most clearly affirmed through the basic fact of women's reproductive experience" (13). Kroetsch's novel affirms this moment of "women's reproductive experience" among women's experience of all kinds. In this novel, there are so many babies conceived in such innovative ways as to make the men often redundant, as though Kroetsch takes the distance between men and babies, indeed the male role as father and sperm-provider, and magnifies it to the point of absurdity.

In *The Canadian Postmodern* Linda Hutcheon claims that Kroetsch challenges "unexamined humanist notions such as centred identity, coherent subjectivity, and aesthetic originality. He offers instead decentred multiplicity, split selves, and double-voiced parody" (161-62). One of the ways Kroetsch's novel challenges the "centred identity" is to question assumptions about how babies are conceived and also to delineate, in often comic terms, who is taking responsibility for the babies once they arrive. The narrative expresses a fascination with fecundity.

Kroetsch creates a matriarchy where the rule of estrogen, of women and babies—mostly baby girls—is the only world that makes sense. Thus he proposes an antithetical world to the one established by Cohen where male babies are necessary for establishing a rural dynasty.

All the Lang women, apart from Vera and Tiddy whose boys die, have daughters and the daughters also have daughters. The only functioning, sensible people are women. As Gunilla Florby sees it, "*What the Crow Said* exaggerates the division between male and female, which Kroetsch sees as typical of prairie literature, to the point of parody" (73). Elsewhere Kroetsch elaborates his theory of the "grammatical pair in the story-line (the energy-line) of prairie fiction": horse/house, masculine/feminine, on/in, and motion/stasis ("Fear of Women" 114). Kroetsch upends this construction by trivializing masculine motion, often directed in the novel toward absurd accomplishment, and sustaining a sense that the women do all the important work, not the least of which is the work of reproduction.[8] Kroetsch, then, not only acknowledges O'Brien's "alienation of the seed" (30), but he celebrates it. The women dominate this text, both with their ability to get pregnant and their ability to get on with life without the men who copulate but fail to take responsibility. Vera summarizes the view of the Big Indian women: "Men are a bunch of useless bastards" (123). For example, their Schmier game continues for 151 days and stops only because Tiddy visits them in the shack where they are covered with festering sores and gangrenous flesh. She invites them home for "some homemade bread. Fresh out of the oven...homemade butter and homemade apricot jam.... Some fresh pancakes.... Fresh eggs" (126). The women take over and look after men who have become worse than infantile.[9]

While the men are occupied with card games and building giant ice towers, the women are getting pregnant and looking after the babies and the farm. The baby is the result of sexual desire, secondary to what Linda Hutcheon calls Kroetsch's specifically male-gendered "version of the procreative urge" (170), constituted in possibility rather than actuality. Hutcheon acknowledges that in Kroetsch's work "the erotic energy of sexual desire... itself becomes like writing: potential acts of creation, unpredictable, exciting" (170). The "potential acts of creation" ignite the pages of *What the Crow Said* as the babies are conceived in altogether unpredictable, magical ways. Kroetsch, then, uses babies to trouble the narrative. In the opening sentences of the novel, bees impregnate Vera Lang. Tiddy's baby has two fathers, and Anna Marie's is the result of her experiments with the semen pipette. An amputee, who can feel and also use amputated parts of his body, including his genitals, impregnates Rose.

Susan Rudy Dorscht, in *Women, Reading, Kroetsch*, finds that "the subject of *What the Crow Said* is the unnatural. After all, the world of the text is one in which bees seduce and impregnate women, futures are remembered, crows speak, summer never comes." Kroetsch's text "asks us to reread the 'natural,'" to welcome the "bloody confusion" because it is "made to be misread" (72). Kroetsch creates a world that explores its own assumptions, even assumptions about conception and birth. He makes it possible to read the baby as nothing short of a miracle: conception and birth and care of babies are things that men within the novel are unable to appreciate, or even really participate in.

Anomalies abound in this novel, particularly anomalous babies. Leibhaber is himself the first of many babies in the novel, becoming infantile after lying in the frozen June snow. We read that, "he was incontinent: he pissed the bed every few hours, shit himself once or twice a day.... Tiddy took to putting diapers on the man. She rubbed his frost-burned skin with baby oil, dusted his behind with baby powder" (37). When Liebhaber, emerging from his infantile state, finds Tiddy in the kitchen, he conceives a baby with her (a baby who turns out also to be anomalous). There is some confusion about whether John Skandl, also with Tiddy in the dark kitchen, might have fathered the child. And although Tiddy's baby "was the most beautiful baby ever born in the Big Indian General Hospital. He was too handsome to look like anyone" (61), he remains silent throughout his brief life. When Tiddy's baby cries, "he made no sound, a condition of silence he was to maintain throughout his life" (62). Tiddy's baby cannot express himself; even in crying he is silent. Critics agree that the novel explores possibilities of expression, potentials of meaning. The baby is itself a site of potential meaning, a silence one can never really penetrate. Kroetsch's text "offers, not finished, coherent, unified story… but traces of unfinished, indeed unfinishable, text" (Dorscht 73), making a definitive reading about babies difficult. In fact, deliberately avoiding definition and consistently subverting parameters, Kroetsch's interest in "play" emerges in the variety of ways that he depicts infants. He states in *Labyrinths of Voice*, "It's interesting that we play the game, isn't it. There is a double thing that goes on even in the statement.... *Play* resists the necessary rules of the *game*" (50).

Kroetsch's determined resistance to conventional representations of infants makes it difficult to ascertain their significance in a text that plays with signification. Infant consciousness is inexplicable and Kroetsch fills up that mysterious space with "words of his choosing." The combination of ordinary events with fantastic or extraordinary elements involves the reader in a kind of collision. In this text, what is real keeps clashing with what is understood to be impossible. Not bound by the regular parameters of infant development, or even infant conception, Kroetsch plays with the imaginative possibilities to produce a text whose meaning is persistently elusive. Kroetsch's magic realism is significant as it relates to Canadian literary babies because of the surreal manner in which he explores the unknowable. For example, Kroetsch's use of the crow who either speaks for the baby or does not, a fact "that was never clearly determined" (64), underscores the idea that one can never clearly determine what a baby might be thinking. It is a construction that makes evident the self-reflexive nature of the endeavour. The crow's first words to Liebhaber, its insults and suggestion that he hook his "dirty big toe onto the trigger of a borrowed shotgun, and hope for the best" (65), does seem to come more from Liebhaber's own mind rather than from JG's, since he is the one "complaining bitterly that Tiddy was whimsical, persnickety, high-hatted, stuck-up" (62-63). It is possible that Liebhaber's own despair is speaking to him through the crow, making the infant even more mysterious.

What the Crow Said must be included in an analysis of representations of the infant because it is unique for the humour with which it treats men's alienation from the reproductive process. And coincidentally or not, it is only after the publication of this novel that infant representation by male writers changes drastically in the 1980s and 1990s. In a study on representations of the infant, Kroetsch's novel stands as an astonishing, effulgent deviation from the norm. While the male characters do not form strong ties to the baby, babies nevertheless impose themselves upon the world of the farm, grounding the women who care for them, imparting a vitality that the men lack.

Women's writing about babies during the 1960s and '70s explodes in its investigation of the work of reproduction. The writing is intimate, inquiring into the traditional connection of women's biological function to intrinsic weakness and inferiority. Much of the writing reveals women's struggle to distance themselves from the bonds imposed on them through their own biology by a patriarchal system—a patriarchy that claims ownership of the infant even while it negates the value of the woman's labour at all stages of fetal and infant development and nuture. This is evident on a sociological level, both in the decline in the birth rate and in feminist rhetoric of the 1960s and '70s. Feminist theorists tackle the problem women have reconciling childbirth with their ages-old domination by men. In *The Politics of Reproduction*, Mary O'Brien discusses the negation of women's work in delivering a child and posits a dialectical process that governs reproduction, a dialectic that is "genderically differentiated" (21). The difference in approach to childbirth according to gender is evident in the literature of these decades; men approach birth far differently from women, in life and in literature. O'Brien also posits two preconditions for theorizing the dialectical process of reproduction. The first is that reproduction is not a "'pure' biological process" but is affected by historical forces (21). This is evident in the tremendous social changes of the period. Further, O'Brien argues that contraceptive technology has brought about "a fundamental historical change of the kind which Hegel called a world historical event" (21). The birth control pill offered women the opportunity to "choose parenthood," or not, creating "a transformation in human consciousness of human relations" (22). This choice enabled women to gain some protection against what Simone de Beauvoir calls "women's inferiority" which lies, she says, "in the immanent nature of childbearing" (78). If, traditionally, women's weakness has been connected to the biological functions of pregnancy and birth, then clearly some of women's vulnerability is elided by new contraceptive options. The work of de Beauvoir in the 1950s profoundly influenced the new generation of women coming to terms with biology. Mary O'Brien explores the views both of de Beauvoir and of Shulamith Firestone, who, according to O'Brien, "believes childbirth to be barbaric" (9). The revolutionary consideration that women might divorce themselves permanently from the function of reproduction was something scientists were already exploring in their experiments with new reproductive technologies such as *in vitro* fertilization.[10]

But the connection between biology and inferiority does not tell the whole story. Binaries abound in women's writing about babies. While the baby has throughout the century been represented in ambivalent terms, it did not preoccupy women writers to the extent that it begins to in these decades. Women were writing more about the baby than they ever had before, specifically in light of continuing political movements for women's equality with men. The infant comes to be seen as the enemy for women who want to live independently, a site of struggle for women between power and weakness, between joy and despair. Of most prominent concern to women writers is the simultaneous opposition and connection of the self and the other, from which all other binaries grow.

In *Desire in Language*, Julia Kristeva articulates the question, "What does it mean to give birth to a child?" (10). Although Canadian writers weren't necessarily reading Kristeva, this is the question that occupies the artistic sensibilities of women writers in the late 1960s, '70s, and beyond. Women writers give expression to the experience of childbirth, to the strange conjoining and radical separation of self and other. The fetus, although often configured as the weaker, dependent part of the woman, acts on its mother *in utero*. Kristeva says of this action:

> Cells fuse, split, and proliferate; volumes grow, tissues stretch, and body fluids change rhythm, speeding up or slowing down. Within the body, growing as a graft indomitable, there is an other. And no one is present, within that simultaneously dual and alien space, to signify what is going on. "It happens, but I'm not there." "I cannot realize it, but it goes on." Motherhood's impossible syllogism. ("Motherhood According to Bellini" 237)

The growth of one subjectivity within an other is a mysterious undertaking, inexplicable, silent, and yet clearly momentous. Babies grow inside their mothers. It's a process that some women writers have a heightened sensitivity to, a sensitivity to inner and outer worlds, and an intense drive to answer the question of what it means to give birth to a child. The baby's growing presence and subjectivity, the ways in which it owns and acts upon the mother and those around it, become experiences that find utterance in literature.

With regard to representations of the infant, two issues are at work in the writing of Canadian women in the 1960s and '70s. One is the reclamation of voice, and by voice I mean the ability, the right, and the means to give expression to personal experience. Women writers in growing numbers offer resistance to male perception concerning the significance of babies. The second issue is an extension of the first and concerns the exploration of "motherhood's impossible syllogism" (Kristeva "Motherhood" 237), the inner/outer dichotomy that forms the mother's connection to the infant, the infant's connection to the mother, as well as all of the resonances of this relationship. There has been a great deal of critical inquiry into motherhood in the context of feminism, but what is most surprising is the lack of critical attention paid to fictional representations of infants in light of the extraordinary and irrevocable changes they provoke. Where mother-infant interaction in the earlier works of the twentieth century had been depicted by both male and female writers as something best gotten over with quickly, the writing that emerges during the 1960s and '70s represents motherhood, and, if you will, fetushood, as disruptive to the hegemonic patriarchal structure. Writing about the uniquely feminine experience of mothering a baby becomes a means of expression that empowers women. It is interesting that in the decades most politically resistant to the notion that biology is destiny, women writers explore their own subjectivity in its relation to an other that is the baby. In novels where women writers explore the mother's connection with the growing fetus and the new baby in detail, male distance from the reproductive process becomes insignificant.

Postwar novels of the 1940s and '50s explore the shame and humiliation that women feel for having conceived and given birth to babies in contravention of accepted moral codes. Male writers who are complicit with patriarchal structures—whose work in society is to ensure proper paternity—have written many of these novels. The disruption of such structures occurs in the 1960s and '70s with investigations of the rich interrelations between fetus and mother, and baby and mother. This is the palpable, vital relationship that both Adrienne Rich and Julia Kristeva have written about. Rich cites the mother's reaction to her infant as an example of the mother/child dialogue that is

> crystallized in such moments as when, hearing her child's cry, she feels milk rush into her breast; when, as the child first suckles, the uterus begins contracting and returning to its normal size, and when later, the child's mouth, caressing the nipple, creates waves of sensuality in the womb where it once lay; or when, smelling the breast even in sleep, the child starts to root and grope for the nipple. (*Of Woman* 17)

The child cries, the mother's breasts fill with milk. As the infant sucks, the uterus contracts. Such a connection is biological, instinctive, and exists apart from language, before language, yet it is no less crucial for that. Without language the child learns through "the mother's eyes, her smile, her stroking touch…you are there" (Rich, *Of Woman* 18). This is a relationship that stands apart from considerations of shame or legitimacy. The baby simply is. And its effects are potent.

Even before birth the fetus has already been at work changing the mother's body in preparation for a radical splitting of the subject in the process of creating a new one. Rich, for example, describes how, "in pregnancy" she sensed the embryo not, as in Freud's terms, "decidedly internal," but rather,

> as something inside and of me, yet becoming hourly and daily more separate, on its way to becoming separate from me and of-itself. In early pregnancy the stirring of the fetus felt like ghostly tremors of my own body, later like the movements of a being imprisoned in me; but both sensations were my sensations, contributing to my own sense of physical and psychic space.… The child that I carry for nine months can be defined neither as me or as not-me. Far from existing in the mode of "inner space," women are powerfully and vulnerably attuned both to "inner" and "outer" because for us the two are continuous, not polar. (*Of Woman* 48)

Socially, questions of shame and illegitimacy may arise, but biologically, such questions do not signify. A pregnant woman is aware of life going on within her and she is aware of the external effects. The infant's life and her own are, in fact, connected and contiguous. This awareness is profound and mysterious, growing, as Rich says, with the growth of the baby regardless of whether the mother is married or not. The affirmation of this intense connection fractures sociological concerns about legitimacy.

Often the relationship between infant or fetus and mother is one where the question of who is in control is difficult to answer. Rich's analysis of the profound nature of pregnancy and motherhood permits a reappropriation of the experience that both empowers women and enslaves them. While the infant depends on its mother for life, for nourishment and care, the mother, in choosing to nurture the fetus/infant, permits her own enslavement to bodily changes, different dietary requirements, different clothing, less energy, more fatigue, cranky bowels, intolerant bladder, stretch marks, and swollen ankles. Overarching all these submissions is the submission to the medical conveyor belt of physician care which, in the 1960s and '70s, was almost exclusively male physician care during pregnancy. The mother's life is not her own. In many ways, the baby is in charge.

Several women writers of the 1960s and '70s explore this question of ownership and power in the relationship between the baby and its mother. It is significant that each of *A Jest of God*, *Mrs. Blood*, *The Edible Woman*, *Surfacing*, and *The Honeyman Festival*, deals with pregnancy, placing the pregnant woman in a particular social position—where she is beyond the excitement of courtship, where certain life decisions have already been made, and where options are closing down rather than opening up.[11] In constructing the figure of the unborn infant, each of these books, although generically different, inquires into a specific construction of the woman.[12] While women in these decades acted politically and socially to resist being defined by their ability to reproduce, many of the novels published nevertheless deal specifically with women in the middle of the reproductive process. Women writers assert themselves as people who know about pregnancy and about babies. They enter a conversation without ultimate answers that explores the complex issues surrounding the mother/infant bond as these writers explore women's connection to babies within the literary world. It turns out to be a connection that empowers, that gives women a voice—sometimes constrained, but always articulate.

Women writers give voice to the particular concerns of women as these relate to sexuality and to pregnancy. They begin to question social constraints about legitimacy during these decades when social mores are increasingly challenged. In Margaret Laurence's *A Jest of God*, for example, the protagonist, Rachel Cameron, considers her reproductive options when she feels certain she is pregnant. The novel explores issues concerning illegitimacy from a distinctly female perspective that is complicated by love and constraint. If, as Diana Brydon asserts, Margaret Laurence provides a "composite portrait of Canadian women in the middle of this century" (184), then it is also true that Laurence extends such portraiture to the infant, as her writing destabilizes the power of social taboos against illegitimacy. Although this novel is written twenty years after Roy's *The Tin Flute*, things have not changed much for the single mother or for the baby. Rachel experiences the same fear and anxiety as Florentine. However, unlike Florentine, she gives serious consideration to the possibility of keeping the baby, of flouting social convention in the face of her mother's stiff dignity and in the face of the town of Manawaka. The enormity of Rachel's decision is manifest in Laurence's characterization of her as a docile daughter who never gives her mother any worries. Rachel's docility is not uncomplicated, however, and although there is no actual baby, its very possibility changes her life. As Nora Foster Stovel says of the character, "Margaret Laurence was a sexual pioneer in *A Jest of God* because she explores female sexuality and challenges the old double standard. By depicting a woman's sexual awakening and examining the forbidden issues of contraception, abortion, and single parenthood, Laurence makes feminist history" (13).

Laurence is careful to establish Rachel's character along certain lines. At age thirty-four, Rachel feels that she has to be on guard against the tendency to become "odd" (8). She has already found herself beginning to "brood" (8). She is a single woman who lives at home with her mother, whose big outing of the week is to go to "Tabernacle" with another single woman. These aspects of her life speak of Rachel's conformity to community expectations about what her life should be. Rachel's voice is a quiet one. Her reticence extends to her relationship with her mother and her boss. She is compliant, outwardly at least, and if she rebels in her thoughts it is to no effect. When her mother coerces Rachel into doing what she wants, Rachel either complies or insists on her own way, but with a great deal of discomfort. For example, when Mrs. Cameron suggests that Rachel's orange scarf is "a little bright" (46) for her green coat, Rachel refuses to change, but she is caught whether she complies or not. She says, "I won't change. I don't like the pink scarf. But now I won't feel right about the orange one either" (46). Laurence constructs Rachel as someone who pursues the path of least resistance. When she thinks she might be pregnant, the shock and the potential for public shame are that much more powerful because of Laurence's creation of her personality as extremely meek. She is not someone to flout the conventions of her small prairie town and yet the thought of the infant growing within her gives her power, an ability to come to a decision no matter what the consequences. And she is certain that the consequences will be dire.

One of the consequences for Rachel will be, according to Jonathan Kertzer, her voice. "Voice has symbolic significance in the novel" ("Margaret Laurence" 281). Kertzer refers to the "elaborate network of references to barbaric speech, spells, prayers, prophecies, holy words, ecstatic utterance, and the gift of tongues," asserting that "Rachel associates words with all that is hidden, true, and shameful" (281). Rachel has an overt life that she lives in the eyes of her mother and coworkers, but she also has a secret life that is associated with sexual fantasies which she attempts to repress and an emerging voice within that she also fights against. She often has to coax herself to say nothing in response to her mother's jibes. As her mother reiterates that Rachel is a "born teacher" (23), a title that frustrates and confines Rachel, she tells herself to "Stop. Stop it, Rachel. Steady. Get a grip on yourself now. Relax. Sleep. Try" (23). Rachel's secret, rebellious life also shows traces of erupting in her suppressed laughter at her mother's outrage because of a neighbour's illegitimate twins. Rachel is also afflicted with chronic headaches and insomnia, signs that the stresses of quiet conformity are barely contained in her body. Finally, lying in bed and unable to sleep, Rachel conjures an image of a man whose "features are blurred as though his were a face seen through water" (25). Rachel's fantasy and subsequent masturbation suggest that her grip on "proper" spinsterish behaviour is tenuous. These unexpected behaviours foreshadow a larger break with the social norms of Manawaka. Rachel knows her body, is familiar with its longings which function as a source of disruption to her carefully crafted persona. This is a disruption that the infant itself, though it is only imagined, will augment.

In spite of the "scene" she fabricates for herself when she cannot sleep, Rachel says that she "can't bear scenes" of any kind (53); the experience at the Tabernacle of falling down and speaking in tongues is, therefore, overwhelming and appalling to her. She is shocked by the sound of her own voice, "Chattering, crying, ululating, the forbidden transformed cryptically to nonsense, dragged from the crypt" (42). In the Tabernacle Rachel is overcome by a voice she cannot recognize as her own. One "ululating...dragged from the crypt," dragged, in essence, from its burial place deep within herself. The heat of the room and the feverishness of the occasion compel her to utterance, a crying that she has kept hidden within. That she should succumb to the atmosphere, that she should make a spectacle of herself, mortifies Rachel. She informs Calla that "more than anything" she detests "hysteria" (44). This word choice, considering the etymology, is interesting. "Hysteria" comes from the Greek, "hystera" referring to the uterus or womb and once characterized as "suffering in the uterus, womb: because women seemed to be hysterical more than men, hysteria was attributed by the ancients to disturbances of the uterus" (*Webster's Dictionary*). Rachel particularly loathes an emotional excitability thought at one time to be connected to the uterus. The irony is that Rachel's uterus will turn out to betray her in more ways than one.

Laurence verifies a sense of community standards through the upright Mrs. Cameron who can refer only euphemistically to the disaster that has occurred in the Stewart family. The disaster is, of course, Cassie's illegitimate twins, born while she has "been away" (64). Mrs. Cameron says, "It's dreadful for her mother, a nice woman.... The girl isn't married and no one even in prospect" (64). The notion that two illegitimate babies are worse than one subjects Rachel to a "powerful undercurrent of laughter" (64). It is Rachel's laughter that offers a sign that she will find a way to resist the imposition of silence. The laughter, although an undercurrent, is at least present. Twins, she thinks, must be in her mother's eyes "twice as reprehensible as one" (64). Cassie's intention to keep the babies is, for Mrs. Cameron, "the awful thing," an unfathomable decision based on "thoughtlessness" (64). Mrs. Cameron says, "I thank my lucky stars I never had a moment's worry with either of my daughters" (64). This foreshadows Rachel's imminent unwed pregnancy, and it also establishes the nature of community gossip. The "fall" of the Stewart girl buttresses Mrs. Cameron's sense that her family is superior. Stacy is already respectably married. Rachel notices her mother's use of the past tense in "thanking her lucky stars." At her age Rachel is presumably no threat to her mother's notions of propriety.

The contradictory forces in Rachel's personality, her need to conform and her need to rebel, clash in her affair with Nick Kazlik.[13] Once she has a relationship with him and suspects that she might be pregnant, she can no longer be the woman she has pretended to be. Rachel had believed that the sterility of her character itself would prevent such an unlikely occurrence as pregnancy. "I can't believe it could happen though. A thing like that—to grow a child inside one's structure and have it born alive? Not within me. It couldn't" (124). Rachel reveals volumes about her character when she uses the word "structure" in reference to her own body. The word connotes architecture rather than flesh. Rachel's life has not been one that, as Kristeva writes, explores "the complexity of the female experience, with all that this complexity comprises in joy and pain" ("Women's Time" 207). Far from it. What complexity there is in Rachel's life occurs in the silence of her bedroom or within her own thoughts.

Laurence's book, published in 1966, three years before the legalization of abortion, broaches some risky topics. She writes frankly about Rachel's sexual desire and satisfaction, and she explores the real longing Rachel has, when her period is overdue, to consider the thing, the pregnancy, itself "by itself," which, considering the sterility of her life, "seems more than [she] could ever have hoped for" (165). Considered on its own, what Rachel wants more than anything is to have this baby that she believes herself to be carrying. Her love for Nick gives her this certainty and this affinity with the baby. If she had despised him, she claims, she could not have borne his child. The value of the baby, then, is contingent for Rachel on her feelings for its father. As such, its value is immense.

However, because she lives in Manawaka, because she is the daughter of her mother, she must face the fact that the child, indeed, "can't be borne. Not by [her]" (166). Rachel imagines her mother's insistent and interminable reproaches, the town's gossip, and her own unbearable position. She understands that she must destroy the child:

> I know I have to do something. I can't bear it. I have to get rid of it.
> I guess that is the phrase which is used. Get rid of it. Like a casual
> itch which one could scratch and abolish. I have to get rid of it.
> Excess baggage. Garbage.... I have to get it out of me. (169)

Rachel is caught between two extremes: she cannot bear the child and she cannot end its life. She tries to compare the baby to an itch that she "could scratch and abolish." The text communicates both her sense of urgency—"I have to get it out of me"—and her anxiety—"I can't bear it." She wonders if she could not perhaps act as her own "angel-maker" (179), using a knitting needle to bring about an end. She has heard that babies are "surprisingly difficult to kill," that "no delicate probing would ever dislodge" them (179). In the same breath, she is fascinated by the implications of the word "lodge." She has given the baby lodging: "How incredible that seems. I've given it house room. It's growing there, by itself. It's got everything it needs, for now" (179). Again, one senses an architectural metaphor at work. Rachel wants to "house" the baby, provide the shelter it needs since it has "everything" else "for now."

The juxtaposition of the tectonic image with her more organic sense that a baby is "growing there" suggests that Rachel is becoming more alive in spite of her dread. The possibility that she is pregnant is already transforming her life. She is fully engaged with the duality of illegitimate pregnancy. She imagines both the shame and the constraint, and she also imagines herself in labour and delivery; she imagines herself to be a mother, potentially freed from the demands of her own querulous

mother. Like a swinging pendulum, Rachel vacillates between understanding the need "to get rid of it" and the longing to have the child, to
connect in a vibrant, vital manner with life. No sooner does she assert
the necessity of abortion than she changes her mind. The infant is
already a presence exerting force:

> It will be infinitesimal. It couldn't be seen with the human eye, it's
> that small, but the thing will grow.… It will have a voice. It will be
> able to cry out. I could bear a living creature. It would be possible.
> Something you could touch and could see that it had the frame-
> work of bones, the bones that weren't set for all time but would
> lengthen and change by themselves, and that it had features, and
> a skull in which the convoluted maze did as it pleased, irrespective
> of theories, and that it had eyes. It would be possessed of the
> means of seeing. (169)

The baby will have a "framework of bones," a composition that is
simultaneously architectural and organic, and it will have breath and a
voice. For Rachel, who has been so ashamed at her own public "crying
out," the thought that her infant will "have a voice" is a powerful one.
Moreover, the thought that she could "bear a living creature" is both
astonishing and empowering. Considered apart from the proprieties of
her time and place, the thought is thrilling to Rachel. The possibilities for
life, for the growing child and its potential, are, for Rachel, undeniable.
The baby exerts the force of its subjectivity by virtue of its existence, by
virtue of her knowledge that this incomparable, unknowable "other"
grows within her. Her incredulity is generated not only by the fact that
there should be a baby inexplicably growing but also that it should be
growing within a body she assumed was too sterile to cultivate life. The
mere possibility of this baby changes everything for Rachel.

Rachel is transformed despite the fact that her period has stopped
because of a tumour, not because of a baby. Stovel claims that "Rachel
has not delivered a child, but she has given birth to an adult self" (68).
Other critics have agreed that having faced possible motherhood,
Rachel becomes the mother and climbs out from under her own
mother's thumb.[14] But most have focused on Rachel's relationships
with Nick and Calla and their power to change Rachel. Although these
factors do alter Rachel and contribute to her sense of self, nothing does
so more than the infant she imagines herself to be pregnant with. The
text resonates with references to the biblical Rachel crying for her children, and critics have made much of Laurence's Rachel and her need

for fulfillment. But what they have neglected is the power of the baby to transform Rachel into someone who can mother her mother. She can do this only after she has been through the trauma of even an illusory baby. Once she has faced that, she decides that they will move to Vancouver to be closer to Rachel's sister. When Mrs. Cameron embarks on a litany of her health complaints, Rachel meets every objection and stands firm. Her phantom pregnancy has altered her perception of herself and her own potential to a remarkable degree. The very thought of the baby has taken her over and enforced a previously unknown maturity.

Writing by women in the 1960s and '70s about the baby pushes at socially proper limits of what it is speakable. Laurence explores issues of illegitimacy and abortion in *A Jest of God*. Audrey Thomas's *Mrs. Blood* is noteworthy for its visceral detailing of a woman's experience of miscarriage. As Laurence Ricou says of Thomas's work, "it must be the most feminine novel in Canada" ("Phyllis Webb" 205). Critics have discussed the confessional/autobiographical nature of Thomas's fiction, and the weaknesses and strengths of this type of writing.[15] Whatever side the discussion falls on, and it varies from critic to critic, the fact remains that Thomas's *Mrs. Blood* provides significant insight into one kind of representation of the infant—that is, the infant who will not survive gestation to be born. Much research has been done recently on the effects of miscarriage and new attention is being focused on the significant loss to the mother when the baby she is carrying dies.[16] But Thomas's novel is the first to explore, in an extended way, women's personal anguish for the loss of a developing baby. It is valuable because it so unreservedly delineates the nature of Mrs. Blood's personal catastrophe. The infant is again configured in terms of a binary opposition between the constraint it imposes—the narrator must lie still to try to save it—and the desire she has to make her infant survive.

Her name itself is something that requires pause. At the novel's beginning, the protagonist says "Some days my name is Mrs. Blood; some days it's Mrs. Thing" (11). The main character is defined either by her blood, which flows with her incipient miscarriage, or by the objectification she feels because of her life's circumstances. The two names reduce her to the functions she performs. She bleeds and she is acted upon. Mrs. Blood/Thing is motivated by love for the baby within her, fear that it will die, and fear that she also might die. Thomas's narrator is both double-named and double-voiced, on the one hand, constructing herself as a quiescent fetus-serving being, on the other, vividly inscribing women's experience of pregnancy, miscarriage, and birth. This story combines the powerful metaphors of blood and milk to juxtapose the connection of birth with death, in this case, the death of the infant before it is born. As Anne Archer writes of Thomas, "procreation...is equated with blood, death, and denial" (217). Thomas's novel is valuable because, while it is intense and at times overburdened, it is nevertheless a sustained, unapologetic female perspective that explores the contradictions that are inherent for women in pregnancy, birth, and motherhood.

Thomas's Mrs. Blood lies flat on her back in an African hospital. She says, echoing Descartes, "I am here because I bleed" (14). Because she bleeds, Mrs. Blood identifies with all women of childbearing age; the novel iterates the experience of this group. Images of blood and death permeate the novel and act as an alarm sounded by Thomas, insisting that attention must be paid. Thomas forges a connection between blood, copulation, birth, and mortality, all vital human activities which, according to Mrs. Blood, "are horizontal occupations that occur between clean sheets" (118). Thomas speaks here to the fact that society casts clean sheets, in a sense, over life's most significant events. That is, social decorum prohibits the frank discussion of "vital human activities," particularly the ones that affect women. Thomas comes out from behind the "pale blue plastic curtains" (14) where most of Mrs. Blood's treatment and bodily functions are performed, offering a revelatory utterance that foregrounds the experience of women in one of their most essential activities.

Part of that experience is loss of power. In the hospital Mrs. Blood loses more and more control over what happens to her and over her reactions. She is afraid that she is becoming like the mad women she once cared for, that if she loses complete emotional control and starts to cry, she "would be carried screaming to a place far worse than this" (36). Thomas reveals the association of madness and femininity with the use of the term "hysterical" (172) to describe the women's condition. Mrs. Blood says that the women she had cared for were not "real women to [her], you know, screaming, kicking monstrosities" (172). This, now, is the end she fears for herself. Already weak, Mrs. Blood fears that the next step for her is madness, complete self-negation. Even the presence of the other women from the European compound renders her helpless "like some enormous baby in a cot" (28). Her prone position requires that she look up to visitors, particularly visitors who are "brave and competent and healthy" (29). Mrs. Blood longs to be "a hardy annual, not something wilting on a too thin and bloody stalk" (29). The novel probes women's heterogeneous responses to the state of being pregnant with all its weakness, love, and strength.

In this exploration of the weakness and indignity suffered by pregnant women, Thomas presents an image of Mrs. Blood waiting in the hospital "for the iron shot" (14), and thinking about Joseph, her house help, at home. The juxtaposition of male and female lives is stark. Mrs. Blood's buttocks are tensed in anticipation of the needle. She wonders about Joseph, who might be "relaxing on the back stoop, smoking *Tusker For Men*, not aware of his buttocks at all, but only aware of the silent, ordered house behind him, maybe the smell of the bread baking, and the feel of the first drag on his cigarette" (14). Joseph is a man, not pregnant, not bleeding, enjoying something as simple as a cigarette—a cigarette made and marketed for men—without having to tense his backside against what the next moment will bring.

Thomas gestures toward the medicalization of pregnancy and the manner in which it further denies women power. Mrs. Blood longs to carry her child safely to delivery and fears that she will fail. She refers to the baby as "my nutmeat, my centre, my dying darling" (26). She is caught in stasis. If she moves, the baby will miscarry and die. If she does not move, Mrs. Blood fears she will go mad. Her maternal body is in danger and she therefore submits to the authority of Dr. Biswas. Her commitment to the child's well-being enforces compliance, a compliance so great that Mrs. Blood is never named in the novel, although her doctor is. She knows him only by his title and by his last name in spite of his intimate knowledge of her body. Dr. Biswas's authority is gentle. We are told that he is "young and delicate and intellectual" (47), often playing word games with Mrs. Blood and calmly reassuring her on his daily rounds. When she is first admitted, he says that he will "have a little look," but that she "should stay here for a while." Mrs. Blood replies, "'Do I have to?' (and my voice thin and high—the voice of a child at the dentist's)" (47). Mrs. Blood's fear is evident, as is her regression to an almost child-like whining. While motivated by love to save her baby, the cost to her as a subject—a woman engaged with enacting her own life—is clear.

Thomas underscores the fact that pregnancy is a condition fraught with hazards, not the least of which is the powerlessness that it imposes upon women. Dr. Biswas and Mrs. Blood discuss the best way to learn French. When Mrs. Blood suggests that the way she learned the language, through the repetition of correct but rather useless statements such as, "J'entre dans la salle de classe," was a nonsensical approach, Dr. Biswas contradicts her: "But why is this nonsense? You have learned French following certain rigid patterns.... I think the old methods have a great deal to recommend them" (90). Dr. Biswas is a proponent of rigid patterns and old methods, the same patterns and methods that made it impossible for Mrs. Blood to learn to speak French effectively. Although she agrees that "we must stick to the patterns," in fact, Mrs. Blood needs to break those patterns in order to gain a voice, to speak on behalf of herself and her child.

Biswas's authority contrasts sharply with the style of the "officious" Dr. Shankar who has a loud voice and who always wears his rubber operating room boots on rounds and is terse with his patients. Thomas composes a compelling contrast at the level of sound in the names of the physicians. Dr. Biswas's name is composed of softer sounds while Dr. Shankar's clanks harshly.[17] Mrs. Blood knows he became a gynecologist because he likes power: "his boots tell me about him" (94). Dr. Shankar's authority sounds in every step he takes, but whether that male, medical authority is loud or quiet, it nevertheless persists and demands compliance. When Mrs. Blood was born her mother recalls that "they put a bit of gauze over my eyes. I think they did it always, then. Just to make sure everything was all right, you know, before they let the mother see her baby" (138). This information shocks Mrs. Blood, but emphasizes medical dominance over childbirth. The mother has no choice; others decide for her whether the baby meets a standard of acceptability.

Yet Mrs. Blood also valorizes women who "do" birth well. She recalls being "really proud" of herself when Nicholas was born because she was "not at all afraid" and when her husband came back, she "was sitting up eating tea and toast and the sun was streaming in the windows" (87). She approves of the absence of fear, the quick recovery, the complicit sun which shines after Nicholas's birth, as some kind of affirmation of her own harmony with natural forces. Mrs. Blood refers to primitive women who "squat in the fields" to give birth (118), suggesting that she longs for a primordial birth experience where the birthing mother is empowered by the act of giving life to the infant, an act that liberates women from the victimization of the horizontal. What Mrs. Blood longs for is an experience that celebrates natality, that enables her to focus on the baby, to engage actively and purposefully in the job that will bring the baby into the world. Instead, because of the imminent loss of a baby, Mrs. Blood renders herself passive, attempting to save it. And she is frustrated by her passivity.

Most compelling is the novel's navigation of the dichotomy women feel between strong attachment to the baby before and after it is born, and the sacrifice of pregnancy and childbirth. The baby is born through the "red-ring" of the mother's pain. Thomas describes the birth in fierce terms:

> They come out, if properly, head first and downwards, diving into life through the blazing red-ring of their mother's agony, as though through a hoop of fire. They are held up and admired and patted on the back as though they, and not the broken, spent thing lying on the table, were the heroes.
>
> And once you have caught them, held them up and slapped them into breathing
>
> You cannot throw them back.
>
> Earlier, when just a cipher—under seven inches like a trout—perhaps they could be thrown back; only thrown back not to thrive and grow but to become nothing, an excrescence.
>
> Dive for life they do, as you or I, braver or younger or in another clime, might dive for pearls.... And the bloody thing in the bed or on the table smiles and forgets the horror and the outrage and holds out her arms to receive her violator, her hero, her fish, saying, "This is my body which was given for thee. Feed on me in thy heart by faith and by thanksgiving." (182-83)

Writing of the baby's struggle for life, Thomas inverts the term, "hero," which, she writes, is misapplied to the newborn baby. Then, when the mother "smiles and forgets the horror and outrage," she holds out her arms "to receive" the baby who is both her "hero" and her "violator." The mother is "the broken, spent thing lying on the table" whose life "was given" for the baby's. In a very literal fashion, Mrs. Blood is giving her life up for her baby. This is something she does out of love. But clearly, she is not unequivocal about childbirth, or about the baby. "Once you have caught them.... You cannot throw them back." The infant's cells, as Kristeva says, fuse and split. Moreover, the presence, as Rich describes it, gradually grows and takes over the woman's body. These are not met with indifference or unambiguous welcome. In her anger and suffering, Mrs. Blood's subjectivity is intimately connected to the infant; it is a connection that is not smoothly enacted. These are the decades when women writers emerge from behind the "blue plastic curtains" (14) that conceal life's functions, especially pregnancy and childbirth. Women writers, Thomas among them, explore their understanding of their biology and radically alter perceptions of the baby. Far from demystifying the infant, or women's response to it, this novel problematizes the complex discourse of the body and the baby.

It's a discourse that includes some anger for men who have not been aware of the immense courage of women and all that they endure. Thomas returns again and again to religious imagery, referring to Christ at the Last Supper who commands the disciples to eat and drink in remembrance of him. Mrs. Blood equates her broken, bleeding body with Christ's. Wine is, in her case, the blood that "dries sticky on the sheets and in the secret places" (21). She herself is being consumed for the redemption or life of the infant. The communion metaphor also suggests that Mrs. Blood wants to bring about a deeper connection with her husband, Jason. She orders herself:

> Say your beads and be silent. And call out to Jason who has no ears, "This is my body," and fling back the sheets and cry out to him who has no eyes, "And this is my blood." And take his head between your hands and force it down, crying, "Drink this, eat this in remembrance of me," and afterwards cry, "Bow down," and cut off his head with the beautiful silver blade of the fury and pain you have been hiding underneath the white vestments in which you clothe yourself and behind the white altar upon which you sleep. (91-92)

Having invoked silence, Mrs. Blood calls for an immediate transgression of that silence. She feels an urgent necessity to "call out" to her husband who, without ears, is clearly unable to hear her, and to violently throw back the sheets to show him her blood even though he has no eyes, no means of perceiving what the significance of that blood is. Similarly, she would force his head down so that he tastes the source of the bleeding, compel him to drink and eat, an image at once sexual, dominating, and eucharistic. It might be construed as invitation to share in the experience of the miscarriage except for Mrs. Blood's "fury and pain" which are conceptualized as a "beautiful silver blade" she might use to decapitate her husband. This is a call to arms, an expression of female rage too long hidden behind the chaste "white vestments" with which women have clothed themselves. Both the author-

ity of the church, as represented by the "crumbling wafers," and the
authority of the male, whom Thomas's character would force to drink
her blood, are "crumbling" (92). Mrs. Blood would force her husband to
face the essence of her suffering in the loss of their baby.

Thomas's novel articulates both women's weakness and women's
strength as they pertain to the baby. Mrs. Blood/Thing does not succeed
in pre-empting a miscarriage. However, the concern of *Mrs. Blood* is the
articulation of women's complex response to the infant, both before
and after birth. Barbara Godard finds that while Thomas is "not a feminist in the strict sense of the word [however one defines 'strict'],
Thomas nonetheless works to advance women's knowledge of themselves...and this dedication to the real is political in a broad sense"
(202). Like the work of other women writers of these decades, Thomas's
work challenges perception of pregnancy and babies. Her representation privileges the "real": the way babies really are, the way babies
really affect women. And what's most interesting is the way that the
ideal is folded into that reality. The baby the narrator carries is always
already her "nutmeat" and her "darling." These are sentimental terms
and yet Thomas's portrayal is of a mother-infant connection grounded
in an all too painful and bloody real.

Thomas is part of a larger movement of women writers who focus
attention on this relationship in such a way as to lay groundwork for
the increasing significance of the baby. As Lorna Irvine says, childbearing "is actually and metaphorically central in women's narrative" (35).
What has been missing in the analysis of women and childbearing,
however, is the child itself, an undeniably unmetaphoric being. Irvine
responds here to the notion put forward by Susan Gubar that "the startling centrality of childbearing in the künstlerroman of women represents a response to the hegemonic texts and contexts of our culture that
either appropriate the birth metaphor to legitimize the 'brain children'
of men or, even more destructively, inscribe female creativity in the
womb to insult women whose productions then smack of the *re*petition
of *re*production, its involuntary physicality" (qtd. in Irvine 35). On the
contrary, Thomas's novel explores the actual deliberate work of pregnancy, the living fact of the baby and the mother's connection to it. In
the work of "labour," that is, the delivery of a baby, according to Mary
O'Brien and Di Brandt, there is a "social importance" (Brandt 13) that
must not be negated, must not be concealed underneath "white vestments" or behind curtains. Thomas's Mrs. Blood refuses to accept nega-

tion, in spite of the passivity she accepts in her efforts to save her baby. As Irvine claims, "the space is not always clean and it certainly is not well-lit"; however, by writing the baby so provocatively, Thomas's narrator "turns it into legend" (36). Thomas foregrounds the infant, the mother's real work to nurture and save it, and the impact it always has upon her.

As Thomas's Mrs. Blood is involved in a doubling of voice that represents the duality inherent in the figure of the baby, so also does Atwood's *The Edible Woman* explore the tension between the baby as object of loathing and object of desire. Atwood's depiction of the baby is significant because it dissects all that is most loathsome about women's connection to this small figure. She examines the disarray caused by women's vulnerability to biology, mocking both the women engaged in pregnancy and baby care and those who are appalled by it. She writes what people know to be true about babies, that they are untidy and malodorous, that they cause disruptions to otherwise well-planned and ordered lives, and that they limit women's capacity to fulfill themselves intellectually and socially. Nevertheless, what is most compelling about this satiric exposé is the undermining work of the subtext so that even in Clara's vegetable-like existence, which her connection to her babies forces upon her, there persists a strain of engagement with infants at the level of the ideal that is subversive to the narrative's overt unfolding. Atwood has said of Simone de Beauvoir and Betty Friedan that "they got a lot right, for me, but there was one thing they got wrong. They were assuring me that I didn't have to get married and have children. But what I wanted was someone to tell me I could" ("Great Unexpectations" xvi). She articulates here the driving force behind Kristeva's inquiry into women's desire to have babies, which for decades has been considered counter to feminism.

Marian's friend, Clara, in *The Edible Woman*, represents all of the chaos, entrapment, and mind-numbing engagement with bodily extrusions associated with pregnancy and babies. Seen through Marian's eyes, Clara's life is nightmarish in its encounter with the viscera of motherhood. For Marian, who is obsessively concerned with being "all right" (3), with being orderly in her approach to life, "efficient for Ainsley's benefit" (4), on time for work, polite to the sanctimonious landlady, accommodating to her lover, the chaos of Clara's life is almost unbearable. Clara's house, even the walk up to the "doormat-sized lawn" that "had not been cut for some time" is disordered because of her children. Marian has to step over the "nearly-decapitated doll," around the baby carriage where there was "a large teddy-bear with the stuffing coming out" (24). The inhabitants of the house are also in this same semidecaying state where the forces of entropy seem expedited by the presence of small children. Joe answers the door "after several minutes...harried and uncombed, doing up the buttons on his shirt" (24). Clara is in the back yard which Marian and Ainsley can find only after "stepping over some of the scattered obstacles and around others. We negotiated the stairs of the back porch, which were overgrown with empty bottles of all kinds, beer bottles, milk bottles, wine and scotch bottles, and baby bottles" (24). Motherhood, indeed parenthood, is no easy feat. It takes numerous and varied bottles to sustain both the parents and the children of this household.

Clara is "holding her latest baby somewhere in the vicinity of what had once been her lap" (24). Atwood's description is unsparing. Marian examines Clara as though under a microscope, as though she were a creature alien to Marian's experience or understanding. Clara's seven-months-pregnant body is compared to a boa constrictor "that has swallowed a watermelon" (24). Interestingly, Clara's head in proportion to her body seems "smaller and even more fragile by contrast" (24). Marian perceives Clara as a "strange vegetable growth, a bulbous tuber that had sent out four thin white roots and a tiny pale-yellow flower" (25). The roots are Clara's arms and legs and the flower is her head. As such, she appears to be barely sentient, much less intelligent. Based upon Marian's observation of Clara, the answer to Kristeva's question of what it means to give birth to a baby is that one must live on the outskirts, turn oneself, or be turned by babies, into a vegetable. It means becoming monstrous. To cap the picture, Clara is also barefoot and her latest baby is whimpering. Marian feels helpless, acting only as a "witness, or perhaps a kind of blotter...absorbing a little of the boredom" (25). However, it may be possible that Marian is the only one who is bored. Certainly Ainsley encounters the same event; however, when she leaves Clara's, it is with the firm decision that she wants to have a baby.

Atwood's representation of the baby is unusual because of the sarcastic tone she uses, which constructs the baby in terms that are much less than ideal and which has more to do with the way women really talk about their babies. There is no sense of wistful longing for a baby, and certainly no immediate sense that Clara finds in the baby a source of meaning and value. On the contrary, Clara refers to the baby as a "leech," or a kind of creature similar to an octopus, "covered with suckers" (25). The baby stares at Ainsley, drools, and wets on her dress, an act Clara takes in stride as she removes the now-howling infant from Ainsley's arms. She calls the baby a "goddamned fire-hydrant," a "stinking little geyser," and accuses her of "spouting" on "mummy's friend." After this incident, Clara denies that there is any such thing as "maternal instinct," insisting that she cannot fathom how people "can love their children till they start to be human beings" (27). The suggestion is clear that infants are less than human. Atwood writes to comic effect, allowing Clara's voice to desentimentalize discourse about babies. There is, for the first time in Canadian fiction, no sense that the babies are precious. On the contrary, the chaos of the home, the whining baby, the pregnant incapacity of Clara, the dishevelment of Joe, are compounded by Arthur, the toilet-training toddler, who is Clara's "little bugger," "little bastard," and "little demon" (28). Clara deprecates her children, their bodily functions, and her own responsibility to deal with them. This is a lavishly unsentimental picture of babies that speaks to Clara's resistance to stereotypes about motherhood. Compare Clara's "fire-hydrants" with Gabrielle Roy's depiction of Rose-Anna and her baby in whose presence she feels beatified, or even to Audrey Thomas's Mrs. Blood who refers to the baby as her "nutmeat." These divergent descriptions demonstrate a change in cultural discourse, in the sorts of ways one can talk about babies. As well, Atwood's Clara demonstrates a certain ironic distance from her offspring.

Yet Atwood also presents complementary if not interconnected views of the power of the infant to alter Clara's life. One view is that Clara's voice, while heavily laden with irony, can clearly function only on a foundation of real love and care for the babies she gives birth to. On the other hand, there is also a strong sense in the text of repugnance toward the life that Clara lives as a mother. Even the dinner itself, "wizened meat balls and noodles from a noodle mix, with lettuce" followed by "that new canned rice pudding" (29), seems to reflect the couple's weariness and diminished capacity. This may be repugnance only through the eyes of Marian, but it seems clear that Ainsley, too, is affected by the way that Clara parents her babies. It troubles her to such an extent that she wants to have a baby in order to show how it ought to be done correctly.[18]

Compounding the sense of chaos and exhaustion is the information that Clara's pregnancies are unplanned. Clara "greeted her first pregnancy with astonishment...her second with dismay," and that now, "during her third, she had subsided into a grim but inert fatalism" (30). In spite of the widespread availability of contraception and the fact that abortion was legalized the same year that *The Edible Woman* was published, Clara seems unable to control her fecundity. Indeed, she seems unable to act either on her own behalf or on anyone else's. This lack of control is something that appalls Marian whose need for control is so rampant that she endures throughout the novel an increasingly obsessive eating disorder. Clara's own metaphors for her babies "included barnacles encrusting a ship and limpets clinging to a rock" (30). Marian pities her and so do readers. Atwood's comically desperate revelations of parenthood leave them with no other option.

The ambiguity in the text emerges after Clara's third baby is born. What has been a fairly straightforward representation of the infant as the source of all chaos alters somewhat when Clara describes the birth. She compares the delivery experience to a sort of messy Christmas, "with all that blood and junk" (129), but the process fascinates her, particularly when "the little bugger sticks its head out." When Marian visits Clara in the hospital, even she notices the very suggestive "curved metal rod suspended like a large oval halo above the bed" (129). While Atwood carefully avoids romanticizing the birth experience, nevertheless the text explicitly evokes comparison with the Virgin Mary and the birth of Christ. Clara draws the analogy with Christmas, complete with the birth of a baby and a mother sporting a kind of halo. Furthermore, Clara feels "marvellous; really marvellous" (129). Clara's fascination contradicts all that has come before it. As Kristeva suggests in "Stabat Mater," the power of the Madonna's image, "one of the most powerful imaginary constructs known in the history of civilizations" (163), imparts to women the sense of synergy with some sublime force. In Atwood, an elusive undercurrent contradicts even Clara's coarseness in regard to her babies, which opens up the text to the love babies engender in their mothers, often in spite of the mothers themselves. While babies can, as evidenced in Clara's life, enfeeble women, wreaking havoc on their bodies and exploding what order there is, nevertheless, Clara is captivated:

> I watched the whole thing, it's messy, all that blood and junk, but I've got to admit it's sort of fascinating. Especially when the little bugger sticks its head out, and you finally know after carrying the damn thing around all that time what it *looks* like; I get so excited

waiting to see, it's like when you were little and you waited and
waited and finally got to open your Christmas presents. (129)

Atwood satirizes Clara's approach, attempting to derogate birth by
comparison with Christmas. One hardly imagines the virgin birth in
Bethlehem to have been a typically messy one, and yet this seems a failure of imagination. Imagine Mary waiting for the birth of the Saviour,
having been visited by an angel, having endured the pregnancy, the
census, the stable, and then able to see "what it looks like." While
Atwood maintains an ironic tone, there can be no doubt that Clara considers the infant to be a gift. Clara's discourse works ironically to under-
state the joy that she feels, having "waited and waited and finally"
receiving the gift.

Clara's is a joy that Marian cannot grasp. She feels the reproductive
possibilities presented by her own gender are "suddenly much too
close" in the room where these "white-sheeted outstretched women"
(129) resemble nothing so much as corpses. For Marian, giving birth is
just another way of dying. Clara is ensconced in a feminine world from
which Marian feels entirely removed. She offers to bring Clara something to read, but Clara refuses because she would not be able to con-
centrate for listening to the women around her. The discourse of the
maternity ward is fascinating to Clara but revolting to Marian. Clara
says,

> Maybe it's the hospital atmosphere, but all they ever talk about are
> their miscarriages and their diseases. It makes you feel very sickly
> after a while: you start wondering when it'll be your turn to get
> cancer of the breast or a ruptured tube, or miscarry quadruplets at
> half-weekly intervals; no kidding, that's what happened to Mrs.
> Moase, the big one over there in the far corner. And christ they're
> so *calm* about it, and they seem to think that each of their grisly lit-
> tle episodes is some kind of service medal. (130)

The representation of women's connection to birth, to babies, and to
their own bodies is again, inscribed in a satiric mode. While this enact-
ment of pregnancy and birth can be said to reduce women to stereotypical complainers, compelled by amorphous hormones to become no
more than the sum of their various ailing parts, nevertheless, one imagines Mrs. Blood on this ward, contributing to a strictly feminine discourse on the hazards women bear when they bear children. While she
is funny and irreverent, Clara is both conscious of, and complicit with,
this stereotyping, finding that she is herself "producing a few of [her]

own ailments, as though [she] has to compete" (130). Fertility, birth, motherhood, and infants themselves emerge as the subjects of a strange kind of feminist interdependence as Clara participates with the women who give voice to their experience. This is what Mary O'Brien called the "unifying female sociability attendant on the birth of a new life" (10).

Clara foregrounds women's experience, specifically as this experience relates to babies. These conversations have doubtless been going on for millennia. What is different about writing by women of the 1960s and 1970s is the medium. Kristeva writes in "Women's Time," concerning how women "might try to understand their sexual and symbolic difference in the framework of social, cultural and professional realization, in order to try, by seeing their position therein, either to fulfil their own experience to the maximum or—but always starting from this point—to go further and call into question the very apparatus itself" (198). If one aspect of the "apparatus" is the symbolic order by which the "penis…gives full meaning to the *lack* or to the *desire* which constitutes the subject" (Kristeva, "Women's Time" 198), then Clara and the other women seem not only to be fulfilling their own experience by speaking it, but further, they seem to be calling "into question the very apparatus itself."[19] They construct themselves not as women experiencing lack but as women engaging in a discourse about their own experience, which is constructed around the baby who provides a connection at once pleasurable and natural. The "apparatus" that constructs women as "other" is centred on the penis as the site of lack and desire, women's lack of and desire for. Instead, these women challenge that representation. If babies make women weak, they also make them strong. If biological determinism has constructed women as "other," and the "second sex," then biology, the capacity to give birth, to know "the other within" marks them also as astonishingly gifted. Atwood's Clara embodies the discourse of the real and the ideal, at times coarse, and at times astonished by the baby. In spite of her frailty and lack of organization, she is nevertheless caught marvelling at the experience of birth, at the appearance of the gift, the baby that is hers. And it is a marvel that she speaks along with the other women in her room. This is not a room of her own; it is a room that women share because they have given birth. While the voices are shared within the closed realm of the maternity ward, Atwood presents these discussions for a public readership who may laugh at them, but who may also pause to consider their veracity.

Atwood's portrayal of Marian, according to Darlene Kelly, leaves her without an escape, "ending where she began" (331). Kelly's assertion that "the most enduring historical aspect of *The Edible Woman* [might] be [its] portrayal of a woman's place in the sixties as no place at all" (331), is one that I take issue with. Atwood's text is eminently important for the attention it calls to babies as they are really experienced by some women, with all that experience encompasses satirically and unsentimentally. Nevertheless, she offers the merest suggestion of an answer to the question of the baby's significance.

Atwood satirizes stereotypical notions of femininity, of motherhood, and of masculinity and she does so democratically. No one is spared. The central, unnamed character in Atwood's *Surfacing* also explores the nature of motherhood in a manner much less humorous, much more haunting, than Marian's encounters in *The Edible Woman*. The narrator leaves her first baby with her ex-husband, aborts her second, and, at the novel's end, redeems these losses through the conception of a third infant. The narrator attempts to re-envision her life and the losses she has sustained. There emerges an increasing sense of sorrow in the narrator who, like Marian, becomes less stable as the story progresses. William Closson James claims that Atwood's text relates "a solo voyage, a descent into the depths of the self under the auspices of the animistic deities of lake and rock," and that the narrator "reenacts an Amerindian vision quest" (71). Critics have written extensively about *Surfacing*, reading it in Jungian terms "as a process of individuation" (Augier 11), as a primitive "female initiation into the destiny to give birth" (James 178), as "a descent to an underworld that affirms the instructive value of the Freudian unconscious" (Davey 163), and as a book fortuitously written "at the right time" and also in "the right geographical setting" (Delbaere-Garant 8). While the novel is all these things, it also tracks a narrator whose life has been marked by loss, the loss of parents, of a husband, and primarily, of her babies. The novel, published in 1972, is one of the first sustained engagements with some of the outcomes of more access to abortion and to women's consciousness-raising. It navigates, as well, the terrible tension between desire and rejection that comes to bear on the woman's relationship to the infant and it offers at the end a representation of the infant as a figure of redemption that will restore something of what the narrator has lost.

In *Surfacing* the infant cannot be considered apart from the complex social and ideological context in which it appears. While there are cer-

tainly complex contexts for representation in general, the time of publication of Atwood's book coincides with some of the most explosive in
Canadian cultural history when the conventions of legitimacy and
potential for reproductive choice are being challenged more forcefully
than ever before. Thus, babies appear in some writing by women in
more tangled ways that demonstrate an increasing candour about the
intricate and often uneasy relationship between women and babies.

Atwood configures the infant as a source of strife for the narrator
who has left one baby with her former husband and aborted another.
These are acts that shape her thinking and place her, at the novel's
opening, in an apprehensive frame of mind. She "can't believe" (7) she
is on a road that will return her to the site of her childhood, evoking
strong feelings about the loss of her own children. Instead of offering
safety, this land that is both "home ground" and "foreign territory" (12),
will disturb her perception of herself and the decisions she has made.
Like Mrs. Blood and Clara, this narrator speaks in a voice that is doubled, edged with grief and longing for redemption through the figure
of the baby. What is first known about her is that she has left a child.
She waits for "Madame to ask about the baby," and anticipates the lie
that she will tell about leaving him behind in the city (25). She understands that leaving her child is "an unpardonable sin," both in the eyes
of the community and most particularly in the eyes of her parents, but
her feeling is that the child was never hers. She refers in a general way
to her stupidity (31), but she does not clarify whether she refers to the
marriage, the birth, or to the divorce and abandonment of the child. For
the narrator, her ex-husband's baby was instrumental in her own objectification. During her marriage she "felt like an incubator" (37). Pregnancy is a state imposed and monitored by her careful husband who
"measured everything he would let [her] eat, he was feeding it on [her],
he wanted a replica of himself; after it was born [she] was no more use.
[She] couldn't prove it though, he was clever: he kept saying he loved
[her]" (37). Her claim that her husband used her to produce a "replica"
is destabilized by his insistence that he "loved" her. His purported control of her and his professed love for her put into question her reliabil-
ity as an accurate judge of her own experience. She thinks this lie
allowed him to believe in his own righteousness while leaving her permanently in the wrong. In any case, her compliance with these desires
renders her powerless, distancing her from the child of her body to the
extent that she can never identify the baby as her own (37). Moreover,

her husband's actions commodify the infant because he regulates all aspects of its development.

In order to spare herself both pain and explanations, the narrator does not tell her friends about the baby and does not keep photos of it "peering out from a crib or a window or through the bars of a playpen" (52). Most compelling about these absent photographs is their implicit reference to images of separation and containment. The photos she imagines, the ones she denies herself possession of, are all pictures of the baby set apart from her, contained behind the bars of a crib, separated by the glass of a window, or through the prison-like bars of a playpen. She does not envision pictures of herself or anyone else holding it, in proximity to it, giving it love. There is also the image of the "chicken-wire fence" in the front of her father's house, which "is a reproach, it points to [her] failure" (37), a failure to provide a dynasty for her father. In contrast to these images of separation, however, are images of connection that the narrator is equally scrupulous to counteract. Moreover, as Jacques LeClaire finds, "the image of the foetus in the womb is an image of sanctuary and the surfacer's betrayal is connected with the notion of catching and enclosure" (18). The womb itself turns out to be a kind of enclosure that traps the narrator and her babies. The metaphors for connection, the baby as "Siamese twin," as her "own flesh," as "a section of [her] own life" (52), are immediately followed by verbs suggesting an enforced and official disengagement. The baby was "taken away... exported, deported...sliced from [her]...[her] own flesh cancelled" (52). She attempts to restrain her grief and her sense of longing for the baby, reminding herself that she has "to behave as though it doesn't exist, because for me it can't.... Lapse, relapse, I have to forget" (52). There is a multiplication of imperatives in this section of text: *I have to, it doesn't, it can't, I have to*. This word choice emphasizes her sense of connection to the baby and her negation as a mother. Moreover, her feeling of powerlessness emerges in her discussion of the birth process itself.

The narrator contemplates the future possibility of the development of an artificial womb, wondering how she "would feel about that" (85). It would, she thinks, be an improvement on the hospital where one is shut in, where

> they shave the hair off you and tie your hands down and they don't let you see, they don't want you to understand, they want you to believe it's their power, not yours. They stick needles into

you so you won't hear anything, you might as well be a dead pig,
your legs are up in a metal frame, they bend over you, technicians,
mechanics, butchers, students clumsy or sniggering, practising on
your body, they take the baby out with a fork like a pickle out of a
pickle jar.... I won't let them do that to me ever again. (85-86)

In the context of the previous discussion concerning the development
of an artificial womb for producing babies, it seems clear that this passage is about the narrator's experience of a forceps childbirth rather
than of abortion. In either case, the lines are drawn between "they" and
"you"; there can be no mistaking who owns the power over this
woman's labour and delivery. Not only is she the object of technicians,
mechanics, and butchers, but also the baby emerges into the world of
no more importance than "a pickle out of a pickle jar." Agency belongs
to those who control the process, which further alienates this mother
from the product, the infant itself. She does not, in Kristeva's phrase,
"call into question the very apparatus itself" ("Women's Time" 198).
Instead, in her recollection, she submits. She has participated in a birth
which, as Mary O'Brien states, "transforms woman, in every sense the
agent, into a patient" (10). Her only resistance is to assert that she will
not allow this to be done to her again. What the language also does is
remove fault from the narrator so that whether she is giving birth or
having an abortion, and the text is somewhat ambiguous, she can, by
objectifying herself in her recollection, allay some of the guilt she feels
toward the baby.

   Atwood articulates this vital feminist concern: the right to make
choices about the birth process. Her notion that such power is an intrinsic aspect of the mother's ability to bond with the baby speaks against
the jurisdiction of the male medical community who "shave you," making the birthing woman appear prepubescent, who tie hands and stick
needles. This appropriation of power negates the mother-infant relationship which, writes Sara Ruddick in *Maternal Thinking*, "is emblematic of promise" (206). Ruddick argues that "in the language of natality,
'birth' signifies a reciprocal relationship of woman and infant. This relationship is indeed marked, as the philosophers suspect, by the dissolution of boundaries" (210).[20] However, in the narrator's case, the experience of birth has been compartmentalized in her perception, so that she
considers the baby's father as the real parent and herself the fraud.
Boundaries have been maintained and, far from entering into a reciprocal relationship with either the child she left or the one she aborted, she

is cut off from any connection. Anesthetizing the mother, limiting her movement and her power, works against both the mother and the baby.

In this narrative of loss and redemption, the absent baby haunts the woman. When the narrator is under the water and comes across what she thinks is a dead body, it evokes memories of the infant she had aborted. She says that she had seen it "in a bottle curled up, staring out at [her] like a cat pickled; it had huge jelly eyes and fins instead of hands, fish gills, I couldn't let it out, it was dead already, it had drowned in air" (153). She sees the "pickled" infant—note the echoes of her previous description, "a pickle out of a pickle jar"—suspended above her, "like a chalice, an evil grail" (153), an image in Western culture evocative of the legendary cup used by Christ at the Last Supper. It is an image that carries, therefore, a sense of death with it. She understands that this vision is inaccurate, that she never saw the child. She recalls how "they scraped it into a bucket and threw it wherever they throw them, it was travelling through the sewers by the time I woke" (153). This time, the ubiquitous "they" are not at work in a hospital, but in a "shabby" house, before the legalization of abortion, full of "the smell of lemon polish, furtive doors and whispers" where "they wanted you out fast" (153). The effect is the same. The narrator is again the victim of the depersonalized "they." She feels "amputated" and "emptied." The "non-nurse" with the "acid" armpits (154) renders her powerless, as does the married man who gets her pregnant and then kindly arranges for her to have an abortion while he attends his child's birthday party (155). Her degree of volition is ambiguous in the text. On one hand, the narrator says that she was left with no choice:

> He said I should do it, he made me do it; he talked about it as though it was legal, simple, like getting a wart removed. He said it wasn't a person, only an animal; I should have seen that was no different, it was hiding in me as if in a burrow and instead of granting it sanctuary. *I let them* catch it…that made me one of them too, a killer. After the slaughter, the murder, he couldn't believe that I didn't want to see him any more…. Since then I'd carried that death around inside me, layering it over, a cyst, a tumour, black pearl. (155 my emphasis)

The ambiguity in the text is evident. Even while insisting that "he made" her do "it," she understands that, ultimately, it was her decision to "let them" take her baby from her. The man compares the baby to a wart, something about which she should have no feelings other than to consider it an inconvenience, as he does. However, she sees the abortion as a failure of mercy and her complicity with it as an act of murder that plants death, the ultimate negation of agency, within her.

In order to redeem this implanted death, the narrator senses that she must act in accord with the natural world. When the men on the launch bring news of her father, her friends think she "should be filled with death," that she "should be in mourning" (170). In fact, the narrator feels that, "nothing has died, everything is alive, everything is waiting to become alive" (170). Redemption is at hand as the narrator plans to turn death into life. She seeks a means of accomplishing her ends that will clearly invest her with power, and control, and identity. Animal-like, the narrator is in "the right season" (173). Once Joe "trembles" and the act is complete, she "can feel [her] lost child surfacing within…forgiving…rising from the lake where it has been prisoned for so long" (173). Such a genesis will allow her to have control:

> This time I will do it by myself, squatting, on old newspapers in a corner alone; or on leaves, dry leaves, a heap of them, that's cleaner. The baby will slip out easily as an egg, a kitten, and I'll lick it off and bite the cord, the blood returning to the ground where it belongs; the moon will be full, pulling. In the morning I will be able to see it; it will be covered with shining fur, a god, I will never teach it any words. (173)

This is a compelling dream vision of an idealized birth, one that Mrs. Blood and Clara both refer to, that sees women as powerful and self-sufficient. And it speaks against what Lorna Irvine has called "a quintessential Canadian cultural journey into the forests of Quebec" (151). Such a summary is dismissive in the extreme. Atwood's narrator is not merely on a "Canadian cultural journey"; she is in the process of making peace with her babies.

What is most fascinating about Atwood's construction of the ideal is the narrator's idea never to teach her child words. In an ideal space she would preserve it from entering the signifying system that has disempowered her to such an extent since "the release of the baby, this time, will not deliver it into hostile hands…but launch him [sic] on his natural course" (Leclaire 18). The narrator yearns for an impossible birth experience that is indeed reciprocal, where she performs the labour of birth and the severing of ties. There is no question in the narrator's mind that she is pregnant. Joe no sooner "trembles," or reaches orgasm, than she "can feel [her] lost child rising within [her], forgiving [her], rising from the lake where it has been prisoned for so long, its eyes and teeth phosphorescent" (173). The image of the infant rising phosphorescent from uncharted depths to reinhabit its mother speaks to the narrator's desire for restoration and forgiveness. For the narrator, hope is indeed bound up in the infant. This chosen pregnancy restores to her a connection to the rhythm of life that will enable her to come to terms with the death of her mother and father and the losses of her other two babies. The decomposing heron suggests to her that change in all its forms must be accepted. She says, "my body also changes, the creature in me, plant-animal, sends out filaments in me; I ferry securely between death and life, I multiply" (180). Between the death of her parents and the loss of her two other babies, the life of the infant growing within her, real or not, provides for her a fulcrum necessary to stability. She compares the baby growing inside her to a goldfish "undergoing its watery changes" (206). She considers that it might very well be "the first one, the first true human...born" (206), because of her decision and because it grows knowing its connection to the "primaeval" (206) natural forces that brought it into being.

The construction of the infant is complex in this novel, intimately tied to issues of women's power. Atwood's narrator in *Surfacing* leaves one baby because it is born under her husband's control, aborts another at her lover's insistence, and of her own will generates a possible third that ultimately restores to her a sense of herself as an agent in the world. While her actions become more and more bizarre—withdrawing from her friends, from the cabin, and finally from anything manmade—she seems on the edge of severe psychosis. However, having undergone a "vision quest" (James 71), cutting herself off from the civilization that imposed its rule on her, she has come to a point where she will "refuse to be a victim" and will "give up the old belief that [she] is powerless" (206). She returns to the cabin and puts on clothes. While it may seem that the baby has compelled her to social conformity, in fact, the baby empowers her. She will grow it and give birth to it and nurture it as independently as she possibly can. The baby galvanizes her decision to *be* without being a victim. She returns to society but with a new resolve. She "tenses forward" (207), on the brink of returning both to Joe and, ultimately, to a place of trust. This is what she does for the baby and what the baby does for her.

The baby's de facto command is also evident in Marian Engel's *The Honeyman Festival*. Minn expresses the powerful nature of the birth experience, the woman's precise connection to life at its most vital. The

story traces twelve hours in Minn's life as she prepares for a party. Elizabeth Brady describes the book's structure: "Each of the thirteen chap-
ters has a central action, an intrinsically insignificant activity drawn
from Minn's domestic routine" which act as "Proustian triggers to
memory" (203). It is remarkable, if not ironic, that Brady summarily
dismisses the activities of Minn's domestic routine as "insignificant"
because primary among these routines is the care of babies. Indeed,
Minn herself is pregnant. The novel begins with Minn in the bathtub,
her "globe" of a belly rising "above the waterline to meet the spotted
ceiling" (1). The image is of a woman hugely pregnant, pregnant to the
ceiling, carrying, as she herself admits, "a very big baby" (2). It's not just
Minn's belly that is large. The baby dominates her every move and
thought, dominates the entire narrative. Lorna Irvine says that the
novel "focusses on the female body," that the pregnant body is "so
dominant...throughout the novel that it seems to encompass the earth.
It is celebrated" (153) in a celebration that "marks the female text" (153).
Christl Verduyn similarly argues that the novel depicts "female worlds"
and Engel's own "commitment to writing about women's experiences"
(64). Engel is among many emerging female writers during the 1960s
and '70s who engage with the subject of women and babies.

The feminist movement was becoming a powerful force when
Engel's book was published. The notion of a woman staying at home to
have babies and care for them had begun to move away from being the
accepted norm.[21] Engel joins Atwood, Laurence, and Thomas, creating a
space for the dichotomies engendered by infants in the women who bear
them. Her work is unique in its devotion to "the solidity of the flesh...the
insistent temporal demands of the developing baby" which in fact shape
"the narrative space and time" so that they "become the female body"
(Irvine 153). She accomplishes this in a manner that negates neither the
value of the infant, nor the value of the mother who is more than an
incubator. Engel's construction of the babies in the novel is singular
because Minn is married and already has several children. She is also
intelligent and articulate, a woman who "question[s] the dichotomies of
the male world, which does not correspond to [her] experience in life"
(Verduyn 62). She is eminently involved with her babies and at the same
time self-consciously aware of the ambivalence they provoke.

The overwhelming power of the novel is its articulation of the vitality and virtual necessity of the baby. The baby growing within Minn is,
in her terms, "real" (94). Minn defines this, saying, "What is real noses

up to you, winds around your neck refusing to let go.... She rubbed her belly and that was real. And right.... The baby still kicked and jerked. Another go-all-day-resist-sleep-zonk-collapse one. He'd fit with the others. They were real" (94). The baby's materiality is undeniable. It is vigorous, insistent, powerful. Minn never entertains the notion of terminating it, though its existence creates for her what Adrienne Rich calls "a hoard of ambivalences." According to Rich, the female body, "with its potential for gestating, bringing forth and nourishing new life, has been through the ages a field of contradictions: a space invested with power, and an acute vulnerability...a hoard of ambivalences, most of which have worked to disqualify women from the collective act of defining culture" (*Of Woman* 90). Engel's Minn is living the inherent contradictions of pregnancy and motherhood in terms of sorrow and joy, power and weakness, and yet, she is also defining, reflecting, and refracting infant culture. She examines both the positive and negative aspects of pregnancy. On the one hand, pregnancy makes Minn extremely happy. She feels more sexually aware and more grounded in what she considers to be real life. On the other hand, pregnancy also strictly minimizes her spectrum of experience so that "sin" becomes "a chocolate bar at a bus stop; adventure, a forbidden bath" (3). As well, the baby's growth inside Minn makes her feel "draggy and discouraged" (3). Pregnancy makes the stairs seem longer, makes the children seem heavier, and makes her feel unable to bend to pick them up (38). Before its birth, the baby clearly impacts Minn's life in ways that sap her energy, circumscribe her sense of purpose, narrow her experience, compel her to be focused on the goal of giving birth. Its survival and growth are the pre-eminent concerns of Minn's life and they are concerns that, nearing the end of the pregnancy, Minn is beginning to resent. Because she is carrying the baby, she considers herself to be in a state of "suspension" without "action or direction" (47). She feels that "everything is confused and flaccid. The child floats in its placenta, covered with meconium like new white cheese" (47). As Irvine asserts, "Like *Mrs. Blood*, this novel also seems suspended, operating in a hiatus that represents the waiting for a birth" (153). The infant physically constrains Minn so that she has difficulty getting into her car and when she finally does, "her belly pushe[s] the horn" (67) so that the baby seems to be audibly sounding its existence. Minn is frustrated with waiting. She keeps checking for "show," for a sign that labour has begun so that she might end the waiting. She longs to know the baby as separate from herself. She wants "even the sprint to warm the bottle, the terrible effort to soothe the colicky child. To deal with something live and squirming and visible," that she might see the baby's "wrinkled articulated feet" (47). Minn contemplates the baby as other: "Towards the end, she thought, it's more a thing than a part of yourself. It ripples with a motion you did not cause. It is an appurtenance of a child, not quite your own body now" (1). Engel articulates the strangeness of the interior yet separate nature of Minn's relationship with the baby, the relationship of fetus to mother, a dyad that nourishes a new life, a new "hope of the world" as Hannah Arendt calls it, but that also severely circumscribes Minn's life.

The narrator describes the surprising nature of Minn's fertility which is itself an ambivalent force:

> Just over four years ago, fertility had taken them by storm. Louisa made them happy, even being pregnant with Louisa made them happy.... They wanted to make love all the time, and felt free to. So after Louisa was ambulant, they launched into what turned out to be Bennie and Til.
>
> And since condoms puncture, dutch caps fly greased into the furthest dusty corner of the bathroom on their coiled spring rims, pills reduce the libido and increase the protruding veins, this one was to be born wearing a Lippes Loop for a lorgnette in June. (2)

Such rampant fertility withstands the technological advances intended to broaden a woman's sexual choices, establishing a tension between the vigorous abilities of nature and the woman's attempts to thwart it. The tension is most clearly delineated when Minn describes her pregnant state, the happiness she feels, the opportunity and freedom to make love.

She sets these "natural" feelings in opposition to the technical difficulties associated with preventing pregnancy. These difficulties read like antics in a script from "The Three Stooges": punctured condoms, gymnastic diaphragms, mood-altering medication, and an IUD monocle. Controlling the maternal body is no easy feat, whereas conceiving the baby is easy for Minn, as easy as gravity. While part of her enjoys it, part of her also understands that, as Rich has said, pregnancy makes women vulnerable. Minn wants to warn her girls that

> They will end up strapped on a table in a delivery room, their hands tied to the bedsides. Bodies in two halves, sheets above and stirrups below; at the head an anaesthetist telling clinical jokes; at

the waist, men working. Their privates sealed off and shaved and sterilised, delegated to professionals. The men will work well, and tell them it's for the good of the child, but something.... (8)

The image of women's powerlessness in the hands of a medically ordered system of birthing could not be clearer. The unfinished "something," indicated in the text by ellipses, is provocative here. Minn is thinking about a contradiction, about men in control of the arrival of the baby, about men who have never been pregnant, never known the child within, known only the external manifestation of its data, telling her what ought to be done for the good of the child. The woman's body is cut in half with the men working below the waist and an anaesthetist working at the head, nullifying intelligent decisions, appropriating control. Minn would almost prefer to "squat in a field and do it alone, though not with placenta praevia" (9). Minn envisions an opportunity to have the baby alone. She is feeling some contractions, "small bands of fear or taboo circulating like elastics. Not dilation. Nothing so large and satisfying. Mean little jabs of viciousness" (120) that presumably come from the baby itself. She considers the possibility of squatting, panting, and ejecting to "get it over with" (121):

> Magine [sic] having it on your own, here. Pulling it out raw into your own hands, biting the cord instead of a cop's bottom, could you? After screaming at kid mess could you face your own crap? The darkly inevitable connections that cheat us of air and fancy. Let it open, it isn't wooden, let it give, shunt life out. Emit that object, the valued and valueless child.
> Life is cheap, now. Though we fail to admit it. (122)

Engel, Thomas, and Atwood all configure the process of the birth of the baby as an extreme choice between being dominated by doctors or being alone in a field. Even Laurence's Rachel would prefer to manage the birth on her own, though this is more a function of her desire to escape social stigma than to avoid medical intervention. Such aloneness reasserts the primal nature of the relationship between the birthing mother and the baby about to be born. These women writers all enter imaginatively into a space where birth is a voluntary labour and where the baby can be celebrated. To give birth to a child is to be exposed to unprocessed, unsanitized experience, to watch creation and bite through one's own connection to it. Could a woman do it on her own, without medical intervention? Could she face her own "crap"? The force of the birth process, the pain, the raw nature of the experience, cheat women of "air and fancy," of the luxury of breathing, of modesty, of possibility. The baby itself—"life" shunted out—is an "object" at once "valued and valueless." This evocation of birth, from a specifically female perspective, acknowledges the essential nature of the undertaking as well as the contingent value of the baby.

Minn's baby will not be born in a field. She submits to male authority although such submission is detrimental to Minn's state of mind. Dr. Mordie, Minn's gynecologist, "liked fertility," and "had a joy in him when he probed a belly or yanked a baby out of one" (3). But while he is happy enough, he is clearly in control of the birth process and not at all reluctant to force his opinion on Minn. He expresses his disgust with "soft women" who were out of shape and failed to get proper exercise and this affects Minn's self-perception, and denigrates her identity as a multigravida. He tells her she is eating too much, that she ought to do more housework for exercise (3). Unfortunately, Minn's view of her pregnant self complies with Dr. Mordie's opinion. She feels, after looking at herself, that

> She was ugly, ugly and hairy with it [the baby]; rippled with fat. Blue fingers of stretch-marks held up her belly. Later, they would fade to pale striations, silver tracks of glaciers or snails. And there would be there, again, the negroid pigmented line from navel to mons. Something primaeval and sinister about that, hidden where you could not crane to see it, your body pulling a fast one. (3)

The baby has marked Minn's body for as long as she lives. The "pale striations, silver tracks of glaciers or snails" inscribe the baby's existence on Minn's body. She blames her weakness on the "small parasite" who is perhaps "supping, gathering its strength for the voyage out" (8). This description focuses on the details of the infant's invasion of the mother's body. The infant does not respect a flat stomach and Minn, while somewhat appalled by this, nevertheless catalogues the extent of the destruction. The baby grows within and leaves its mark without, evidence of another powerful subjectivity growing where Minn indeed cannot even "crane to see it." Minn's body is ripely pregnant and, although she cannot accept its beauty, acceptance does come from a surprising source. Ben sees her naked and reaches up to touch his mother, "murmuring softly, 'Fur, fur.' That made it all right again, when nothing before had helped" (8). Minn can come to terms with the "fast one" that the baby inside her body is "pulling" with her son's help. Ben accepts his mother's appearance, helping her, at least for a moment, to transcend her own self-perception.

Engel writes against the tendency to see both the work of the mother and the infant itself as unimportant. This is a tendency that has permeated critical thinking to the extent that a female critic analyzing *The Honeyman Festival* could, as recently as 1987, summarily dismiss Minn's work in pregnancy and caring for her children as "intrinsically insignificant activity" (Brady 203). Engel tackles with humour and intelligence the problem of perception as it relates to the job of mothering. Minn is like Clara in her frank assessment of her job as "an engineer of alimentary canals" (32) whose days are composed of "stuffing" her children at one end and "tending" the other (32). Minn analyzes the value of her experience, of her children with their inescapable demands. When she changes their wet diapers in the night, she feels most revealingly that at "times like this they seemed all the world to her, richer and better than anything because they were newer. She was caught up in a fallacy she recognized. She had to think of them this way because it was the only way to make breeding tolerable" (69). As a woman of her time, a liberated, intelligent woman, Minn must find some way to convince herself that growing babies is a valuable occupation, that the baby is in itself valuable. But it is a construction she finds difficult to maintain.

She is not only physically limited by her belly, but she is also limited in terms of the world's perception of her. She endures people's judgement of "a pregnancy not socially acceptable in the days of anti-population crusades" (10). People are shocked by the number of children Minn has, people who speak "of three children as if they were forty" (10). The notion that a woman who is already a mother to three children would voluntarily produce yet another is horrifying to some of the women of Minn's society. Even Minn's mother's response is condescendingly negative. Upon hearing, or rather seeing, for herself that Minn is pregnant again, she says, "It's hardly necessary to have so many these days" (80). Her mother then observes that Minn, although not yet due, is already "as big as [she] was with the twins," and she states doubtfully that she hopes Minn's doctor "knows what he's doing" (80). She worries that Minn runs the risk of having a Downs' Syndrome baby, as she herself did. Minn's mother is surprised that her daughter would risk another pregnancy in light of the possibilities.

Engel conveys Minn's precise understanding of the difficulties in which she is enmeshed because of the infant. The baby's existence sometimes leaves Minn feeling "swathed in pregnancy and despair" (11) as though the two conditions are coequal. The baby's presence is felt on every page as Minn struggles with her role as mother, which compels her to live in disorganized squalor. She dusts her home with the hem of her skirt, while rejecting Jane-Regina's second-hand baby trousseau even though it is "exquisitely coffined in uncrumpled tissue paper" (26). Jane-Regina is an interesting counterpoint to Minn. She visits as part of her volunteer service for the Junior League, stopping by on a scheduled basis to keep Minn's spirits up with a stream of gossip and advice. Not only is her tissue paper uncrumpled, but her life is, too. She has one child, lots of money, and a nice, if unfaithful, husband. Jane-Regina's daughter has the benefit of a nanny to assume the mothering role. But Jane-Regina's cleanliness and perfection are not admirable. Minn mocks her because she is a member of "a whole race of women whose shoes and handbag match" (19). The thought is enough to send Minn, great with child, into a depression. Her matching handbag and shoes, her kid gloves, her superficiality, her complaints about her maid and her husband distance Jane-Regina from a visceral engagement with life as it is embodied in the baby. Minn seems honest, expressing the experience of many women, feminists of the 1970s who become mothers and find themselves facing the mess, as Atwood's Clara does, that comes with babies. In *The Honeyman Festival* children "are real and they occupy a privileged position both in Minn's world and in Engel's imaginative universe" (Verduyn 84).

Engel creates a protagonist who contends bravely with obstacles that are often tediously undermining. Minn grapples with negative responses from Jane-Regina and from her mother. Moreover, since her husband is away in Katmandu, she also bears the greatest responsibility for her children and for the baby within. When she is tired or depressed, she has to rely almost exclusively on her own resources to keep looking after herself and nurturing her children. The baby is a constant, demanding presence that both connects her to real love and real life, and also erodes her limited strength and what she sometimes feels is her limited hold on sanity. Minn treads an ambivalent path between these two poles. On the one hand, she is shocked when "the deep, selfish and murderous desire to be alone and independent again"

(5) emerges in her dreams. On the other hand, she is incapable of understanding love apart from her love for the children:

> She thought a lot about love now that she had children. She wondered how so many people could be wrong about it, how they could say there were so many sorts of it, and there seemed to be only one, a well of feeling in the back of your personality, in the bowels of your personal earth: you tended your supply carefully, tried to get in order later to be able to give, for it worked better when it was primed, but it was all the same stuff: the kids seething like insects in the playroom and Minn sitting mending just outside the gate so they wouldn't grab the wool away, and love shining like the sun. (101)

Like Roy's Rose-Anna, Minn connects this profound love with the metaphor of a "well of feeling in the back of your personality." The usage of "bowels" suggests the depth from which this feeling arises. The children are "insects seething" and Minn sits, keeping the fabric, the "wool" away from the children so she can continue to mend whatever ravages the day has imposed. Minn connects her experience of love to her essential relationship with her children. Her knowledge of the inescapable and often maddening demands of babies exists concomitantly with her knowledge of love. Minn gives utterance to the myriad difficulties of pregnancy and birth, but her discourse is also permeated by a sense of joy.

Engel's work charts historically new textual territory that involves, according to Christl Verduyn "the mapping of new spaces, located for the time being at the margins of representation and reality" (65). In taking up the job of re-visioning women's real lives as mothers, Engel moves the work of motherhood from the margins to the centre. And with the movement of the mother comes the movement of the infant as well. Engel's writing necessarily demands that attention must be paid to the marginal role of infants and all that they inspire in terms of both love and exhaustion. If, as Verduyn writes, gynesis is "above all a process entailing a reconceptualization and reincorporation of that which has both eluded and engulfed the master narratives" (65), then clearly a necessary part of that reconceptualization has to do with the infant, which constructs the maternal body as maternal. Mary O'Brien claims that "it is from an adequate understanding of the process of reproduction, nature's traditional and bitter trap for the suppression of women, that women can begin to understand their possibilities and

their freedom" (8). One cannot consider or reconfigure the mother
without having a look at the baby. Verduyn's understanding that what
"has both eluded and engulfed the master narratives" is the story of the
"m/other, or (maternal) woman" (65). Engel constructs a maternal narrative of pregnancy through the unflinching gaze of Minn, but she also
affirms the significance of the infant itself, the inexplicable joy that its
presence provokes in spite of the mess and hardship. As Kristeva
argues, women who experience pregnancy and birth "find it indispensable to their discovery, not of the plenitude, but of the complexity of
the female experience, with all that this complexity comprises in joy
and pain" ("Women's Time" 205). As women writers, Audrey Thomas,
Margaret Atwood, Margaret Laurence, and Marian Engel all interro-
gate the "complexity of female experience" as it relates to childbirth.
While the male writers of these decades, Matt Cohen and Robert
Kroetsch among others, do not grapple extensively with the infant, or
with the experience of men and babies, the women are clearly motivated to explore their investment in the figure of the infant.

These female narratives have several aspects in common. They all
deal with the pregnant body and its concerns, including the birth
process. The desire to give birth in a field alone emerges in these texts,
for example. Childbirth is a primordial endeavour, where the labouring woman is moved by a rhythm she cannot control, one that brings
forth the mystery that has been growing within her.[22] The "natural"
birth fantasy recurs only within the socio-historical context of radically
reduced infant/mother mortality rates because of the very medical
protocols, including asepsis and fetal monitoring, that the characters
wish to escape. The characters long for independence from the constraint imposed by typical medicalized birth such as the shaving of
pubic hair and the use of stirrups and forceps. They also desire a birth
experience free from social taboos surrounding legitimacy or paternity; rather, these women imagine an experience that reinforces their
power.

Finally, and what is most compelling, is the double-voicing that
occurs in all these novels, a duality that navigates the contradictions
intrinsic not only in pregnancy and birth, but also in what it means to
be female. None of the writers backs away from the complexity of
childbirth and its effects on women. In fact, their sustained engagement with the inexplicable happiness that comes with pregnancy and
babies, and the fear and exhaustion and loss of personal space that

come as well, speak to their courage. They articulate in a literary forum women's profound connection to biology, to the hope of the world and its personal cost.

Furthermore, in foregrounding pregnancy and the life of the infant as it grows inside a woman's body, these writers pave the way for an expanded understanding of the complex effects of infants upon the maternal body. As the babies develop in the bodies of Mrs. Blood, Clara, Atwood's anonymous narrator, and Minn, their impact is indisputable. The infant disrupts the lives of these women, invading them as both foreigners and newcomers, stretching the shape of their bodies, challenging them with a connection that provokes both constraint and love.

In speaking their experience, women writers of 1960s and '70s focus attention on the effect of infants on the women who bear them. While writers are at work, as Toni Morrison sees it, "describing and inscribing what is on the national mind" (14), they are also structuring that "mind" to an extent, inquiring into constructions both of the feminine and the masculine as these relate to babies. It's compelling that, in writing that includes babies by both men and women, the figure of the father is emotionally, if not physically, distant. The feminist movement of these decades will begin to help men broach the distance between themselves and babies and lay the groundwork for richly varied manifestations of infant subjectivity. Rich claims that the infant becomes "hourly and daily more separate, on its way to becoming separate from me and of-itself. In early pregnancy the stirring of the fetus felt like ghostly tremors of my own body, later like the movements of a being imprisoned in me" (*Of Woman* 48). That imprisoned being emerges as a powerful force in the lives of women, a force that writers in the 1980s and 1990s will reckon with.

CHAPTER 4

Wider Truth: Infants in the 1980s and 1990s

The wider truth seems to me to be that our culture has so dismissed the power and importance of parental love, so derided the vitality and beauty of motherhood, so denigrated the tender feelings of the father, that the miracle is that there is anyone left who stumbles on the knowledge that the nurturing of new life is so much more terrifying, painful, exhilarating, illuminating, enraging, exhausting, wonderful, and important than investment banking.

— Michele Landsberg, *Women and Children First*

L andsberg's view of childrearing in our culture is an inclusive one, referring as she does to "parental love," and not just maternal love. Moreover, she gives equal time to the "vitality and beauty of motherhood" and to "the tender feelings of the father." Those feelings have been essentially ignored in literary representations of the infant until the latter decades of the twentieth century. Making space for fathers' profound feelings of attachment to babies marks yet another transformation in the way babies are represented. In recent literature men have begun to write in more detail about babies, speaking into that silence about their own sense of devotion to them. Robert Munsch's children's story, *Murmel, Murmel,* is a telling fable of late twentieth-century attitudes toward babies. In Munsch's tale, a girl finds a baby down a dark hole. She picks it up and, knowing her own limitations, she tries to find a grown-up who will take the baby and love it. The child stops several men and women, all of whom insist that they are far too busy doing, among other things, investment banking, to care for an infant, or that they have no idea of what one does with an infant. Finally, a man who owns a fleet of trucks agrees to love the baby. He claims that she is just what he needs. He already has everything else. The baby is a site, as usual, of rejection and acceptance, but in this case, the baby is clearly situated as a figure of redemption, that which can take people away from materialistic endeavours (which the book's illustrations trivialize) and can lead them into relationships of love. The truck-fleet owner is radiant when he holds the baby, smiling and apparently astonished. What makes the story interesting is that it is the male character who recognizes the baby as exactly what he needs. This is unusual in the context of relations between male characters and babies in previous decades.

This chapter examines the differences in late twentieth-century representations of infants by male and female writers. The fictional representation of a strong relationship between men and babies is a recent phenomenon and reveals something new about how people think about babies. It is also a relationship that has not been the sub-ject of literary study in spite of its evidence in the literature itself. This chapter focuses on Leon Rooke's *A Good Baby* (1989), Thomas King's *Medicine River* (1989), and three of David Arnason's short stories (from *The Circus Performers' Bar*, 1984, *The Happiest Man in the World*, 1994, and *The Dragon and the Dry Goods Princess*, 1994). These titles stand out from several works by men because of their exceptional encounter with the baby.[1] The number of titles written by men that include babies has demonstrably increased. However, the ones I've chosen for study are important because they illustrate a momentous change in the way men write about babies. This is a change not only in the quantity of babies written into the literary text, but more importantly, a change in quality. The babies have more concrete value in these texts; they are uniquely valued, even precious to the male protago-nists. And it's a preciousness that is eloquent in the texts, moving engagement with the baby away from the world of women and into the world of men.

Women writers, on the other hand, have been writing within a dichotomy. Their writing is, throughout the century, characterized by a double-voicing that represents the figure of the infant as a locus of ten-sion. In the 1960s and '70s, women's writing reveals a compulsion both to explore the minutiae of pregnancy and babies as these impinge on women, and as well, to reject the biological destiny of motherhood. The urgency women feel to understand the effects of childbirth, babies, and childcare, and often simultaneously to escape them, is evident in fiction. As fiction becomes more frank and more detailed, infant representations shift within a shifting ideological context that both subverts the power of biology and also revels in it. Women writers begin to write candidly about pregnancy, labour, childbirth, and the often-tedious drudgery of the demands of small infants. In these texts the infant is a primary figure of constraint for women. But the infant continues to be a figure that inspires overwhelming love, as well as a profound and satisfying sense of complicity with primordial creative forces. The tension between these two poles is manifest in this discourse of the real and the ideal. The significant change that occurs in women's writing of the 1960s and '70s is their acknowledgement that the drudgery and the tenderness that babies create are equally real and equally valid. That, indeed, these apparently conflicting responses are integral to understanding what the baby means.

Such writing challenges the patriarchal apparatus that has constituted the domestic sphere, the women's sphere (including the care of infants), as less important than the work outside the home that men do. As Jeffner Allen and Iris Marion Young write in *The Thinking Muse*, when "men set themselves up as the one, the subject...men constitute women as the inessential, the other. Much of women's experience can be understood as an encounter with such oppression, whether in resistance to it, in complicity with it, or both" (5). While women's experience can hardly be defined in terms of childbirth, this nevertheless is, for women who bear children, one of life's defining acts. More interesting is the fact that women use their connection to babies to institute their own discourse. As we've seen, writing by women in the 1960s and '70s demonstrates an overt resistance to the invisibility of women's culture, particularly as it relates to babies. The influence of such writing cannot be underestimated and plays a tremendous role in the major change that occurs in the fiction of the 1980s and '90s when the fruits of the women's movement, as it affected the production of literature in Canada, became evident in writing across genres about the baby. From Laurence to Atwood to Thomas, women writers assert their experience, resisting the hierarchy that constitutes them as weaker, and using their relationship with the infant to give expression to a powerful voice. On the contrary, during most of the twentieth century, in writing by men, infants, when they occur in the texts at all, exist as sidebars to the main action of the story. Men's lack of relationship to infants is evident in the huge silence in the texts.

However, an interesting development occurs in writing after 1980. While I acknowledge that this is a rather arbitrary date to attach to literary study, I can find no examples in Canadian prose fiction of such writing before 1980. I'm referring to writing by male writers about babies, writing that shows a sustained engagement with the figure of the infant, where the infant moves to centre stage, occupying the emotional heart of the novel. And what's most fascinating about this is that men's writing about the baby also challenges that same old patriarchal construct that configures women as other largely because of their capacity to give birth and all that such a capacity entails in terms of weakness and constraint. So that instead of diminishing domestic work, including the work of caring for babies, the male protagonists in these texts are privileging it. No matter that their participation in infant care is overtly reluctant. The fact remains, particularly in literary works by Rooke and Arnason, that these men care for babies in the same or better ways as the mothers. This is a stunning change that seems to occur once women's right to equality is established in political and social discourse, and once men have been invited into the delivery room.[2]

In their book *Becoming a Father*, Jerrold Lee Shapiro, Michael J. Diamond, and Martin Greenberg describe how "the father's role in childbirth and early parenting has shifted dramatically" over the past thirty years (3). Dr. Michael Lamb characterizes this recent development as an evolution from the breadwinner role to that of the "nurturant" father (Lamb 27). In Western culture, men are more involved than ever before in the raising of babies. In 1975, Dr. Lamb pointed out that theorists have, in the past, undermined the role of fathers. He claims,

> There is a peculiar tendency to infer sequentially that, because mothers are the primary caretakers, they are more important than fathers, and thus that they alone deserve investigation. This rapidly becomes translated into a belief that mothers are uniquely important. Fathers can hardly be expected to maintain a belief in their importance when they are continually being told of their irrelevance. (29)

This sense of the father's irrelevance is evident not only in studies that foreground the significance of mothering to child development, but it also filtered into the fiction of past decades where the lack of father-infant interaction is all too evident. But the writing of the 1980s and '90s demonstrates a remarkable departure from the model of paternal indifference. Shapiro, Diamond, and Greenberg attribute much of the change in father-infant relations to the women's movement which operated as "a powerful political and social force that has called into question many of the previous assumptions about...gender roles" (5). The change grows out of the women's movement because of its insistence on equality in relationships, including parental relationships. Feminist writing of the earlier decades articulated the materiality of women's connection to babies, but also challenged men to become more involved in the singularly rewarding experience of child rearing. But this involvement carries compelling ideological nuances with it.

This role of caregiver has been lately redefined for fathers. For example, in her article "Bringing in Fathers," Diane Ehrensaft describes the role of psychoanalysis in constructing "conceptions of parenting and child development." She says that,

> in almost every psychoanalytic and psychological formulation of development, it is taken as a given that the mother is the first primary attachment figure for the child in early life. Fathers hardly exist, except to offer support to their wives. Whole theories and paradigms are built from this premise: the oedipal drama; the stages of separation-individuation; the development of a self. In the past two decades feminists have questioned these formulations. To take as immutable or universal the female mother as *the* single significant other in the young child's life is erroneous. It is a socially constructed, not a biologically determined reality. (45)

Ehrensaft scrutinizes the social construction of women as the primary nurturers of babies. In order to do this, however, she ignores the strong biological connection between mother and baby, including the inarguable fact that women grow babies inside their bodies and that many of them breast-feed after their babies are born, further sustaining the infants' lives in a strong "biologically determined reality." But, in her examination of gender roles, she does speak to the notion, emerging in these decades, that men have an equally important role to play in having babies and caring for them.

Articulating this role, exploring the nature of male engagement with babies, are Rooke, King, and Arnason, who inquire into the father's role in nurturing babies. They explore the intense and subtle nature of their male protagonists' relationship to infants. Often what emanates from these books is a profound sense of wonder, an attachment to the infant that is remarkably appealing. It almost seems as if these relationships are less complicated than women's because of the voluntary nature of the men's involvement. Where women writers have explored feminist resistance to the non-voluntary work of mothers, male writers depict male protagonists who choose to make a connection with babies. If it is true that "the uniqueness of a creature or thing depends on the manner in which we conceive our relationship with that creature or thing" (Perelman and Olbrechts-Tyteca 90), then clearly what is happening in recent Canadian fiction is a reconception of the infant in relation to men. Men—male writers, male protagonists—begin to see the figure of the baby and specifically men's relationship with the baby as unique and therefore valuable. Writing by men in the 1980s and '90s explores this relation in a personal, intimate fashion that privileges the baby as a source of meaning and of love. The writing is surprisingly unequivocal in its encounter with the baby during this time. The men seem unencumbered by the resentment that women have had to come to terms with, arising from Western culture's insistence that women shoulder alone the domestic responsibilities of child rearing.

Three salient aspects emerge in men's representations of infancy. The first has to do with the infant's power to redeem the male protagonist, to draw him into community, and to create meaning for him. As one man says in Thomas King's novel *Medicine River*, "A person should do something important with their life" (200). The "something important" turns out to be the baby and the men's connection to it often lifts them out of their ineffectual lives and moves them toward significance. Second, the male protagonists are engaged in their relationships with the baby by the force of the baby's gaze, which is significant from both a cognitive development perspective and a psychoanalytic one. Finally, the fact that these are male protagonists preoccupied by infants marks each of these texts as a departure from what has been the concern of male writers in previous decades.

Prior to this shift toward men becoming caregivers, women and children were described as the primary dyad. Nancy Chodorow argues that the infant's "original relation to the mother is for self preservation" (63). That is, the mother satisfies physiologically based drives, giving the baby the food it needs to survive. The basis then for formulating an entire theory of infant development that is centred on the infant's primary connection to the mother occurs because the mother is the one generally who is equipped with milk to feed the baby. From this stems the insistence that mothers are primary while fathers are secondary. But the emergence of men as not merely helpers in caring for infants, but primary caregivers, permits them to form a dyadic bond of their own with the infant. As Alan Fogel says, "at the most basic level, human interaction is a sharing, and [babies] are biologically equipped to give their caregivers just this feeling"—that is, the feeling that interactions with the baby, whether the caregivers are male or female, forge a vital connection. Fogel continues, stating that the "newborn's appearance, smell, and sound are very powerful stimuli for the adult" (114). These stimuli cross gender barriers inviting, indeed, compelling, a connection between caregiver and infant.

The new relationships emerging in literature between male care-givers and infants reveal a strange alteration in power relations between men and women. While the sociological phenomenon of intense male involvement in caring for infants is attributable in some degree to the women's rights movement, it is also a complex encroach-ment on women's experience as it has been articulated. Women have only recently spoken explicitly to this intimate relationship with babies, a new voice that reveals, as it always has, a degree of tension between the desire for them and the desire to be unrestrainedly engaged in the world at large. Women have explored sexual difference at its most extreme—the capacity to grow and give birth to life. Donna E. Stanton writes in her essay, "Difference on Trial," that women's essential capac-ity to "give life/love to another is concretized through the metaphor of the pregnant body" (165). Babies' attachment to women has tradition-ally been the source of women's perceived weakness. Instead of accept-ing this, women begin writing about the pregnant body, about the changes provoked by the baby both before and after birth. Such a dis-course endows women with power through the very thing that consti-tuted them as "other." According to Stanton, "the maternal metaphor exemplifies women 'getting within,' seizing, powerfully manipulating male discourse on women" (168). As such, women's connection to babies endows them with power, with a voice that, up until the 1980s and '90s, had been exclusively theirs.

What does it mean, then, that men, now generally in Western cul-ture acknowledging women's equality, make inroads into assuming a role that they themselves once constituted as specifically and exclu-

sively female, other, and secondary? Men are no longer simply "helping out" with the baby's care. Often, they are taking over and while this
takeover may have been what women have wanted all along, and
while the benefits of father involvement are documented in sociological study, nevertheless, men's writing about babies marks a certain kind
of voice appropriation, a voice that women had only just established
for themselves. The involvement of men in the care of babies involves
them in a shifting power relation. If male writers navigate this new
world in stories that often display significant sense of wonder, men
become, as in the Robert Munsch stories, the ones who recognize
what's really important. While the women are involved in investments
and big business, the truck driver recognizes—becomes aware of what
he has already known—that the baby is exactly what he needs.

Because it does not speak for itself, what we know about the baby we
know from observation. The baby in literature exists much as it does in
real life. We endow babies with attributes, filling the silence of their consciousness with what we think must be happening. We are helped in this
process of understanding the baby not only by its behaviours, its murmuring, reaching, crying, smiling, and so forth, but also by its relations
with others. We understand it as someone's son or daughter; we see its
responsiveness accelerated by the mother's presence or by the father's
and we draw conclusions concerning its feelings about the person. Similarly, the baby as a literary construct exists and is understood by its relations with others. The infant's developing relations with male caregivers
offer new insight into its significance. While there have been examples in
past writing of men who take care of babies—Charles Tory Bruce's *The
Channel Shore* and Sinclair Ross's *As for Me and My House* come to mind—
these relationships are briefly described, limited to a couple of sentences
or paragraphs. It's clear that the male protagonists care for the babies, but
it's equally clear that such care has not sustained pages of exploration.
Social perception of infants as the responsibility of women likely resulted
in the dearth of consideration given to babies by male writers. Babies
have not for men been the "something important" that they have to do.
However, the baby's relationship to the male protagonists in current
writing enriches its representation in new ways as it redefines and recon-
structs not only the figure of the baby but also the traditional view of
male behaviour as being less involved in the infant's care. The metamor-
phosis that occurs is fascinating. Men begin to perceive the infant as
something important, and that caring for it is, in many ways, vital. And

the infant itself takes on new value. This reconstruction also involves male protagonists in a renegotiation of roles with their female counterparts as the ones who are capable of nurturing babies.

In Leon Rooke's novel *A Good Baby*, Toker is not the biological father of the baby; however, his active interest in the baby in a caregiving role, while initially reluctantly offered, redeems him on many levels in the world of the text, invites him into community and, more importantly, into peace. Thomas King's Will, in *Medicine River*, finds himself reluctantly coaxed into familial relationships through the agency of baby South Wing. David Arnason is the most forthright in his articulation of the father-infant relationship in such stories as "My Baby and Me" and "Angel, Baby," among others. These authors' male protagonists cathect to the infants and their lives are changed whether they are biologically related or not.[3]

The literary exploration of father care is relatively new to our culture, almost a novelty. While women have been, as Chodorow has asserted, socialized to accept the primary caregiving role (qtd. in Ehrensaft 45), men's commitment to this role involves them in a reconstruction, a redefinition of themselves as father. The baby is, of course, vital to this redefinition, acting as an agent in the lives of the men who nurture it. There is a textual duality where the baby is both subject and object of power. The infant's characteristics, its (admittedly limited) ability to communicate, its helplessness, and its inherent charm work to invite characters into a relationship formerly the reserve of women.

The reconstruction of Raymond Toker begins when he meets a "good" baby. Toker is not the biological father of the baby; however, his adoption of a caregiving role changes his life for the better. Branko Gorjup finds that Rooke writes about love "central and sacred to all relationships among individuals, as well as to those between individuals and the world, the working of which depends on the interconnectedness of all its constituent parts" (272). Prior to his encounter with the baby, Toker's life is characterized by a lack of relationship and almost no sense of connection to the world. The baby is the catalyst that will bring him to that interconnectedness. The story is undergirded by an extension and subversion of the notion of salvation through the birth of a special baby. Indeed, as Michele Kaltemback claims, "the baby's unnatural abilities come into play whenever a special fleeting moment of unison has been reached. Hence the Christ-like quality of the baby: it brings people together in a universe where everything seems to be pulling them apart" (42). The baby occupies the point of convergence of this text; the forward motion of the narrative leads all the characters to it. As the title indicates, the good baby is at the centre of the forces at work in the text, forces that include an exploration of evil and the surprising goodness in the people who come into contact with this "good" baby. The baby redeems Toker and, indeed, affects all the people with whom she comes in contact.

In his essay on Leon Rooke, Keith Garebian argues that the world according to Rooke is "not 'given' but depends on the kinds of assumptions we bring to it, and it is best not to bring too many" (132). Garebian's warning against coming to a reading of *A Good Baby* with preconceived ideas about babies is appropriate, for Rooke presents us with a baby whose survival seems unlikely, whose abilities are amazing, and whose saviour is reluctant, to say the least. The question of who saves whom also arises in this narrative since the baby, as newborn offspring of a murdered mother, is in need of rescue, but Raymond Toker, her rescuer, is also in need of redemption from the purposelessness of his own life and the ghosts that haunt him. As Gorjup sees it, "Rooke's story is simultaneously ancient and contemporary. It holds a mirror to our complex and compromising age of self-consciousness and self-doubt. It asks the question, how can we hope to redeem ourselves in that which is most threatened and most fragile?" (272).

The baby is that "which is most threatened and most fragile" in the context of the novel whose unfolding provides an answer to Gorjup's question. The hope of redemption lies in relation with the baby. Rooke explores the necessity of redemption that seems unbound by considerations of specific time or place. Like Sheila Watson's *The Double Hook*, the characters in Rooke's valley occupy a microcosmic space that seems to await the arrival of the baby. Of course, it is Toker himself who will be most affected by that "most threatened and most fragile" infant who turns out to be much tougher than expected. Rooke is a pioneer in creating a literary space for men's involvement with babies. The narrative explores the nature of good and evil and is centred in Toker's response to the baby, his increasing attachment to her, and his wonder at her abilities. Rooke also explores two kinds of fatherhood in the text. As Peter Cumming claims, the novel offers "a grotesquely dysfunctional rural community" that grounds the conflict between "two men embodying the worst and best of manhood.... One man epitomizes father as sperm factory; the other becomes a nurturing parent" (97).

Leon Rooke rewrites a gospel of salvation through attachment to the infant girl whom Toker carelessly totes around in a burlap sack. While biblical allusions in Western literature can hardly be said to be unusual, Rooke's reclamation is unusual in its daring. He develops a world of abnormal, if not grotesque, characters who align themselves with good or evil as they align themselves with the baby's welfare. I use the word "daring" because of the story's challenge to what we have come to believe is a postmodern questioning of values as absolutes, particularly values of right and wrong. While these extremes are mitigated to a small degree in Rooke's development of character, for the most part, he paints a picture of good guys opposing bad, the guys in the white hats, though poor and unkempt, and the guy in the black hat, evil incarnate. This is where Rooke broaches the unusual in contemporary literature. As Garebian describes it, "Rooke is himself abnormal in his fiction, venturing into spooky corners of the mind and soul, laying bare the troubled, fogbound spirit of characters caught in a world where evil proliferates" (171). Rooke has ventured into an exploration of good and evil, extremes of which are unusual in a decade when many were coming to the conclusion that good and evil are relative terms. Relativity does not necessarily apply to Rooke's fictional world. *A Good Baby* is a story without the sort of moral greyness in life and in art that has come to be expected. Herein lies its force.[4]

Rooke's juxtaposition of good and evil seems designed to subvert the stereotypes surrounding our perception of how infants should come into the world and how they should be treated once they are here. But through his resistance to a cliché response to babies, Rooke creates a sense of wonder and engagement that are more powerful for the context in which they are evoked. Traditionally, babies invite protection because of their helplessness. Their arrival causes change that most often occurs at the level of personal behaviour and attitude. People most often respond tenderly to infants, cooing, making faces, seeking response. They tend also to want to protect them. However, the codgers who malinger at Cal's general store begin talking about cunnilingus with the baby, transgressing conventional writing about babies. Out of such a slough is born wonder.

The story resonates with biblical images. *A Good Baby* both works within and resists the tradition of writing about the baby as a type of saviour. Against the traditional maternal narrative, Rooke creates what amounts to a paternal narrative.[5] There is no Virgin Mary who "treasures all these things in her heart" (Luke 2:19). Instead, Rooke uses a male protagonist and caregiver. Further, there are no angels heralding the child's birth and no wise men, strictly speaking, who come to worship. However, the baby's aunt sees visions of her sister with Truman and comes in search of her. Although poor, hungry, and cold, she pursues the trail as she envisions it and meets up with another visionary, a blind man, a Samaritan who gives her his coat, warms her, and helps her. Such writing "evokes the supernatural, the magical, the mysterious, the spectral, and the horrific" (Gorup 270), which all seem significant for the baby born under less than auspicious circumstances.

The mystery and magic surrounding the birth in Rooke's book recalls the paradigmatic mysterious birth of Jesus. According to the New Testament, Christ is born to Mary, a woman who is betrothed but not married, whose fiancé sticks by her—even though according to Jewish law he would be within his rights to accuse her of adultery and divorce her—under orders from God (Matthew 1:19-21). Christ is born during census-taking time. Bethlehem is crowded and the hotels are full. A young woman, hugely pregnant and possibly in labour, is offered shelter with the animals in the stable. The story of the birth of this baby is laden with images of hardship and lowliness that are depicted in tension with the grandeur of the annunciation, the solemnity of the wise men's arrival, and the threat of murder from the king. Such imminent danger foregrounds the importance of this particular baby and propels the gospel story forward.

Similarly, Rooke's baby is born under the curse of death, born without the benefit even of a stable for shelter. The mother of this child is, like Mary, unwed, but has no real expectation that the man who fathered the child will "do right" by her (7). But unlike Mary, she barely outlives the birth of her child. This baby is born under a bush during both a chase scene and a dark and stormy night. The young, pregnant mother, running for her life from the father, manages to give birth and hide the baby before the father slits her throat. It's important to consider the gothic elements of Rooke's text, the filthy backdrop against which the baby's appearance shows in stark contrast. Augmenting the atmosphere of desolation, filth, and decay is the young girl's understanding of life's hopelessness, that she "ain't never known anybody.... Able to hep hisself. Or herself either." Hers, however, is not a hopelessness that drives her to despair. Instead she is numb, resigned to her fate, to her own sense that the "baby's rattle and God's fist" were "part and parcel of your every infant's cradle" (15). Truman enjoys the power he has to kill her whenever he chooses: "it tickled him, this prolonging of the caretaker's mercy" (16). He refers to himself as "the caretaker," an "ordained minister" who has had a vision of God (23-24). But Truman is filthy, with his bad teeth "and this slickness on them almost like a pus" (1). When the girl kisses him, his skin is "rough and broken, smelling of cigarettes, of salt and grease and some indefinable aroma, and in his sweatlines her tongue could distinguish tight wads of dirt. She could feel on her tongue the grit" (10). His unsavouriness is palpable. Once the girl senses Truman's intent to hurt her, she begs him to wait, to let her first have her baby (23). Truman has no such patience so the girl garners the strength to run even though active labour has started. Her instinct to give her child life overwhelms her fear of Truman, of the night, of God's fist descending. Into the darkness, filth, and violence comes an extraordinary baby.

Toker is an unlikely hero. He is without resources and without hope until he saves the baby. He is not just unemployed or poor. Rooke foregrounds the poverty and isolation of Toker's life, this man who lives in the hole in the ground where his house once stood, virtually buried alive, in order that the transformation caused by the infant will be all the more startling. Rooke consistently juxtaposes contrary and unexpected elements delineating the contrast between despair and hope. If Rooke is given to extremes, Toker is no exception. Roby addresses him as "Raymond Toker, burnt-out, had-a-sister, living-in-a-hole-in-the-ground" (31). Living, as he does, in the burnt-out foundation of his house, he is a man without ambition who offers himself to the sawmill when his "spending money was getting close to zero" (185).

This sense of transformation from hopelessness and lack of connection to hope and affinity recurs in novels written in these decades. While the change from isolation to kinship is also evident in Bruce's *Channel Shore*, there are a number of factors at work. Grant seeks out Hazel to mitigate the shame of her unwed pregnancy by marrying her. When she dies he is forced to nurture the baby, and although he does this with care, Alan's babyhood is negligible in the text, enduring for a mere sentence before he is walking and talking. What sets Rooke's novel apart is Toker's "maternal" relationship with the baby. Not only does he care for her but he also begins what Peter Cumming calls "tentative steps towards feminization and 'male motherhood'" (96). Miraculously, this baby stays hidden until Raymond Toker shambles by and

begins to tote her around like a strange Santa Claus, looking for a home
to leave her in.

The baby transforms Toker. Once he picks her up she begins to act
on him in ways he had not expected. While he flirts with Roby, the baby
who is only one day old, squirms and wiggles her way out of the burlap
sack she is in to "take the sun" (37). We are told,

> Its head was up high, erect, and riding the small valley of its shoul-
> der, the arms fully extended from its body, like wings, Toker
> thought. Only a smidgen of its belly was touching grass, the chest
> lifted, the legs elevated too, and shooting straight out from the
> apple-roundness of the buttocks. Feet pointed, the heels up like
> high rudders. It was some kind of ballet-type baby, or winged
> sculpture—an airplane. It looked ready to fly.... The baby lifted its
> head higher, smiling at him.
>
> It's a goddam wonder, he thought. A newborn baby hardly got
> bones.
>
> The baby went on with its flying. (37-38)

Toker's life has been one without many wonders of any kind. That the
baby performs such a stunt, appearing to fly, astounds Toker and his relationship with her begins to change. The text offers an accumulation of
details. Toker takes everything in: the high head, the "smidgen of belly,"
the "apple round buttocks," and the smile. He is clearly captivated.
Instead of only having himself to talk to, he now has the baby, the "god-
dam wonder" for a companion and he will never be the same. While he
continues to complain about the "wrench" she is putting in his day (41),
he also confesses to her that he has been "a long time between women"
(41). As well, he tells her he fears that, in spite of his efforts to find the
baby a home, "not a soul" would have her (41). In short, he embarks on
a conversation with the baby, a relationship that starts in resentment and
grows into love, a love that is undergirded by the instinct to protect.

Rooke's novel contains echoes of Munsch's *Murmel, Murmel* where
the characters unanimously reject the infant who is finally adopted by
one unique man. Toker first protects the baby from Mrs. McElroy, back-
ing away from her and getting "set to run" because he "could see this
woman would talk the baby to death" (43). Next he refuses to stop and
see if the "dirt-lappin" Priddys would take her because "before mornin
they'd have [her] out earnin they's keep. Out trappin and shootin,
[her] nose behind a plow" (45). Toker's protectiveness shows his growing care for the baby. When he encounters Truman at Cal's store, Truman studies the baby "for prolonged seconds" (87). When Truman does

reach out to touch her, Toker's response is unambiguous: "Toker whipped back" (90). The evidence mounts that Toker will not likely give the baby up to anyone, least of all to Truman. Even Cal's wife, Sarah, asks to keep the baby. "She'd cried and begged and promised to look after her with her every fiber" (206). Again, Toker refuses because Cal himself, though "decent enough," would not give the baby "the hugs and kisses a good baby required" (206). Though Sarah believes that the baby would "make a man" of Cal, in fact, as Hindmarch perceives, Toker "means to hold onto that baby" (226).

Toker's connection to the baby is further evident in the way he carries her over his shoulder in a sack through which "once in a while he felt a kick" (45). The suggestion here is obvious. Toker takes on the role of nurturer, even appropriating a substitute womb. While the baby seems content with her "ride," as he calls it, Toker himself also points things out to the baby, "the yeastin clouds" (45), whippoorwills, beetles, and gnats (47). He tells her about his life and the abuse he suffered from his father and mother; he tells her he will buy her a popsicle when they arrive at Cal's store. He engages in a discourse of self-revelation and observation with the baby, revealing his interest in her, as well as his own loneliness and need for kinship. Whether or not he knows the rhythms of his voice soothe her, his conversation throughout the walk to Cal's, as well as his actions in cradling "the squenchy-eyed baby" (51), and comforting her during the rain, disclose his growing tenderness for the baby, a tenderness that will be more fully exercised.

While Toker tells the baby to put on her "best Sunday manners and [she would] be breast-cradled by mornin" (60), the text makes it clear that no one who offers will seem suitable to him as an adoptive parent. As various women offer to take the baby off his hands, including Sorrel Jeff and the madwoman, Dolly Bellhop, who offers to buy her for three dollars, Toker finds grounds for refusal. Not only does he refuse to let Dolly take her, but Toker is also surprisingly jealous because the baby looked "so all-fired happy" when the woman was holding her (195). Instead of distancing himself from his charge, Toker moves closer and closer. When she is on the floor in Cal's store, Toker again notices details of her physical appearance, that her nose needs "reaming," that her head was "way bigger than her body," and most particularly he notices the top of her head. He says,

> You kept wanting to rub it, hardly believing the perishable nature of that crown. The palm of your hand won't hardly satisfying; you

wanted to nudge your cheek up against it. You wanted to nuzzle
it, to let your lips graze. To ask yourself how, in this world, a thing
come to be so soft. You rubbed it and the softness spilled all inside
you, made your own bones crumble. (73)

Examining the verbs and adjectives Rooke uses involves one in an
exponential erosion of defences. The words pile up on top of one
another: rub, nudge, nuzzle, graze, soft, softness, crumble. There is a
danger of slipping into treacly sentimentality in attempting to write
about the softness of babies. Leon Rooke navigates the difficulties
inherent in creating a tactile experience that circumvents the cliché.
Part of the reason this passage works so well is that the baby has been
handled roughly. Its flesh has been "blemished all over where ants and
mites, bugs, no doubt even wood ticks had taken their plugs out of its
hide" (38). That the baby should have been so exposed transgresses one's sense of what is proper. Nevertheless, Rooke uses such transgression to fine effect, now inviting one to be seduced by softness, a per-
ishable softness that "spills all inside you," a necessary softness that
compels one to seek out more, even as Toker does. The softness of the
baby releases the softness of Toker, no small feat for a man raised as
roughly as he has been. Rooke juxtaposes the profound contiguity
between such exquisite softness and the filth that abounds in Toker's
environment so that Toker begins to "crumble." Toker knows the grime
of his own life, the decision he made to live in a hole in the ground, and
he perceives that his care of the baby has been barely adequate. Toker
knows that he wants "to git down there and claim some of that softness
for his own self" (73). This is powerful, redemptive softness that invites
nuzzling and wonder, and it is ultimately the baby's softness that
erodes Toker's determination to give her up. It is Sarah who says to
Toker, "You look like you've plummeted down a well. You look plain
lovesick" (74). Toker begins to love the baby in a way that he does not
fully fathom. And he begins to love her at length, the kind of love that
takes pages to explore in a discourse that, even while it incorporates a
realistic view of the infant who is blemished and bitten, is nevertheless
illuminated by the refulgent language of ideal love.

The satisfaction for which Toker yearns is the satisfaction of the
mother-infant bond, a bond he reproduces in his own "mothering" of
the baby girl. Not only does Toker transport the infant in a womb-like
sack through which he feels her kick, but he also participates in a
domestic baptism by giving the baby a bath. Thus, he assumes the roles

both of mother and priest, or "father" and grows even more attached
to the baby girl although he takes awhile to realize it. The narrator says
that, "Toker wondered what it was he felt about this baby" since "all a
baby was was worthless" (74). Nevertheless, when Cal tells him that
she is too young to smile, Toker smiles himself, watching "the baby
smile" (74). In spite of himself, his gaze is more and more involved with
the baby. Her gaze moves even Cal's acrimonious wife, Sarah, to a surly
kindness, offering the baby milk and an old dog toy, and Toker a place
to bathe her. The baby's bath is crucial to the story. Rooke relates the
scene in words that purposely slow everything down. He leaves physical gaps in the text and uses repetition, consonance, and assonance to
decelerate the narrative. Details accumulate. The language is soft and
soothing:

> The baby watched him do it.
>   It watched with wide open eyes, turning its face to wherever
> Toker sailed the cloth, smiling as Toker held the cloth over the belly
> and squeezed the water drip-by-drip over the rippling flesh.... It
> giggled and gooed as Toker lifted the two legs in one hand and
> soaped its bottom. As he spread its legs and tentatively, bashfully,
> opened its crevice and washed there.... The baby liked it.
>   You could maybe see some personality in a baby, you let your
> mind bend that way.... A whimsical bit of a thing was a baby. (78)

The baby's whimsicality, her unexpected softness and the force of her
gaze compel Toker to form a tie with her, not umbilical in nature but no
less profound for that. The force of that gaze is something that infant
development researchers have studied to a great extent. For example,
according to Alan Fogel, "newborn infants are much more sophisticated
in their visual behaviour than people had thought previously" (97).
Rooke's baby engages Toker through her capacity to gaze and through
her softness. He remarks on the baby's bottom, how it "seemed molded
for the fit of a hand" (79). When he sprinkles powder on her, she
laughs. She "whooped out great volleys of mirth, and all the time it
seemed to Toker that the baby was maintaining a steady watch on him.
It seemed to Toker that the baby's big I-don't-want-to-miss-nothing
eyes never once left his face" (79).
    This gaze between Toker and the baby is crucial to the development
of the relationship between them. As Jackson and Jackson describe it,
"Eye-to-eye contact...plays a significant role in infant behaviour" (97).
Selma Frailberg concurs that "vision affords the sighted child an ele-

mentary form of initiative in human partnership…. From the responses of the mother of a baby under 2 months of age, we can say that the baby woos his mother with his eyes. He elicits social exchange through the automatic smile in response to the human face gestalt" (221). Cognitive development theorists have concluded that infant gaze is important "as a cardinal attachment behavior. Gaze also serves a signal function in human interaction. The onset of visual gaze, as a signal, indicates a readiness and intention to engage in an interaction" (Stern 189). These infant researchers develop a view of infancy that is dynamic and permits infant agency and engagement; it contradicts the Lacanian view of the infant as "outdone by the chimpanzee in instrumental intelligence" (1). On the contrary, the infant actively engages with its environment using a variety of strategies, not the least of which is the capacity for eye-to- eye contact. While Stern is writing about babies of around the age of three months, it is no surprise that Rooke's rather magical baby, precocious as she is, would already be performing engagement behaviour.

The baby engages Toker with her gaze, watching him perform all the acts of care. Her presence redeems him from ways formerly shiftless. He has a reputation for having "lit up the Crossroads" pub (119). He lives in a burnt-out hole in the ground where his house burned down with his sister in it. He walks through places where "scumwater" fills "his imprint even as he lifted bleak heel" (106). Yet the baby has such an effect on him that he feels hope. Even though "he hadn't done anything with his life," even though scumwater sucks at his footsteps, Toker believes that "he might come to open field" (106), to a place of possibility. This place of possibility includes a future with Roby who has seen the baby fly (243) and been awestruck by the vision. Toker also envisions a future for the baby, whom he calls "a worldbeater" (242). He will build her a house in the clouds "with roof windows that opened to the heavens, and windows that looked out at everything else" (289). Because of the baby, Toker climbs out of his hole and looks up.

The place of possibility, the notion that the "something important" that a man should do with his life is to care for a baby, recurs in King's *Medicine River*.[6] This novel privileges familial/community connection and the role of Baby South Wing in accomplishing this connection in Will's life. Critics have focused on the role of the trickster in King's writing and certainly Harlen Bigbear fulfills that role.[7] For example, according to Herb Wyile, Harlen "is at once a force of chaos, meddling in Will's life and complicating the life of the community in general" and he "can also largely take the credit for Will's finding a sense of community, place and family" (110). However, while Harlen does contribute to Will's ongoing interest in Louise, Wyile ignores the importance of the infant in cementing Will's attachment to the community and affirming his growing sense of kinship. From the masculine/fatherly point of view, Thomas King represents infants in ways that are informed by Native culture. The infant is valuable as a marker of family heritage and cultural survival, but mostly, in the late twentieth century, the infant is valuable as an object of love.

King establishes Will's relationship with South Wing in the familial context of his Native heritage, which foregrounds personal relationship. King is also important to understanding fictional representations of infants in Canadian writing because although his writing is particular to a Native cultural community, he also speaks to the general anxiety and specific wonder that fathers experience when they interact with babies. As Percy Walton has argued, "King's text rejects the culturally exclusive endeavour that has marginalized the Native as Other, and privileges instead an inclusive and collective process that does not rest upon cultural superiority/inferiority" (78). *Medicine River*, then, is about the process of Will's "immersion in the community" (Wyile 111). And it is in the context of extending the definition of family that King's novel enhances understanding of the infant as a subject.

Immersion in the Native community at Medicine River means expulsion from the city. Toronto is the place of museums, art shows, poetry readings, Harbourfront, and restaurants that serve mostly bean sprouts. It is also the place of Will's personal betrayal. Although Toronto offers Will access to material success as a photographer, he is isolated there, betrayed in love by a married woman trying to find herself. But when Will returns to Medicine River, the infant, South Wing, involves him in an extended family relationship that woos him into its fold. While this immersion takes place in a Native community, as Walton notes, it is an inclusive rather than exclusive community.[8]

In *Coyote Country: Fictions of the Canadian West*, Arnold Davidson quotes Atwood on the "Great Canadian Baby," relating the reference to King's *Medicine River*. He argues that South Wing "allows Will, the half-native male protagonist...to get a better fix on his life and to begin to resolve thereby the large questions of representation that have long troubled him" (190). These questions have to do with Will's own sense of exclusion from connections, both to his family and his community. At the beginning of the novel, he is in a state not unlike Cohen's Erik in *The Disinherited*. However, as a result of his connection with the baby South Wing, when Will takes the photographs of Joyce Bluehorn's "big" family at the end of the novel—photographs in which he himself is included—he discovers that his community *is* his family and he is smiling in the pictures (216).

Like Toker, Will is not South Wing's biological father. Nevertheless, he becomes involved with her shortly after her conception. The novel is constructed in flashbacks that reveal Will's estrangement from his father, his mother, his brother, and his people. He is, like Raymond Toker, a solitary man. His relationship with South Wing will end his solitude and redeem the loss of his father. King once said in an interview with Constance Rooke that "there's the sense that Will's father never took responsibility for his sons. So when South Wing is born, Will takes responsibility for her" (72). Although Will attempts to resist Harlen's matchmaking, insisting that he cannot "start seeing Louise just because she's pregnant" (31), he is nevertheless drawn to Louise Heavyman. King characterizes Louise as a strong, independent, career-oriented woman who, although pregnant, is not interested in marriage. Harlen tries to arrange male care for Louise in the form of Will.

Will is curious about Louise's pregnant body and he begins to become protective of her, "opening car doors" and holding her arm when they "cross an icy street" (35). His involvement grows when Louise takes his hand and puts it on her belly. She says, "Here, Will.... You can feel her kick" (35). The baby invites protection and conversation. Louise and Will talk "mostly about babies" (34). He says, "I helped her watch what she ate. I even gave her a little help with some names" (35).

Will becomes more involved with Louise and with her baby because he wants to, as though his care for them encourages some aspect of himself yet to be discovered. King writes about Will's sense of connection in a casual tone. Will feels no apparent urgency to stay at the hospital when Louise is in labour; his remaining there seems almost haphazard except that it represents his staunch refusal to obey her request that he go home. He is there when the baby is finally born, and he is there to perform the symbolic act of naming the baby after the sign designating a place in the hospital. As Davidson explains it, the name "South Wing derives from a mistaken identity and a joke mistaken for earnest" (191). When the nurse asks him about names, Will jokingly replies that they "will probably call her South Wing" because the sign on the wall—"south wing" is all he can see (40). Moreover, he does not quibble with the nurse's assumption that he is the father, "Mr. Heavyman" and he dons the official hospital gown.

His surprise at what he finds when he sees South Wing is unmistakable. He says that, "all you could see was her face and eyes. I thought they would be closed like puppies' or kittens', but they weren't. They were open, and she was looking at me" (40). He names her and makes what is probably her first eye contact, a contact that impresses him: "That little girl kept looking at me, and I just sat in the rocking-chair in the nursery" (40). Between Will and South Wing is a gaze that creates a relationship, one that encompasses Will and draws him into community. He does not clarify his relationship with the baby to the nurse. He is content to rock the infant and share a mutual gaze.

The gaze of the baby is magnetic for Will throughout the text. Its initiation surprises him and its sustained interest compels an enduring response. In short order he envisions a future with Louise and the baby. He thinks, "Maybe it wouldn't be so bad. Maybe it could work out" (41). He lingers at the hospital the next day, taking gifts for the baby whom Louise has named Wilma, though it is a name that no one ever uses. Will lays his head against the glass window of the nursery to watch "South Wing sleep" (41). When the nurse asks him which baby is his, he points to South Wing and says, "That one" (41). He makes his claim when he is certain no one can hear, but it is a claim nevertheless.

This claim is further established when he visits Martha Oldcrow at Harlen's insistence to look for a birthday present for South Wing. Martha asks Will if he is her father because, she says, "that little girl needs a father." Martha questions Will's credentials for this role:

"You see her born?"
"I was there."
"Okay. That'll do. You love her?"
On the way back, when we crossed the river again, I was going to drown Harlen.
"Sure."
"Don't sound sure."
"I love her." (141)

Martha accepts Will's declaration and his position as nominal father of South Wing. She gives him a handmade rattle and with it, a song that she expects him to learn and sing to South Wing. The song and the rattle comprise the gift of Native heritage passed down from one generation to the next.

King emphasizes the baby's capacity to forge a connection between Will and his community. Even though Harlen brings about Will's and Louise's coincidental gift of the rattle to South Wing, the gesture has several effects. Will not only becomes a type of father to South Wing, but he also enters a deeper relationship with Louise, and with his heritage. After the birthday party when Will goes in to check on South Wing and change her diaper, she plays "with the rattle, watching" him. He recalls the morning of her birth, puts her back in bed, and stays with her all night, trying "to remember the song" (143). He becomes, then, part of Joyce Bluehorn's "big family" (203), where "by Native definitions, a big family is everyone—every cousin's cousin, every brother-in-law's ex-wife's new stepchild. The distinctions don't matter" (Davidson 195). South Wing alters Will's perception, draws him through her gaze into a compelling caregiving relationship, and constitutes him both as a father and as a member of his cultural family.

The question of whether men are appropriating the female caregiving role emerges in David Arnason's writing. Arnason explores male caregiving in contemporary settings that frequently exclude the mother as a figure of importance. Some of the men in Arnason's stories forge connections with babies to the exclusion of the women who bear them.

In the story "My Baby and Me," Arnason develops the father's growing attachment to the baby in a manner that prefigures Douglas Coupland's *Life after God*. Both these stories concern men who are not at first interested in fatherhood, but who end up abducting their infants when their wives want to separate. Like other writers, Arnason concerns himself with the infant's capacity to redeem people from the material world, a redemption that invites the male protagonist to disentangle himself from past mistakes, as in the case of "Mary Yvette," or from an evil consumer society, as in the story "Angel, Baby." In these instances, the baby is on the side of right, of possibility, of hope, inviting his parents to value the "spiritual" rather than the "worldly" ("Angel, Baby" 77). The infant is a force that regenerates and renews. If, in pregnancy, some women undergo a form of beatification, in Arnason's stories, such a transformation occurs in the male protagonists. Arnason's work is significant because it situates fathers as primary care-givers who bond with the baby, often in place of the mothers.

The father is disconnected in a manner that seems typical in the story, "My Baby and Me." Yet the baby acts on him, drawing him into a relationship almost in spite of himself. The male protagonist's wife, Patsy, announces "her intention to become a mother" (*Circus Performer's Bar* 31). The narrator is sitting, not only passive in the face of the announcement, but also nearly drunk on three glasses of Scotch. Like Toker and Will, this male protagonist is isolated. Having already been married twice before to women who became mothers, he tells his current wife that "babies were messy, dirty things, incontinent most of the time, cranky and bad-tempered. You can't judge just by watching them cooing in strollers. You have to live with one to know" (31). The point is moot since Patsy is already pregnant. The man asserts that he is "a rotten father," an assessment for which he can provide references. He urges, "Just call one of my children and ask them what kind of a father I am" (32). However, his other experiences with babies did not do for him what the infant of his mature years will do. He has lived with babies, but he has not really known them intimately. This is a fact he acknowledges, stating that they had arrived "all in a rush" and that "in those days they pretty much belonged to the mothers" (33). The narrator's connection with his new baby will work to undermine that exclusive ownership of the mothers. He recalls that he "liked to dandle them during the rare moments when they were in a decent mood, and for a while [he] developed a real affection for a couple of them" (33). But the fondness the narrator begins to feel for his children is a point of contention for their mothers. He says the mothers are made "bitter" because of such fondness, that they act swiftly, sweeping "the babies away for dusting and powdering" and putting them in bed, "where they clearly didn't want to be" (33). These mothers act to create distance between the narrator and his babies, inserting themselves as obstacles to the baby's power to create love.

His perspective is interesting because Patsy embodies women's inclination both toward and away from babies. She is the one to announce she wants one and she is the one who withdraws to an extent, using the excuses of fatigue and work to distance herself from the baby's demands. Arnason is working within the genre of the fairy tale, reconfiguring fables to reflect "male neo-consciousness taking shape in the contemporary western world" (*Circus Performers'* back cover). He offers a distinctly male insight into the effects of the baby as it is met with such contrary desires. A man who does not want a baby gets one and looks after it, becoming entangled in his wife's antithetic proclivities.

In the physical figure of the real infant, the narrator finds his repugnance justified, but it is a repugnance that will not endure. When he visits "it" at the hospital, the infant appears much as he expects: "tiny and red…and fiercely bad-tempered" (32). However reluctantly, the narrator takes over care of the baby because his wife is too tired. Although changing the diaper makes him gag, once the baby is clean, he notices that she "brightened up and seemed to be trying to smile" (34). Once again, the gaze of the infant snags and holds the male protagonist's attention:

> I watched it for a while, thinking how tiny and fragile it was, and wondering how I could keep from breaking it. I think it went to sleep for a minute, then it opened its eyes and started to cry again.
> I picked it up carefully, keeping my hand under its head so its neck wouldn't break and making sure my thumb didn't puncture the soft spot on the top of its head. (34)

His care for the infant is manifest. The infant whom he sees and who sees him has engaged his gaze. Not only is the gaze at work here, but also the sense of the infant's softness and helplessness, the same qualities that moved Toker to softness, to the desire to "nuzzle" up to the softness and let it spill inside him (Rooke 73). The infant engenders a gentleness in the whisky-drinking narrator who has characterized himself as a "rotten father," yet who clearly cares for the baby.

Male writers seem also drawn to the notion that individual babies are exceptionally gifted. Either they can fly, or they have a unique capacity for gazing. Arnason's narrator sees the baby, Melody, as an "awfully smart baby, though a little devious," a baby who tricks him into thinking her diaper is wet so he will "come in and pick her up when she was supposed to be in bed" (34). The baby practises deception, according to the narrator, in order to be near him. The baby enacts attachment behaviours as described by Stern and Fogel.[9] The narrator is certainly attracted to this baby girl. Not only does he assume the mechanics of caring for the baby; he also begins sneaking into her room to "watch her when she was sleeping" (34). The baby alters his behaviour and inclinations. He gives up drinking because "there's something just wrong about breathing whiskey into a little pink baby's face" (35). So wrong that when Patsy comes home late from work with gin on her breath, a smell that would certainly "make Melody uncomfortable" (34), it is the baby's father doing the interrupting. He "whisks" Melody "off and powders her and put her to bed" in exactly the same way that his ex-wives did to him. This is a startling role reversal. The text does not indicate an equality of relationship between mother and father concerning the care of the baby. It reads like payback. The father is taking over what has been the mother's role. He does not experience pregnancy or childbirth, but his connection to the infant, a connection solicited and sustained by the infant's gaze and engagement behaviours, is vital. But his love for the baby is complicated by his animosity toward Patsy and the power he can exert over her by being a better "mother" than she is.

At the close of the story, Patsy makes another announcement, this time that she is leaving the narrator and taking the baby with her. She tells him he can see the baby "on alternate weekends without even paying the thirteen hundred dollars" (35). The narrator disappears with Melody and "all the equipment you need to operate a baby" (35). The story's concluding line is "we're going for a walk by the river, me and my baby, my baby and me" (35). The declaration of connection is repeated and, therefore, forceful. The repetition of "me and my baby, my baby and me" also takes on the lilting cadence of a lullaby, one that reassures the baby and the narrator himself.

Arnason's narrator sees the infant as a subject who is able to constitute him as a loving, caring father. The mother is content to work long hours and leave the care to him. When Patsy decides to leave the marriage and take Melody, the father abducts the baby. The narrator has been through three marriages and has lost contact with his other five children. Clearly, he blames the mothers of his other children for this loss, women to whom the babies "pretty much belonged" (33), and who would "sweep the babies away" (33) when he manifested his affection. His blame resonates with Dr. Lamb's assertion that "fathers can hardly be expected to maintain a belief in their importance when they are continually being told of their irrelevance" (29). This father's perspective includes a sense of deliberate interference by his previous wives to underscore his irrelevance as a parent. The story is important for its insight into the bond formed between fathers and babies and for its insight into the possible nature of rebellion against the women in his life who have denigrated his capacity to care for his babies. It's interesting that the narrator refers to his other children as "the" babies, whereas the current child, he says, is "my baby." He is determined not to lose this baby. But then, he has already left and taken his baby with him.

Another of Arnason's stories, "Mary Yvette," explores the fractious relationship of the narrator and his daughter with whom, in his recollection, he has barely been able to get along. The narrator understands that "memory is so inadequate," that his belief in his own gracefulness as an athlete contrasts sharply with his recollected clumsiness as a father: "when I remembered myself with my daughter, I remember a clumsy man, awkward, with too-large hands. A man who never knew quite when to stop and damaged all the perfect moments by wanting too much" (*The Happiest Man in the World* 132). He operates under the strain of knowing himself to be graceful and yet inordinately clumsy in the place he wants most to shine. We can assume that although he feels clumsy with his daughter, he has possibly comported himself, through all the trials she has brought his way, with dignity and elegance. He hints at such a possibility when he recalls fishing with his daughter when she was twelve. They are tied, with four perch each, and he prays for defeat to "whatever gods there are who look out for fathers and daughters" (132). She wins the competition with six fish and offers him a consolation in which he revels.

This story is, like "My Baby and Me," complicated by an absent mother. Mary Yvette's mother, the narrator's wife, is "a distant woman who lives at the edges of my life" and "bears no resemblance to the wife I once had. Not that I remember her very well" (131). Once more, a male protagonist assumes the role of primary caregiver, taking over from an absent mother and becoming the source of love, of stuffed rabbits, and of hurt. Interestingly, this mother, though characterized by the narrator as absent, as someone he can barely remember, is "in the next room" (132). The present-but-absent mother has no impact on the daughter, nor is the narrator interested in any response she might have to the expected grandchild. The text offers no indication of what she might be doing in the next room, nor of any contact she has with her daughter in spite of the daughter's promiscuous behaviour. The narrator effectively silences his wife. Though he admits she offers him "reassurance" (132), he does not say what form that reassurance takes. This wife does not mother Mary Yvette and is not a consideration in the narrator's vision of paradise with his new granddaughter. Instead, she is relegated to the margins of the text. What is striking about these later stories is that while the women are silent, the infants are not. Babies occupy a central role in narratives as male protagonists probe the nature of their relationship to them.

At the story's end, Mary Yvette is pregnant and the narrator speaks as though he himself were gestating a hope for redemption. He says, "I am almost radiant with expectation" (135), and feels that, "Fate's fortunate spiral has delivered me another chance. There will be plenty of time now for stuffed yellow rabbits, for fishing lines and poles, for, yes, love, drawn up like golden perch out of the immaculate water, where I will walk barefooted, free from being, ever again, the flawed and failing father" (135). The references to radiance depict a future for this narrator that is nothing short of gilded: the stuffed rabbits are yellow, the perch is golden, the water is immaculate. The scene is edenic; the narrator walks barefoot, is set free. Again, as in "me and my baby, my baby and me," Arnason incorporates a rhythmic repetition, this time of fricatives rather than words, whispered *f*s—"free from being, ever again, the flawed and failing father"—that John Frederick Nims calls "pleasantly soft" (189). The story ends gently and with hope. The narrator's hope is in the baby to come. Arnason's narrator aligns himself with what Hannah Arendt has called "the miracle that saves the world" (247). He is constructed as a pregnant body himself, "radiant with expectation" of a second chance.

In Arnason's story, a father's daughter's baby offers the protaganist hope of redemption, a chance to relive his life as a father with the benefit of hindsight. The baby who is not born yet is the one with whom he will walk "barefooted," with whom he will catch "golden perch out of immaculate water." The paradisiacal nature of this desire is evident. The baby, he hopes, will redeem past sins by wiping them out. The infant is, in this story, the source of the clean slate, the chance to right important wrongs with regard to the choices he has made with his own daughter. What he wants is impossible since, even if he should execute every fatherly/motherly act with perfection, his memory, unreliable as it is, would leave him feeling that his performance was inadequate (as it had been with his first opportunity at child rearing). There is poignancy to his desire, resonating with the longing people all feel for a clean slate. This is a longing that the figure of the baby seems all too well designed to fulfill.

The clean slate is what the baby, Michael, offers to his parents at the end of "Angel, Baby." Arnason's use of magic realism depicts the baby as both somewhat realistic—he wears diapers, for example, and requires changing and powdering (71)—and also magical. The fusion of the everyday with the fantastic occasions new possibilities for depicting the baby as a saviour figure. The extremes of good and bad evident in Rooke's *A Good Baby* are also present in Arnason's story in a contemporary urban environment; however, the fairy tale mode of the telling (the *once upon a time*-ness of it), as well as the humour, undermine the darker aspects of this story. Arnason creates a fabulation, a redemption story with a magical baby, two decent parents sliding down a slippery slope of materialism, and a character who embodies evil. Michael's father, Randy, sells him to "a man in a black suit" (77) in a deal to save his job. Randy refuses to give up his first-born to the man, a type of Satan. That child is a boy of eight who "had just got his first two-wheeler" (75). Randy is more interested in him, has more of a relationship with him than he has with the baby whom he sees as "a pure run-of-the-mill milk-fed baby" (75), expendable notwithstanding his eccentric habits of flying and reciting the Nicene Creed at eighteen months.

Arnason clearly has a sense of the miraculous capabilities of the baby, even considering the genre. This is a baby who will redeem the lives of these people and who will enable them to see their materialistic lifestyle and understand what is really valuable. The couple who live "Once upon a time in a small suburb of Winnipeg," had decided their two children "would be sufficient" (71). When the third arrives they decide "to love him even though they had not desired him" (71). It is this undesired baby who will act as the angelic saviour in the cataclysm between evil materialism and good love. Baby Michael appears to his mother to be sprouting wings. The narrator says, "when you rolled the baby over on his stomach to powder him, you could see the faint outline of the shape [the wings] were going to take. If you laid him down by the window, you could see hundreds of tiny feathers just below the skin" (71). Carolyn tries to get Randy to see the baby's wings but he is not capable. The implication is that Randy is not capable of "seeing" the baby at all. Babies' "naked bottoms are not [his] cup of tea" (72). For Randy, none of his babies have been "anything to write home about" (72); indeed he admits that he likes "children after they had hair and teeth and could walk. He liked them even better when they could speak" (72). Clearly, Randy is not engaged with his new baby, is unavailable for its gaze. Randy is therefore the one in need of redemption, which baby Michael will confer in a blaze of glory.

Arnason incorporates the image of the forbidden fruit to further underscore the parents' need for redemption. The deal that Randy enters into with the man his wife calls "the devil" (77) confers not only a partnership on Randy, but also a ten-thousand-dollar bonus and membership at the country club. When they go to celebrate with too much champagne and Cointreau (74), his wife Carolyn wakes up with a headache "and her mouth tasted as if she had eaten something rotten" (74). The suggestion that Carolyn has consumed something that is bad for her is explicit in the text. She grows uncomfortable with the lifestyle that Randy's deal has imposed upon her. The evening before the black-suited man is coming for Michael, she and her husband talk: "They decided that the things of the spirit were more important than worldly goods. Carolyn confessed that she hated golf and that the people at the country club were all snobs. The baby was a little strange, but after all, it was their baby, and they had responsibilities" (77).

Carolyn and Randy reject "worldly goods" in favour of "things of the spirit." While Arnason is specific about the nature of the worldly goods, the things of the spirit are rather ambiguous and seem, for the purposes of denying the man in black his forfeit, to be nothing more than ownership of the children. They refuse to give up the baby, or any of their children. When the man in black steals the baby, Michael grows "ten feet tall," with wings that "sparkled in the sunlight and his body seemed covered in gold" (78). Michael, now the archangel, engages in battle with the man who, having shed his own disguise, now shows "his horns and his tail and his cleft feet." He is "thirty feet tall and breathing fire" (78). The battle demolishes houses, a Taco Bell, a pizza delivery van, and turns the mall, "three blocks away" into a cavern (78). The baby's battle with the devil, a devil most closely associated with materialism, destroys these icons of consumer society. When the parents emerge from the house, the baby is asleep on the doorstep, still holding the blacksmith's tongs with which he defeated the man. However, the battle itself appears to have been a metaphorical one, since everything "looked exactly normal" with the exception that "it all seemed cleaner and brighter than it ever had before" (78). The baby's battle has refreshed the couples' view of their own neighbourhood, making the houses seem "newly painted" (78). This time when Randy comments on the baby's unique toughness, Carolyn replies, "'Don't be silly…He's only a baby'" (78).

Arnason's story is a modern fable about the ability of infants to redeem adults from preoccupation with material success, a preoccupation that causes Randy to make compromises to the extent that he is willing to sacrifice his baby for a country club membership and ten thousand dollars. This is something that working parents often feel they are doing on a metaphorical level when their jobs keep them, by choice or necessity, from their children. The story echoes Munsch's *Murmel, Murmel* in the sense that caring for a baby requires one to set aside the single-minded pursuit of money. Baby Michael offers his father a clean slate and the opportunity to notice that he has "a tough kid here" (78).

The same three characteristics that mark the work of Leon Rooke's *A Good Baby* and Thomas King's *Medicine River* are also evident in David Arnason's short stories. The first is simply the fact that the protagonist is a man preoccupied by a baby. Second, the male protagonist's relationship with the baby is redemptive. The third characteristic has to do with the power of the infant's gaze that often works in these texts to initiate an enduring relationship. This is what marks this male-engaged writing as coming from a certain era at the end of the twentieth century. And it is also what marks it as compelling narrative that enriches our understanding of the infant as a subject. The babies' engagement is crucial to giving these male protagonists an understanding of values that take them out of the realm of the quotidian and into a magical relationship not bound by the conventions of legitimacy, or sometimes even gravity. Whether the conventions are realistic or magical, the babies give the men an understanding of their own identity, of their participation in a community, of being part of a relationship where they are seeing and being seen. Unlike novels by women in the 1980s and 1990s, which are complicated by contradictory tensions, the men in these stories respond unequivocally to the figure of the infant. The baby fulfills deep needs for these men, needs for tenderness, connection, and the need to see and be seen.

CHAPTER 5

The Hope of the World

The hope of the world—of birthing woman, mothers, friends, and kin—rests in the newborn infant. The infant's hope resides in the world's welcome.
— Sara Ruddick, *Maternal Thinking: Toward a Politics of Peace*

Sex is about making babies. Whether one individual decides to have them or not, still the next generation is right there in all that spilled seed in all those wet cunts in all those babies' small screaming mouths and shitty bums, the next generation and our death. And our continuance if we can let ourselves have it, the knowledge that tomorrow is of our making, poised on the edge of time and becoming.... Because it is that knowledge of standing on the edge, that return to the infancy of creation, to the creation of infancy that knows creation goes on, that is the profound centre in the middle of sex...from which we recoil and turn away.
— Sarah Murphy, "Putting the Great Mother Together Again"

These two epigraphs acknowledge the importance of babies to adults and the importance of adults to babies in the human capacity to sustain life. It is an acknowledgement that should be redundant and yet, as far as literary criticism is concerned, nothing is more obvious than that the baby's importance has been ignored. This is perhaps part of the process of recoiling and turning away from "the creation of infancy." Babies move in the last half of the century from the margins of literary texts toward more central positions and this is true in writing across gender. But this move is complex because while babies do take up more physical space in fiction, they are "silent" because they cannot speak for themselves and because they have been ignored as subjects of critical inquiry. I wish to argue for a reading that lifts the silent infant from the margins of the textual world and questions the inevitability of its place there. Reading against the grain means noting the infant as a subject in itself with effects and resonances. If the baby is an ideological figure, and I think it is, then it is important to question what appeals are made in its name and what vested interests are being served by the manner of its figuring.

Writing by men has evolved to a point in the 1980s and '90s that shows men are beginning to see the infant as a site of value that gives meaning to life. Increasingly men's writing involves male protagonists in caregiving relationships with infants. This writing sees the figure of the infant escalating toward an apex of indisputable value. That is, insofar as men pay attention to infants, they do so in the context of value and meaning. Male protagonists bond to the infant in significant ways, and realize their own capacity for love and connection through the figure of the infant.

The same is not true for women's writing about infants in this period. Female protagonists in books written by women in these decades continue to wrestle with the effects of the infant on their subjectivity and their ability to act in the world. If anything, the response of these writers to the infant becomes in recent times even more complex than ever before. Women writers are conscious of themselves as split subjects—with the capacity to grow babies inside themselves and give birth to them—and so have a more complex and troubled relationship with these creatures. This relationship requires an analysis of the infant through the figure of the mother or mother type, a relationship grounded in the strangeness inherent in pregnancy. For some women, pregnancy is an invasion of one human being by another; it becomes necessary, then, to recognize that strangeness, something Kristeva devotes some thought to. In an interview with Julia Kristeva for *Books in Canada*, Diana Kuprel asks about Kristeva's notion of *étrangeté*, or foreignness. She wonders if, for Kristeva, the fact that "through birth the world is constantly being invaded by foreigners and newcomers" makes the concept of strangeness "not only personal and political for [Kristeva], then, but even biological" (Kuprel 23). Kristeva responds that "in order to become human, you have to think this biological strangeness, and the way to think this biological strangeness is to narrate it. So the particularity, the strangeness of your narration expresses the initial fact of your birth" (23). Being human means coming to terms with biological strangeness, of one's own birth and, for women, of one's babies. Grown within, object and subject, same and other, the baby gives women intimate knowledge of an interior strangeness that becomes an exterior entity.

Women's writing throughout the twentieth century has been in many ways an exploration of what it means to give birth to a baby. In the early part of the century, this meaning has been intrinsically connected to a sense of the miraculous. Anne feels beatified by the birth of her baby, as do Roy's Rose-Anna, Atwood's Clara, and Engel's Minn. But increasingly, there has been a parallel discovery of the strangeness for women of growing a baby and giving birth. This strangeness has to do with the impact on women's subjectivity of that other subjectivity, and all of the constraints—physical, social, emotional, and financial—that the baby brings with it. The baby is simultaneously a powerful symbol of liberation, fertility, and womanhood. However, the baby, as it is literally embodied in the processes of pregnancy, birth, and child rearing, is also a powerful force that obliges women to alter their lives.

What is most compelling about women's writing about the infant is their resistance to essentializing not only the experience of birth but also to exploring the figure of the baby as a totality. As Linda Hutcheon writes, "in literature by women in Canada and elsewhere today, we find the same radical critique of totalizing systems and so-called universal Truths as is to be found in contemporary post-structuralist philosophy and literary theory" ("Shape-Shifters" 220). Women write about the infant in ways that acknowledge the diversity of representation and the wealth of possibility inherent in this small figure.

In the last two decades of the twentieth century, women writers continue to narrate the biological strangeness of birth and the power of the baby in order to navigate intrinsic dichotomies of subjectivity. This chapter examines writing by women in these decades where babies remain a site of tension between women's desire for them and women's counterdesires to have a personally fulfilling life apart from the hindrances caused by babies. In the 1980s and '90s the infant plays a prominent role in constituting the female characters. In much of the writing by women, representations are multifaceted, some empowering the infant with cognition and agency, some transgressing social taboos about mother love. The texts also explore issues related to the death of the infant through the accidental or deliberate act of the mother. The texts involved in this analysis are taken from a large group of fictional narratives where the baby is a significant figure.[1] They are representative of some diverse approaches to the binary oppositions inherent in the figure of the infant. Barbara Gowdy's *Falling Angels* (1989) and Nancy Huston's *Instruments of Darkness* (1997) both deal with long-dead phantom infants who haunt the characters in the text. The power of these phantoms is in their absence as those affected by the deaths of these babies attempt to come to terms with the loss. Elyse Gasco's *Can You Wave Bye Bye, Baby?* (1999) and Terry Griggs's stories in *Quickening* (1990) and her novel *The Lusty Man* (1995) are considered together because they approach the infant from radically opposing poles. Gasco's writing departs from Griggs's in her exploration of adoption narratives that rely on distancing the baby, objectifying it to accommodate the grief of losing it. Griggs's is a representation of engagement, one of the most blatant annexations of infant consciousness in literature. She imputes consciousness, intention, and subjectivity to the infants in her stories where the baby's significance is paramount. Griggs renders a world view all the more vibrant for its designation of the infant as a person. These two writers, whose work is among the most recent discussed in this analysis, present a provocative divergence in infant representation.

The figure of the infant is a site of struggle in women's writing; it is not the clear-cut symbol of meaning and value that appears in writing by men. The struggle for understanding, for a meeting of power and desire, is evident in the complex nature of texts produced in these last decades of the twentieth century. The baby is clearly separate from the mother, though dependent for its survival. Women problematize their relations with babies in the narratives, investing babies with their own sense of encumbrance and joy. As Toni Morrison says in *Playing in the Dark*, "the subject of the dream is the dreamer. The fabrication of an Africanist persona is reflexive" (17). Morrison refers to African-American representations in literature and the manner in which they reflect the concerns of the author, but the same reflexivity occupies an investigation into representations of infants. The "fabrication" of an infant persona is also reflexive, reflecting back on the writers who create it. How writers narrate babies, how they invest them and dream them, structures the perception of who and what babies are. This is true regardless of gender, but it is clear that some male writers are cultivating a reverence toward babies that reflects a recognition of male isolation and a desire to ameliorate it. Women writers are pulled this way and that, seeing themselves reflected and created, structuring and structured by the creatures they grow within themselves.

In her essay, "Apostrophe, Animation, and Abortion," Barbara Johnson says that apostrophe "involves the direct address of an absent dead, or inanimate being by a first-person speaker. [It] is a form of ventriloquism through which the speaker throws voice, life, and human form into the addressee, turning its silence into mute responsiveness" (630-31). This form of address is intrinsic to studying representations of the infant because the baby remains always silent, particularly before birth. By silent, I mean without articulated speech. As such, infants are invested with characteristics, responses, and even conversations. This sort of investment, as Toni Morrison has stated, reveals that the subject of the dream is the dreamer, the subject of literary invention is the inventor. If what women are writing about infants is reflexive, it becomes crucial to a fuller understanding of the feminine self to examine the representations. As Barbara Hernstein Smith claims in her book *Contingencies of Value*, "no illusion is more powerful than that of the inevitability and propriety of one's own beliefs and judgements" (54). In women's writing about babies, the "inevitability and propriety" of a certain view of infancy becomes evident in the way that the baby's subjectivity is made invisible. Because the baby is often a silent figure, it becomes necessary to investigate how these texts fill that silence since the infant itself does not exist in a vacuum.

Women investigate issues of empowerment and helplessness in these texts. They explore the effects of having a baby as these relate to identity, body anxiety, and power. For many women writers, giving birth has to do with fear and desire. But these are neither straightforward nor singular, especially in texts like *Falling Angels* and *Instruments of Darkness* which are permeated by absent babies. In each story, the mother is complicit with the baby's death. The mother in Gowdy's novel has most likely thrown her baby over Niagara Falls. Huston's Nada reacts to her mother's multiple miscarriages by aborting every baby she starts. Yet, in each novel, the birth of another baby moves the characters toward an almost reluctant redemption.

Gowdy's is a story about a dead baby and a haunted family. The mother's act in throwing or dropping her infant son into Niagara Falls proves to be a cataclysm, the aftershocks of which persist throughout the decades of her other children's lives. Gowdy manipulates point of view when the girls are first told the news, offering a distinctly child-like perspective on the tragedy. This perspective demonstrates the confusion and shock that the girls feel, and it also suggests that this knowledge is the pivotal point from which time will be measured.

Falling Angels begins at what Di Brandt calls "the classic site of the mother's body in Western culture: the cemetery" (19). This mother's body is at the funeral home where her daughter, Sandy, is changing the body's lipstick from pink to what she feels is some other, more appropriate colour. This act speaks to the nature of memory, how the girls spend their lives attempting to construct or create a cohesive understanding about their mother's life, about her agency in her own baby's sensational death, and about the effects of that act upon themselves. Gowdy introduces the three sisters, one of whom has death "on either side of her" (7). Her mother has died and she is pregnant with a baby who will also die. The infant permeates the story, framing it with a return to the scene of the crime.

Death is at the foreground of the novel. As Constance Rooke argues in her book *The Writer's Path*, a

> psychological or philosophical issue underlying the creation of fiction and linking writer and reader is the fact of our mortality. We may or not believe in some form of life after death, but in either case we are haunted by the knowledge that we will die. We are born and begin to take shape as individuals who are invested, to varying degrees, with a sense of mission; we think we are supposed to "make something" of our lives. (6)

The baby functions as a symbol of what people sometimes do to prove they have accomplished something with their lives. The baby is, for a time, a way of pushing against mortality. But what happens if the baby dies? And what happens if the mother causes the death?

Gowdy explores these questions in a narrative that communicates a profound sense of the absurd. The characters behave in ways that might be considered wildly inappropriate, and yet, under the influence of loss, their responses seem valid. Each of the characters is influenced by the knowledge that their baby brother died and that their mother was to some degree responsible. Each of the sisters searches for some means of rapprochement with this lost baby. Norma "absolutely exonerated their mother. Having held several babies, she knew how they squirmed in your arms, how easy it would be to drop one" (18). Sandy does not know what to think; knowledge of the incident itself makes her "wistful" (19). Lou, however, "didn't think it was an accident, but she also let their mother off the hook, because who wouldn't have thrown that damn baby?" (18). Each response corresponds to the girls' frustrated longing for love, a longing that each will fulfill in different ways. Norma wants a relationship with her dead brother and creates one, imagining that he haunts her. Sandy's inability to decide "what to think" pervades her life. She persists in demeaning sexual encounters until she finally becomes pregnant with her own baby. Lou's response is grounded in her hatred of babies and her hatred of her father. The narrator says, "she was glad the baby of him died" (19). Lou, the toughest of the sisters, aborts the baby she becomes pregnant with, an act that seems to resonate with her mother's act of throwing her own baby over Niagara Falls and that permits her unique insight into her mother's possible motivations. She aggressively refuses connection with any baby she encounters because she understands them only in terms of their heaviness; the sheer weight of carrying them is too much for her to bear.

The figure of the infant is complex in this novel. It embodies the desire for love, the fear of rejection, the weight of responsibility, and the impossibility for some women and the necessity for others of bearing them. Norma is the most emotionally raw of the sisters. Overweight and lonely, she reaches out for a connection to her dead baby brother. Her relationship with the ghost of her dead baby brother is phrased in scriptural terminology. She insists on telling Lou how she feels: "Although Norma knows better than to go on, her eyes are full with a yearning that she thinks must be the urging of heaven, so she tells Lou everything. About hearing Jimmy's voice emanating from his picture. About asking his advice. About the day when she felt as if she had become Jimmy...as if Jimmy had entered her" (105). Norma's longing for a saviour is palpable. Her eyes "yearn" and she tells her cynical sister "everything" in spite of knowing the reception she will get. Jimmy inhabits Norma the way "Jesus enters" people's hearts (106). She says "His light is in them, guiding them. Well, it's Jimmy who entered my heart" (106). She turns to the baby as a saviour, something she needs considering the strange family situation in which she lives. Norma believes that their brother, had he lived, would be able to save them, that he would be "brave, courageous and bold" (30), that he would be "gentle as the lamb of God" (30). The transference of Norma's need for bravery and boldness is evident. She reassures his photo the way she herself longs to be reassured, calling him a "poor little baby" and telling him, "Mommy loved you. Did she ever. When you drowned, she turned to drink" (78). Norma attributes to Jimmy the status of the Lamb of God, who, as the Bible says, takes away the sin of the world (John 1: 29). She perceives her family as being in need of forgiveness, marked by a deed that has no explanation—a deed that has prevented them all from "making something" of their lives since life is so precarious, dropped into the abyss in an instant. Norma endows the baby with supernatural qualities that help her to cope with his loss and with the loss of her mother and father's love. Her valuation of the baby is hyperbolic, bordering on religious hysteria. The baby likely does not speak to her or live anywhere but in her imagination. Nevertheless, her yearning for him speaks volumes about her need for acceptance, forgiveness, and protection. When she accepts the fact that she is a lesbian, she achieves the "serenity" and "feels a breathtaking relief" (178), able with that sudden recognition to feel within herself all that she looked for from the dead baby.

Lou represents a view of the infant grounded in a discourse of the real, coarsely rejecting any construction of the infant as ideal. She keeps her distance physically and emotionally from the baby. Lou is aggressively practical. When Norma tells her about conversations with their dead baby brother, she accuses Norma of being schizophrenic. She tells Norma bluntly, "he was only just born when he died. He was a baby. He shit, he ate, he slept" (106). Lou refuses to believe that babies, whether they are dead or alive, have any special value. She is grimly hateful toward other children: "When Lou babysits, she warns the kids to stay out of her hair" (106). When she is hired to care for a baby whose penis is inflamed and infected, Lou must apply cream "from the tip down" (107). Lou tells her friend, Sherry, that this is "the sex part" (107). She appears determined to diminish any quality of innocence that might attract her to this baby. Lou's responses to the infant are complicated by her conflicting desires to keep her distance and to come close. The baby she babysits is a good one who sometimes "gurgles and smiles at her, and she wants to pick him up and cuddle him" (107). However, whenever she does this he tries to suckle her breasts so she stops picking him up.

The baby's tendency to situate Lou as his mother infuriates her. This is a role she persistently rejects. She has seen what mothers are like. Hers is ineffectual, having abnegated care of her children. From a young age Lou has been the one to do the grocery shopping and make sure that her mother has breakfast and lunch when her father is at work. She also mothers her sisters, to an extent, though her care is manifested in angry outbursts. While she has dreams that "she is another person, gentle and innocent, often still a little girl" (80), Lou also knows that she "hates living with her sisters" (80). Lou dreams of being gentle, but the difficulties of her life have compelled her to be angry. She sees motherhood as the ultimate victimization. Her mother is a victim, made infantile herself because of the baby's death. When Stella says she wants to have a baby, that babies "love anyone who looks after them" (108), that what is lovable about them is "how helpless they are" (108), Lou vehemently repudiates this. She says of helplessness, "that's not loveable" (108). Lou disavows the equation of love and helplessness. But, helpless herself under the influence of LSD, she comes to what she calls a ridiculously obvious understanding. She realizes that "the last destination of every impulse, no matter what twisted or frustrated route it might take, is to cut through the crap to the purity of emptiness experienced during your first minutes in the world" (149-50). Lou is torn between longing for a restoration of the purity, gentleness, and innocence she might have experienced as a baby and the infant's disturbing ability to make women helpless. She dons a carapace of toughness as a means of coping with the difficulties of her life, but she cannot escape the sense that there is a pure, gentle, innocent place worth knowing and preserving. This is the site of an ideal infancy that seems to engender in people a preserving expectation of good.[2]

This expectation of goodness is what is violated by Lou's mother when she throws her baby into Niagara Falls, a transgression that Lou struggles in anomalous ways to come to terms with. She understands that her mother's baby would have been abiding in that world of kind expectations, even while he was falling. And in spite of her rejection of babies, Lou still craves that primordial innocence, grounded in kindness and in the assumption of kindness. When the baby she looks after is hurt as a result of her neglect, Lou cries "and tells him she's sorry. She wants to mean it. She wants to love him. She wants to love him and for him to know that she loves him. He's just a little baby, she tells herself. But all she can feel is how heavy he is in her arms" (127). It is not only this actual baby who weighs heavily, but also, clearly, the absent baby whose death has altered her life and her ability to offer love and generosity.

Gowdy returns in her characterization of Lou to this weight of babies, which operates on a metaphorical level. Babies are weighty. As Adrienne Rich has said, "the physical and psychic weight of responsibility on the woman with children is by far the heaviest of social burdens" (*Of Woman Born* 35). The baby Lou cares for is "heavy in her arms" (127). She disposes of her own baby, of its unbearable weight. In coming to terms with her mother's act at Niagara Falls, Lou understands that her mother must have killed the baby for good reason. Having suffered so many losses herself, Lou knows her mother was possibly "just speeding up the inevitable" and wonders "why their mother didn't throw herself, too" (190). Lou is troubled by her mother's life, by the forces that brought her to the point where she could kill her baby.

> Ever since swallowing Maternal Instinct at the funeral, Lou has believed that their mother loved the baby with a mother's blind love. Whether or not their mother threw the baby or dropped him, whether it was an act of craziness or sacrifice, whether or not all these years she has been sorry, it dawns on Lou that sometimes she must have been haunted by the moment at which she was standing at the railing, and there was the thunder of the falls, and her eyes were glued to the water that was on the verge of going over—nothing could stop the water now—and she had that weight in her arms. The moment at which the thing she loved enough to die for, she let die. (191)

Lou understands that the weight of the baby, of its care, of the inevitability of its suffering are too much for her mother. The burdens of pregnancy, childbirth, and childcare are onerous ones for women, and Lou is most aware of this. Strangely, though, she is the one who has the most contact with babies. She takes care of other people's babies, she takes care of her mother who has been reduced by circumstances to an infantile state, and once pregnant, she dreams of babies (152). Lou's first pregnancy test is negative, her second, positive. The effect of the knowledge is immediate:

> Suddenly, she feels nine months pregnant. There is a baby inside of her, but what it feels like is a malignant tumour. She's in shock at the thought that with every second it is replicating its cells.... She regards her stomach. It looks twice as big as it did fifteen minutes ago. It looks evil, like a punishment. It looks like the greatest multiplication of all her sorrows. (161)

It seems clear that Lou cannot on any level bear this baby. The heavy baby's weighty cells are "replicating" every second, making her feel huge, that her stomach is growing exponentially. The baby is a weight that is unbearable.

The constitution of the infant as a site of fear and desire is evident even in Lou, the least likely character to be influenced by desire. As such, Gowdy represents the complexities for women who are pregnant and who must decide what to do. For Lou, the baby is "evil," a "punishment," inseparable from her past and from the manner of its conception with a boy she calls an "asshole" (160). Its weight, its malignancy (160), compel her to have it removed. In the ellipsis in the above-quoted passage, Lou fantasizes about keeping the baby. She looks in the mirror and imagines herself "with white, milk-huge breasts, a little baby in her arms, and Tom compelled to love her" (161). Although she rejects this vision, the result she believes of her "hormones...trying to trick her" (161), the baby's existence gives Lou pause to enter into an imaginative world where she has milk in her breasts and a baby to feed and a man to love her. This image, something she can "see," something that "she would like," is interrupted by a man on the street whom she brushes against (161) and who "growls" at her. For Lou, "the effect is like a hypnotist snapping his fingers" (161) and Lou makes the call for an abortion appointment. In essence, the man's rudeness reawakens her from the ideal and reminds her of what life is really like. And once she remembers, the baby within her stomach looks "like the greatest multiplication of her sorrows" (161).

Lou is acquainted with sorrow. In an act that resonates with her mother's act of throwing the baby over Niagara Falls, Lou determines to kill the baby, to negate it by means of abortion. Her problematic relationship with babies is the result of the death of her brother, obviously. But she also abhors babies because her brother's death is what caused her father to be abusive, "what drove him, part way at least, to every bad, crazy thing he ever did" (6). The love normally given to a baby has never been hers so her resistance to babies is grounded in a kind of self-loathing that compels her to reject helplessness.

If Lou's concept of the baby is shaped by her past, so is Sandy's. Gowdy represents the two pregnancies, Lou's and Sandy's, in terms that are diametrically opposed. Where Lou's is "malignant" and "evil," Sandy, on the other hand, feels that the baby is a "miracle," and she feels "as if an angel touched her." Sandy goes for a pregnancy test even though,

> She isn't uncertain, and she doesn't need confirmation. She goes to
> the drugstore because she assumes that you're supposed to. Then
> you go to a paediatrician. From here on in she is dedicated to doing
> what a mother-to-be is supposed to do. Already she loves her baby
> so much.... Having it inside her stomach feels exactly like a mira-
> cle, as if an angel touched her stomach and a baby began to grow.
> (161-62)

The baby is a point of confluence for Sandy, all the streams of her
life, all her yearning for love flowing in one direction. Her body has
been "claimed" by the baby (161). The baby inside her makes her feel
"clean through and through" (162). Ironically, her pregnancy test
occurs at the same pharmacy and within hours of Lou's. Each of these
will have polarized outcomes. While Lou's baby is an object of loathing,
Sandy's is already an object of fierce love and devotion. Her new baby
becomes for her a type of saviour, someone who will be what she most
needs. The pregnancy provokes a simultaneous yearning and comple-
tion, an emptiness that is persistently filled, a restoration of that lost
source of support. She herself is the restoration. For Sandy, there is no
sense of biological foreignness, only the strangeness of the miraculous.
Her response is uncomplicated by a sense of fear or rejection. For Lou,
however, the baby embodies a foreignness so repellent she must
expunge it from her body. She asserts, "No baby. No mother" (179),
after her own mother dies and after she has the abortion. She will not
be the baby; she will not have the baby.

But Sandy's desire for the baby is unqualified. It is absolute. She is
certain not only that she is pregnant, but that this is the most wonderful thing that could happen. When Lou speaks later about the possibility of abortion, Sandy gazes "down at her stomach so lovingly you'd
swear she could see in" and says "in a far-away voice, 'What a thing to
say'" (182). The statement that such an act is unthinkable comes from
someone whose voice is "far-away" and who, indeed, seems intoxi-
cated with her pregnancy. What Sandy sees when she "sees in" to her
stomach is a mystery so profound it obliterates all her future plans and
reorients her life.

For Lou, the baby is a foreigner, an alien, someone to be treated
with suspicion. For Sandy, the infant is a "newcomer," suggesting fresh-
ness and welcome.[3] These are nuanced words, but they speak to that
duality with which people greet the unknown. Women give birth to
babies who invade the world as foreigners and newcomers. Or they

host babies in their bodies along the same lines. It sounds straightforward, but this newcomer/foreigner binary is an unstable opposition. Lou feels that both her own abortion and her mother's decision to throw her baby to his death are acts of ultimate good. She understands what might have motivated her mother to reject the baby, the weight of him, the possibilities, since she herself performs a similar act of rejection. She imagines that at Niagara Falls her mother felt "that weight in her arms" (191). The girls themselves are burdened by the weight of responsibility for their mother and for each other, each of them investing the figure of the baby with their own fears and desires. Life is a weighty thing, full of responsibility and difficulty, with the certain knowledge of death at the end. If the birth of the baby pushes away one's knowledge of mortality temporarily, then the mother's act seems an acknowledgement that any kind of pushing away is futile. At another level, the baby's death also pre-empts its own suffering and disillusionment, the loss of that "expectation of good" that Simone Weil writes about. It may be self-sacrificial on the mother's part to end her baby's life, and on Lou's part to have an abortion, but it also suggests a refusal or an incapacity to perceive the infant as a "newcomer," someone whose potential life might just as easily be fraught with joy rather than futility. Sara Ruddick claims that the hope of the infant is in the "world's welcome" (217). Gowdy's book reveals a welcome for the infant that is complicated by sorrow and loss, by women's knowledge of the difficulty of life and the certainty of death.

Narratives in the 1980s and '90s by women explore complex mother-infant relationship rendered more polymorphous and more poignant because of women's access to abortion. Both *Falling Angels* and *Instruments of Darkness* explore the impact of abortion. However, Huston's novel is a more sustained engagement with the figure of the infant and the sorrow that some women feel—in spite of their best efforts to avoid it—when they make the decision to terminate pregnancy. Huston points up the tension between women's knowledge of the baby as an unwanted burden and their knowledge of the baby as a significant and valuable individual.

The figure of the baby is represented according to this duality. It is adversarial in these narratives; the narrator constitutes the baby as that which denies women personal identity and even life. But the baby is also what provides a vital connection to life, a connection otherwise lacking in the narrator. Nada in *Instruments of Darkness* holds herself aloof from life in spite of, if not because of, her chosen sterility. She has removed the "i" that would have made her name "Nadia," aligning herself with "Nothingness" (12). She hates flowers, growing things, people who grow flowers (11), and when she considers her lovers, she feels that they spill "their seed into a stomach they know will never stealthily transform it into a pudgy squaller" (13). The text implies that Nada's sterility is voluntary, that she has arranged herself so that she cannot conceive a baby—a "pudgy squaller"—needing to know that her "pleasure would be sterile. Otherwise no pleasure" (13). Nada has arranged her life in such a way as to "recoil and turn away" from what Sarah Murphy calls "the profound centre in the middle of sex" (10). She denies life to her future possible babies, but she also denies life to herself. She claims that her antipathy toward babies is equal to her antipathy toward gardening. But Nada's rejection of her babies is more troubling than she cares to admit. Her persistent attempts to oversimplify the infant's significance result only in that significance being more profoundly felt. She insists, "Getting rid of my babies has moved me exactly as much as flushing down the toilet a beetle found on its back on the bathroom floor, flailing its legs in the air. A tiny distress; finished" (14). Yet there emerges throughout the text a strong sense that nothing is finished.

The novel is structured with a double narrative whose parallel strands are entitled, "The Scordatura Notebook" and "The Resurrection Sonata." In "The Scordatura Notebook" (i.e., discordance notebook) Nada navigates the losses of her own past, the weightiness of both her mother's occupation with babies and her own. But in "The Resurrection Sonata," the historical narrative that Nada is researching and writing, Barbe gives birth to an illegitimate child in the chapter entitled, "The Miracle." I find these designations interesting because they speak to the tension at work in the novel between the discord babies bring into the world and the persistent nature of Nada's interest in them.

Huston inscribes babies who come into the world in the most agonizing fashion and who, once they are here, crush the women who must mother them. There are three scenes related to birth. In the first, the mother dies horribly seconds before a primitive Caesarean section is performed on her. In the second, the narrator, Nada, stands by while her mother nearly bleeds to death in miscarriage. Finally, in the third scene, a young girl gives birth to a baby who dies shortly after. In all three instances, the mothers suffer violently—in lurid colour and in pathetic and terrifying sounds. There can be no doubt that the infant is a site for this narrator of genuine fear. The suffering of the women is depicted in gothic terms. The narrator constructs these narratives within a historical context that includes the threat to maternal life in childbirth. And certainly there is an implicit expectation that childbirth will be painful and messy. But Huston maximizes the negative aspects of birth.

Once again, some sixty years after Grove published *Settlers of the Marsh*, the influence of the mother's experience of too many babies has a negative impact on the daughter who refuses to have any children. Nada's response to the infant is the result of witnessing her mother's loss of identity. Nada's mother, a concert violinist married to a domineering husband, loses what life she has through repeated pregnancies and miscarriages. Like Grove's Ellen, who refuses marriage because she does not want to become pregnant, Nada refuses to give birth to a baby. But at the end of the twentieth century Nada has more options than Ellen, including abortion and tubal ligation. She has, like Ellen, witnessed the difficulty of her mother's life and has borne the brunt of her mother's indifference to her. Like Lou in *Falling Angels*, Nada reacts to this indifference by negating the lives of the fetuses she conceives and by considering them adversaries.

Nada opposes the infant's power to obliterate a woman's existence in the physical hardship of pregnancy and childbirth, and in the constant demands of babies who are "mewling and pewling away in the corner…tearing Elisa's nerves to shreds" (57). Nada sees all the wreckage of repeated pregnancies. She imagines her mother a shy twenty-two year old: "Elisa, her name was, before it became Mother" (156). This annihilation of personhood is, for Nada, the only outcome of contact with infants. Nada's experience of babies is that they rob women of their power, weighing them down and sapping their energy. Like Lou, Nada perceives the difference between being pregnant and not pregnant as an issue of weight. She describes her mother as having been "an aerial creature, a slender, virtually weightless thing in love with sound and movement, accustomed to travelling light" (111). But the same woman, once married, becomes "pregnant, heavy with child, then children, in her arms, in her stomach, at her breast, on her back, three then four then five of us, tugging at her skirts, her hand, her brain with our demands" (111). Elisa suffers under the burden of so many babies; they are ballast that causes strain, forming in her face "the constant expression of effort and surprise" (111). Her prayers to God for strength are answered with more babies, "some alive and some dead, all of them exhausting" (112).

Her mother's life, and her near-death experience in miscarriage, confirms Nada's rejection of infants:

> Being the eldest child, and being, to boot so to speak, a female, it was I who was privy to the regular bedroom carnage, miscarriage after miscarriage as my father continued to knock her catholically up and she in obedience to the pope, Pius XII at the time, refrained from taking measures to prevent it and the sheets filled with blood and trembly velvety black clots of something like human flesh more than once a year, yes, more often than once a year though seven mouths gaped around the dining-room table already.
>
> (Ah! My beetles are so much cleaner, so much drier, and more discreet! At least their murder makes no mess.)
>
> The time she almost died, the blood was literally flooding out of her, she was being emptied of her substance, I was in the room beside her and I heard her screams turn gradually into sighs— almost sighs of pleasure. (30)

The narrator inculpates Catholicism, specifically the Pope's edicts against contraception. She inculpates her father whom she does not depict as being emotionally involved in making babies; rather he "knocks" her mother up, exhausting her and almost killing her with the babies that result. The bedroom is not a site of intimacy, but a site of "carnage" where "trembly, velvety black clots" of miscarriage stain the bed sheets. That the young Nada had to help her mother during this horrible time further accentuates the macabre aspect of pregnancy. Nada's perception of her mother's life is that it is violent and quietly melodramatic. For Nada, there is no joy at all in her mother's life, least of all from the babies that survived, described as "gaping mouths" around the table. Nada insists her mother has lost herself because of the birth of her children.

Nada is horrified by the amount of blood, by the frequent and futile repetitions of pregnancy and miscarriage. Her "beetles," she writes, are much more tidily disposed of. Nada describes the miscarried infant as a clot "of something like human flesh." Nada characterizes the aborted infant as a "beetle." While the inference in both cases is that the babies are less than human, Nada's aborted fetuses resemble nothing so much as beetles. This strategy of dehumanizing the fetus reads as Nada's attempt to distance herself from emotional involvement. In her mother's case the fetus is a bloody clot; in her own, an insect. Nada has opted for murder without mess; her victims are the fetuses she carries. She prefers to make them victims rather than to become one herself. She rejects the invasion of foreigners that Diana Kuprel refers to in her interview with Kristeva, but the tidiness of her abortions turns out to be only a physical tidiness. The babies persist in her consciousness and she is no more comfortable with their deaths than her mother would have been with her miscarriages.

The infant haunts both Nada's story and the story within, the one she is writing called, aptly, "Resurrection Sonata." In Nada's historical narrative of Barbe and Barnabé, the sister and brother twins are born clinging to each other, "embraced, entwined, their limbs affectionately mingled in a tight hug" (20). Huston's second traumatic birth scene depicts the birth of twins born in an embrace of affection that con-tributes to their mother's birth agony and death. The birth is told, not surprisingly, in nightmare terms, overloaded with sensory detail including smells and sounds. The smell of fear is in the air, as is the smell of death. The night is punctuated by "the screams of the shep-herd-girl who used to sing so beautifully" (17). Sensory details over-whelm the event—the smell of death, the sound of screaming, the sight of Marthe's "vermilion" blood. Barbe's mother screams and arches her back; the women pin her down to the floor. There is a cauldron of boil-ing water, candlelight, and finally, Marthe's death (18), followed by a makeshift Caesarean section performed with the hog-slaughtering knife. The images are stark and horrible, evocative of the witches in the opening scene of *Macbeth*. When the twins are finally lifted from the wreckage of their mother, she is already dead. Their position in the uterus has made it impossible for her to deliver them. This, writes Nada, "is why their mother is dead" (20). The two stories overlap in Nada's description of Elisa's near-death miscarriage. In describing the diminishing of her mother's screams, Nada quotes directly from her own account of Marthe's suffering in labour.

In the third and most violent birth scene in the novel, Nada writes about the birth of Barbe's baby. The cataclysm she provokes seems to offer catharsis for her, permitting her to write about her own experience of abortion. Barbe's labour and delivery are again conveyed in gothic terms. She is, of course, alone, with the "lightning bolt transpiercing her." Barbe is the magnetic noun attracting clusters of modifiers: "she is the Earth itself, quaking, splitting, heaving, burning, exploding, disgorging its boiling lava, now the water sac has burst, a boiling geyser spews forth from her innards" (251). The writing is overblown, hyperbolic, indicating that far more than a baby is being born.[4] It's as though all of Nada's sentiments about the abortion of her own baby are delivered in this apocalyptic birth. And not only Nada's experience of abortion. The words she chooses are also evocative of her connection with her mother, as though the experience of her own birth, her symbiotic connection to her mother, emerges in the language she chooses. It is language that is characterized by a violent energy, by a sense of the horror of her invasion of her mother's body and the invasions into her own. Nada's body has been oriented in two directions: toward her mother and toward her babies. Her representation of Barbe's labour and delivery is informed by these profound connections and the losses she has felt in both directions. Finally, Nada says of the abortion that her mother and her mother's cousin

> were extremely deft at extracting my quasi-son, my proto-son, my would-be son, my wouldn't-be son from his abode, his dark cave, gently cutting off his supply of oxygen-giving blood, then wrapping him in tissue-paper and flushing him down the toilet—an inglorious burial for you indeed, Tom Thumb, Elisa's first grandchild, tumbling head over heels amidst the excrement and dishwater through the pipes of the Chicago sewage system, to be unceremoniously spat a few hours later into Lake Michigan. (203)

These are gentler words than the ones she uses to depict Barbe's labour and delivery, but the brutality of the images, the excision of the baby and its ignominious interment, underscore her sorrow.

The novel is an extended apostrophe to Nada's aborted fetuses; she addresses her dead "beetles." There is tension in this depiction of infants as destroyers of women's lives, contradictions that disclose the multiplicity of babies' effects. Nada has had abortions and insists that the babies mattered to her as much as beetles, yet the story is propelled by her own aching sense of loss. Nada perceives the abortive act as murder, and she apostrophizes her lost baby whom she addresses also as Tom Thumb and who appears to her in the night (265). When she returns home after the abortion, Martin, the baby's father, tells her to be more stoical. Nada writes, "I found it obscene to be stoical about the elimination of another human life" (265). She has wondered during the writing of the Barbe story why she should "care about Barbe's dead baby if [she does not] care about [her] own?" (236). The answer is obvi-

THE HOPE OF THE WORLD

ous. In spite of her posture as an uncaring and distant person, Nada
cares deeply, though she must struggle through the parallel historical
narrative before she finds out the truth about herself, that "one need
not *be* matter to matter" (266). She comes to terms with both the loss of
her baby and with the fact that he remains with her. She says, "You matter a great deal to me, my darling. And I apologize for calling you a beetle" (266). The apology and the address itself are in the present tense,
indicating the infant's ongoing presence with her whether she likes it
or not.

Even though the baby is not living, its power to redeem and forgive
is evident in Huston's text. Nada begins the story by asserting that her
secret motto, which she cannot even share with friends, is "I don't care"
(14). It becomes evident that this position sits uncomfortably with her,
that she chooses it out of self-preservation to avoid the hurt that caring
causes. She demonstrates that acceptance is sometimes necessary for
women to move forward in an existence that permits full engagement.
Facing her losses, the loss of her mother and her babies, seems to
strengthen Nada so that she rewrites the ending of the historical narrative. Barbe survives the birth. Although she is sentenced to death for
the murder of her child, her brother, Barnabé, a monk slight enough to
be mistaken for his twin sister, takes her place in the cell and on the gal-
lows. Here Nada writes for Barbe a happy ending where, instead of
being "hanged, strangled, and burned" as a witch (279), Barbe escapes
at the cost of her brother's life, an interesting twist on Nada's own survival at the cost of her brother's life. Barbe becomes "famous throughout the capital as a healer, consoler, spell-lifter, angel-maker and bro-
ken-heart-repairer: around the middle of the century she'll have an
affair with Jean-Jacques Rousseau who is twenty-six years her junior"
(315). This happy ending results from Nada's sense of redemption, her
sense of having asked for and received forgiveness. The two survive,
Barbe to fame in eighteenth-century France, Nada to view Mr. Hartley's hydrangea.

Huston chronicles the struggle of a woman to accept her decision
to terminate pregnancy. The narrative offers a coming-to-terms with
the death of her babies that redeems Nada's losses to an extent. Nada's
title for the chapter about the birth of Barbe's child is called "The Miracle." The miracle turns out to be that Nada herself finds some redemption by playing with Sonya, the neighbour's toddler, and by making
plans to see Mr. Hartley's hydrangea, something she would have

rejected at the novel's opening. She writes, "Every decision to despair is instantly annulled by the face of a child, the smile of a friend, the beauty of a poem or a painting or a flower" (314). There is no doubt that the abortion is the site of Nada's most excoriated loss. Huston's narrative offers a balm for women whose experience of abortion haunts them. In Nada's case the infants she has aborted persist in her consciousness in a way that redeems her life, to engage her with "the face of a child" and with the hydrangea-growing Mr. Hartley.

In many ways, however, Huston's conclusion seems strained. This is evident in the imbalance of comparisons between the "the face of a child" and the "beauty of a poem or a painting or a flower." The equalization of these two things, a child's human face and an object, is disturbing. Furthermore, Nada's address to the infant as "Tom Thumb," a character from a child's nursery rhyme, speaks to a sense that the infant's value is limited in Nada's view. The ideological work of the novel *is* the balm that it offers women who struggle with their decision to terminate pregnancy, and the claim made in the baby's name in this case has to do with the possibility of forgiveness. Recall Toni Morrison's assertion that "the subject of the dream is the dreamer" (17). Clearly Huston creates the figure of the infant so that it is invested with the power to "annul despair" even though it has itself been annulled. If the depiction of an infant persona is self-reflexive, then in this novel what is most necessary is that Nada find a means of coming to terms with her decision to abort—a coming-to-terms that includes a declaration of love for what she has tidily disposed of to find forgiveness that comes ultimately from herself.

Further complexities of women's experience of babies can be found in Elyse Gasco's collection *Can You Wave Bye Bye, Baby?* Many of the stories focus on adoption and are forceful in their rendering of an emotional landscape of distance between mother and baby. The narrators come to terms with the act of giving up their babies and/or the knowledge of having at one time been given up by their mothers. These stories are both disturbing and powerful, in part as a result of the second-person point of view with the narrator addressing "you" when she means herself. This technique has the effect of suggesting a witness to these thoughts and events, a witness of the narrator's own creating. It imposes a distance between text and reader because the "you" is not the reader.

This distance, both literal and metaphoric, characterizes the stories. This is a distance enforced by the narrators' fundamental lack of connection to a mother figure whose absence shapes their response to the babies in the stories. The title story of the collection begins with the startling assertion of a mother's lost love for her baby: "It is surprisingly easy to run out of love.... If someone shook you side to side like a milk carton, they wouldn't know that you were almost out, down to the last drop" (119). This mother characterizes herself as an empty "milk carton," someone who is "down to the last drop" of love. She looks at her baby, "at her soft, unfinished head," and says, "I don't think I will ever really love you" (120). Unlike Rooke's Toker, or King's Will, or Arnason's narrators, this baby's softness does not soften its mother. Gasco's narrator feels and creates an increasing distance between herself and her baby. She begins by leaving the baby alone in the house to go for a walk. The first time she does it she shivers, feels almost "erotic" (120). What surprises her is the fact that nothing "is physically holding" her back, nothing prevents her from leaving—"no elastic band, or choke chain and leash." She is astounded to find that she looks like anyone else out for a walk (120). She is working to cast off the constraint imposed by the baby, something that turns out to be invisible to passersby.

When she encounters a man who punches his dog, she yells at him. He tells her to take the dog herself and he leaves. Significantly, the narrator squints after him feeling that "people should be made to wear license plates. No matter what, you ought to be able to track them down" (121). Tracking people down is important to the narrator whose mother had walked away from her. This is the fundamental exigency of the text. How does one, having been abandoned, be certain of anything, let alone love?

In this narrative the mother attempts to objectify the infant. The baby is an object of curiosity to the narrator, something to take home. She describes how, "it struck you that this was the only occasion where you actually left the hospital with something in hand. Mostly, stuff is left behind. You felt conspicuous with your package wrapped and bound in white like a tiny crazy person being subdued" (123). The narrator has a skewed perception of what, in cliché terms, has been called a "bundle of joy." In her arms, the wrapped bundle of baby suggests to her that the baby is "crazy" and being restrained. The image of restraint is a powerful one; the narrator will continue to restrain the infant, to keep it from her and ignore its claims on her for care.

Gasco's rendering subverts the notion of mother love as it is traditionally conceived. Interwoven with such observations are the narrator's recollections of her own mother's breakdown, of slipping a picture under her mother's bedroom door of "a red flower in a red glass vase…in apology that said simply: Hello mommy" (126). The narrator carries with her the sense of having been an object to her own mother, and an undesirable one at that. Gasco's text addresses with poignancy the question of what happens to a baby, how it is configured, when the mother herself fails to provide "a source of support, a fulfillment of care" ("Place Names" 282).

When the baby cries, the narrator drowns out the sound. She sits on the side of the tub and lets the shower run. The preparation she makes before holding the baby is to sit in the steam until her "skin is damp" (126). According to the narrator,

> You make yourself cold and ready for her. You put her down on her stomach, her forehead pressed sadly into the mattress. Sometimes her head moves from side to side, denying everything. You do not like the way she looks up at you. Her eyes are abnormally huge and she hardly seems to blink. It is the only way she has to take you in. She has not heard the sound of your voice very often…. Soon, it seems she does not cry as often. She is trying to frighten you with her silence. Her hands will reach out and grab hold of your finger if you tease her with it. But this is an uncontrolled movement, involuntary. Her eyes are still adjusting. She cannot make out friend or foe. She reaches for the nearest thing at hand, but it has nothing to do with closeness. (126-27)

The narrator's agency in making her skin damp and cold, deliberately uncomfortable for a baby made comfortable by warm proximity, is most disquieting. It echoes her mother's withdrawal and abandonment. The "you" in the narrative becomes confusing as the palimpsest of the mother's past conduct emanates in the narrator's present encounter with her baby. The ambiguity inherent in the address suggests that the narrator might be rationalizing her mother's deliberate distance.

Moreover, Gasco's repeated use of negation in this passage, "denying," "do not," "hardly," "has not," "does not," "cannot," and "nothing," indicate the extent to which this mother feels a negation of her own maternal connection. If the semiotic is informed by the earliest infant-mother relationship, which finds its expression in poetic discourse as Kristeva asserts, then this language works to emphasize a simultaneous distance and longing, both on the part of the infant and the mother. While it seems to disrupt the "functions and energy discharges that connect and orient the body to the mother" ("Revolution" 95), while indeed, this mother seems intent on disrupting that orientation by acts of her will, nevertheless, such a layering of negation suggests its opposite: that what she longs for is connection, a return to the semiotic through the body of her baby. The semiotic "fights back, making its presence felt through ruptures in discourse" (Sprengnether 213), in this case, with a discourse of negation. That is, while the language explicitly declares maternal-infant disengagement, it also fights against itself, making evident the presence of a primordial longing for affiliation.

When the baby does reach out, her instinct for proximity is not something the narrator finds trustworthy. It almost seems as though she is trying to persuade herself that when the baby reaches up to hold her finger, it is "an uncontrolled movement, involuntary," that she avoids. Soon the baby will avoid it too. The narrator is quiet; the baby has rarely heard her voice. The hugeness of the baby's eyes, her movement toward physical contact, and the movement of her head from side to side, "denying everything," are images that evoke an anguished sense of the infant's helplessness and isolation and of the narrator's own helplessness and isolation. She has become someone incapable of the slightest gesture toward contact. Her inability to love the baby is an extension of her inability to love herself or to forgive her mother.

The austerity of this relationship reflects and informs the complexity of engagement between mothers and babies. This mother seeks disengagement. She keeps walking away, going to bars. She is surprised by the baby's tenacity, "stunned at her determination to stay alive. It seems impossible that she has willed herself here, right into this world, without any encouragement at all" (129). Such tenacity infuriates the narrator who sometimes "wants to shake her out of her dumb sleep" (129). However, she chooses distance rather than aggression. She asks, "Isn't it better to feel this dark-pitted emptiness than the other, the urge to damage and betray?" (129). She withdraws from the baby in order to avoid hurting it, but her withdrawal is in itself a kind of betrayal, not only to the baby, but also to her own instincts. The narrator's desire for distance is not as straightforward as it seems.

Gasco's narrator is troubled by the fact that her own mother has abandoned her. It is a betrayal so fundamental that she cannot form an attachment to her own baby. Indeed, she feels that "There is nothing but the end of the world and a woman walking away. They stumble after their mothers, their arms stretched forward like sleepwalkers, or tiny monsters" (148). The mothers walk away; the children follow with as much sentience as "sleepwalkers," as much intrinsic charm as "monsters." But in the park where she observes this phenomenon, "the women always turn back, always bend and open their arms, baring their conspicuous chest, their heavy longing" (148). The bare chest speaks to the fact that mothers nurture their children physically and emotionally through the "conspicuous chest," the breasts and the heart. The narrator notices a mutual agency. The children follow their mothers like "sleepwalkers," but their very presence compels the mothers to turn and bend and open; their hearts with "heavy longing" are ultimately exposed. This is what the narrator longs for herself, that her mother would turn and bend. This is what she cannot do for her own baby. Instead she divests herself of her belongings, everything she cannot completely understand, searching "for something essential" (145). She hauls her possessions out to the curb in an impromptu, extended yard sale. When the baby is there also, the narrator is unresponsive to the neighbour's joke about purchasing the child.

The story navigates this tension between loss and longing, both embodied in the figure of the infant. Like the other narratives written by women about babies, this story is also characterized by a double voicing. While the predominant voice of the narrator creates distance between herself and her baby, she nevertheless feels her own yearning for connection. The narrator does wish to mark the baby, to "drag [her] hands and fingers across her small body, trying to leave clues. I touched you here. My nails dug here. Pieces of my skin settled on you like baby powder" (148). She wants to leave a record of ownership, if not a license plate, something tangible so that the baby will know her mother has touched her. As well, when she signs the papers putting the baby up for adoption and relinquishing her parental rights, her hands "surprise [her] by shaking, undulating like great white banners of surrender" (153). In spite of herself she is affected by powerful emotions. Her longing for a sign of ownership is evident. She thinks people should have license plates so that one might track them down. She wants to wait "in the middle of [her] livingroom, lying on the floor with [her] arms and legs spread out into an X, as though [she] were a pale painted blotch on some forest tree, a clue someone left to find their way back, something that marks a familiar spot" (153). She herself has been marked, both by her mother and by her mother's absence. Poignantly, she concludes the story waiting to be found.

There is a sense in these stories of history repeating itself, of women who as babies had been given up for adoption and who then have difficulty bonding with their own babies. This is a mother story as well as a baby story, but it challenges one's expectations about the role of each. The absent mother is a profoundly haunting presence that shapes the narrator's response to her own baby. Gasco's grim honesty inscribes a dichotomous view of infants. Gasco writes about the longing for connection by focusing on its absence. The infant is central to the narrative, to the protagonist's consciousness; even while she is trying to make the baby peripheral, she simply cannot. The writing is forceful because of this, and because of the fact that in spite of distancing herself, in spite of treating the baby as a curiosity, the narrator is still implicated in a relationship that will not, regardless of time and distance, be altered.

What Huston's and Gasco's narratives reveal is a continuing engagement with the baby as a destabilizer of subjectivity. The infants disrupt the protagonists' sense of self; it is a disruption that emerges in the language with which they explore their connection to the babies. According to Kristeva, women have a particular understanding of themselves as split subjects: that this is, indeed, a sense most sharply evoked by the experience of pregnancy and birth—that radical splitting of the subject who is the mother by the infant occupier of "that simultaneously dual and alien space" ("Motherhood According to Bellini" 237). Although it is revealed in the symbolic organization of language, although these writers create women who explore in understandable terms their relationship to babies, the exploration is fractured by a subtext of longing, that distinctive mark of the semiotic. Kristeva writes that the semiotic is revealed in "the rhythm of a drive that remains forever unsatisfied" ("From One Identity to Another" 142). The drive for primordial connection to the maternal is manifested in these explorations of infancy. The narrators remain distant from the infants, a purposeful distance that speaks to an even stronger unspoken, unsatisfied need.

Unlike Huston's and Gasco's, Terry Griggs's narrators are not distant from their babies. Kristeva's notion of the semiotic informs Griggs's writing not through absence but through the overwhelming presence of the infant, indeed, of life of all kinds. Leon Rooke has suggested that writers are driven to excellence and innovation in their craft by "the love of the big surprise" (Hancock 109). It's that love of surprise that seems to inspire the writing of Terry Griggs. She writes her way into babies' silence, imaginatively investing them with consciousness and intention. While she is complicit in Morrison's notion that the "subject of the dream is the dreamer" (17)—Griggs is a participant in making infant representation—it seems clear that such complicity does not tell the whole story. Griggs's writing, while it invests infants with attributes, seems to respond to the notion emerging in social-psychological and cognitive studies that infants act as agents. Current studies on infant cognitive development point toward one verdict: that infants have subjectivity, and that they engage in behaviours designed to draw the attention of caregivers.[5] The silence of babies is restricted only to language. Infants deploy a whole range of expression in order to engage with the people and the world around them.[6]

Griggs is absconding with the world. Snakes, dogs, the Holy Spirit, the weather, birth and death. While the prose slips mercurial across the page, what keeps on emerging is a tantalizing concord that insists on involvement in living and breathing, and that insists on involvement with babies. Griggs does not hesitate to appropriate infant consciousness. She sees value in the baby, endows it with insight and action, and fills up the space of its silence with language, the use of which is often intoxicating in its virtuosity. Griggs is the first writer in my experience to create babies who are important as characters independent of—as much as babies can be independent of—their mothers. The baby is a site of surprising possibility, which is not conveyed in terms of a binary opposition. This is because they are not constructed in terms of their relationship to their mothers. That is, Griggs's babies exist as individuals in their own right. They act, think, and feel as individual characters who are more or less attached to their mothers. They are actors and not objects of other people's agency. They exist without qualification and her engagement with them is resplendent. Griggs is a brazen manipulator of sound and meaning. She explores the power of naming, how words structure reality, how they seduce and animate all the matter of the earth, and how even silence is made of speech. And if silence is made of speech, the baby is a production of that medium that both describes and inhabits it. The results are startling.

In *The Lusty Man*, Griggs shamelessly uses the name "Stink" to describe a family that takes a year or so to get "their cowlicks battened down and the shit scraped off their heels" (9) before they can organize themselves to get Baby Stink christened. The Stinks embody white trash, country music loving, "name-calling and nagging, gouging one another with sharp, hurtful words" (11). The Stinks' use of names as assault weapons, as verbal darts, is manifest. On the other hand, the Stronghill girls "were raised on 'Honey' and 'Sweetie' and 'Darling,' a rich confectionery of names doled out generously"(11-12). Language is an unguent that dispenses healing or is a weapon that hurts. If the baby is unhappy, the Stronghills "would apply a soothing verbal balm, massaging him with soft emollient phrases, a cooing and calming language distilled into a tincture of vowels which they dropped into his ears like a warm healing oil" (16-17). Griggs suggests a visual image of the construction of the self in language. She repeats the "*m*" sound, which, according to John Frederick Nims, is used for "warm appreciation. Probably no other consonant is so expressive by itself.… [it] brings the human child the first pleasure it knows—food and the warm presence of its mother" (188). The baby responds to it, is calmed by it, enters into language as language is "dropped into his ears." In the configuration of language as both a weapon and an unguent, causing and soothing the baby's hurts, Griggs creates a metaphor for metaphor, a layering that is sophisticated and provocative, that resonates with the facility of language to evoke, seduce, suggest, create, and destroy. The baby is prelinguistic, unspeaking, but no less influenced and shaped, soothed and healed by the language in which it is bathed by the Stronghills.

In her short stories, Griggs infuses the babies, whether *in utero* or out, with personality, agency, and sentience. In the story, "Her Toes," the baby, Paris, a barely crawling baby, ponders the riches available to him at floor level. His mother's toes come to him "in tumbling footfalls, in rooting litters, piggies popping out of socks, close and many, something a boy could actually reach out and touch" (58). Paris is too young to speak, but his thoughts are configured in speech and his perceptions are subtle. He knows wealth when he sees it. He appears exquisitely and self-consciously connected to his desire for his mother. His jubilation is evident in his fascination with the "tumbling footfalls" and "piggies popping" (58). Her toes are "bounty" (58), numerous and accessible unlike the "dearth" of ear lobes and the "scarcity of nipples, twin pink stars hung too high, halfway to heaven" (58). Griggs delineates the importance to Paris of this reachable part of his mother's anatomy and the longing he feels for connection with her.

When his mother asks him to please leave her toes alone, he acknowledges that he can't, that "he *adored* them. They were his icons. His objects of worship, and the only way he could pray to them was to cling and nuzzle and suck" (59). Clearly, the author's construction of

Paris's toe-fetish is based on his behaviour. This is what observation grants her. But Griggs goes further, letting the reader "know" that Paris is aggressive in his love for his mother's toes, devoted to them. Griggs transgresses the borders of the real by giving the silent, crawling baby language and volition, a forceful agency that directs him to his mother's feet. Paris notices toes. He reaches to touch them, to "sink his teeth into. If he had any" (58). Paris has preferences. Unlike his fascination with his mother's toes, his father's family's toes disgust him. They are "ballooning appendages stuffed bulging into shoes too tight— toes with cleavage! He was always anxious that their feet were going to explode and gag him with rags of flying flesh" (59). The Lerch women, judging only by their toes, are Paris's enemies.

Griggs represents the baby's ability to act as a subject, to distinguish himself from his mother and to know that she is "like the weather and Paris took what he got. It all came from her, succouring warmth and chilly blasts, she was everything. *Hell, I'm just a stupid baby*, he would think, wondering if he was old enough to have that thought, old enough to hurt himself on words" (58). Paris's consciousness is necessarily constructed in language, but the narrator inscribes doubt about his ability to "hurt himself on words" yet. Of course, Griggs works to comic effect, but fundamental to her representation of infants is her understanding of their complexity, their ability to communicate in one way or another, to make choices, to act. She navigates between what it is possible to think about babies, what has been observed to be true about their behaviours, and she extends that possibility imaginatively. What this does ideologically is construct the baby as a subject and a marvellous one, at that. Baby-like, Paris has impressions, not of intent and not clearly of permanence, but his subjectivity is evident. Griggs animates her babies, gives them the ability to think and act and draw conclusions, but Paris still wears diapers and operates within the physically restricted world of a crawling baby. Thus, while she gives Paris language, she does so within the parameters of what we understand to be babyhood.

Griggs is intrigued by infant consciousness, often imagining infants with "visionary powers" (63). Paris's mother, for example, watches him in the back yard, suddenly "still as a statue, gazing beatifically into space. He's seeing angels, she thought, or ghosts. Babies have those kinds of visionary powers, she believed, and they're smarter than you think" (63). Paris's mother may possibly have been responsible for the death of her abusive husband. The narrator hints at this. Clearly Gord's absence delivers her into a world of smiles, "a carefree unravelling of the scowl, the frown. Her look had been revised to one of collusion, of private fun that made [Paris] pump his arms in wild excitement" (62). Her interaction with the baby, her wonder at his being, grows out of her newly found freedom from fear.

Baby Paris has perception. He knows that the man who kept terrifying him is gone and he knows that his mother is more pleasant because of this. Griggs intimates the abuse meted out by Paris's father who jumped out of closets, "roaring, making those monster faces that terrified [Paris]. That made him cringe and shake. A response that Gord seemed to want. And not want. A response that brought the pain, the punishment. Swift and hard" (66). She does not belabour the point, but suggests, by moving the narrative along, that this punishment is not something Paris lingers on.

While Paris and his mother have great range of expression, Paris's father is, apart from roaring, almost incapable of communication. He waves a toy gun over his new baby's crib when the baby "was all of three days old," pointed at the teddy bear beside the baby's head and said, "See, son, like this...BAM BAM!" (63). This is the most he has to say. Gord's inability to communicate seems to be the source of friction in his marriage and this is something, again, that Paris knows. Paris is aware that his "Momma could really get going sometimes, her feet pacing back and forth, her toes clenching and curling when she stopped to drive a point home. And Gord bouncing up and down, sizzling hot 'cause he couldn't put two words together to save his soul" (65). Though he does not speak, Paris is aware of the importance of language, of the advantage it gives someone in an argument. Gord is aligned with the evil Lerch family and is almost without voice. For Griggs, evil is imbedded in ignorance and lack of perception. The baby has neither. But when he does speak, Paris's first words are "Goo, goo" (66), words he immediately regrets since they provoke a rebuke from his mother who is disappointed by his "cliché" use of language (66). Griggs's concern is to endow Paris with the potential for expressing his own thoughts and intentions, to wander at the limits of the unthinkable ("Place Names" 276), and to bring to the fore an imaginative entry into the dynamic space of infancy.

Griggs invites us into a space where language, which many have argued is really all we've got, is deluxe, radiant, loaded. She extends its power to the world of infants, endowing them with consciousness. In her story, "Momma Had a Baby," she uses a yet-to-be-born baby as the narrator. This baby knows about what is going on in the world outside. The title of the story comes from a rhyme children say as they pop heads off dandelions—"Momma had a baby and her head popped off" (182). Nile, at twelve years old, is the story's "love interest," presumably, the love interest of the baby yet to be born. Here Griggs hints at the folkloric conception that babies are born with knowledge of the future, knowledge that they lose when they are born. The baby narrating this story has mature perceptions. She knows that her mother is at a baby shower, a gathering that she refers to as "estrogen city" (182). She also knows that her mother is "terrified of dying in childbirth, and understood her fear to be a restraining band, wide as a strop, holding her baby back" (183). The mother is so frightened of childbirth that she fears she has "marked the baby, that it would be reticent and fearful all its life, and she prayed it would find a source of courage somewhere deep inside itself" (183). She resolves that, boy or girl, the baby will be called Hero, presumably to inspire such courage.

The story is told from Hero's point of view as she waits to be born. In the context of the woman's world (the baby shower) maternal ambivalence about the baby appears. The baby is two weeks late and her mother's concerns about the birth perversely inspire the other women to tell their "inevitable birthing stories. Ancient Mariners all, women trotted out their individual traumas, sparing Mother nothing in the way of still births, hemorrhages, caesarean sections, and marathon labours. Babies' shrill kitten cries repeatedly stabbed the air, and gallons of lost, fictional, and phantom blood sloshed through the room" (187). Like the women in Clara's hospital ward in Atwood's *The Edible Woman*, these women discuss the manifold difficulties of the pregnant body, describing the horror and blood in the context of a celebration of imminent birth, bringing their stories out in order perhaps to console one another, to remind one another of their toughness, their ability to survive. Griggs enforces the contiguity of birth and death even while she describes the distinct difference between the "relentless motion" of birth and the peacefulness of death. Gramma Young dies quietly during the shower: "the drop was so slight, gentle as ash drifting down, it was as if a quieting finger had been placed lovingly on her heart to untrouble its agitated and relentless motion" (186). Though the "relentless motion" ceases in one body it begins with a vengeance in another.

Hero's mother no sooner realizes that her mother-in-law is dead than she is "thrown suddenly in wracking convulsive labour" (189). She rides in the ambulance with her dead mother-in-law and Horace Perdue who "had swallowed his pencil stub while working on a crossword... his emergency eclipsed by the usual female problems" (189). In the juxtaposition of birth and death, as well as the insinuation early in the story that the baby is a result of a sexual liaison between the mother and another man (not her husband to whom she had been married only a few hours before the affair) (184), Griggs engages with the vital essence of life, as Sarah Murphy calls it, "the next generation and our death. And our continuance if we can let ourselves have it" (10). The confluence of matter that brings the baby into existence includes the death of one woman, the pain of another, and the eclipsed suffering of a man who swallows a pencil stub. For Horace, his is an emergency of the first order, one that "women's problems" as usual "eclipse."

This is how the baby describes her own birth:

> I added my weight to the world. Nine pounds, fifteen ounces of pure solid self. Mere minutes after they wheeled Mother into the delivery room, some intern had me by the heels. Well. My first bat's eye view of the situation was not consoling. The room swung muzzy, as though rubbed in grease. Mother lay bloody and limp, a brutalized body cast aside. Pain seared my backside (never trust a doctor), and I let go a river of sound, my tongue a flailing, undisciplined instrument. But I must have known even then, grabbing at the air (I had Albertha's hands!), that the power would eventually be mine to carve that river into the precise and commanding language I needed. For the present, raw underspeech. (189)

Here Griggs wanders along what Kristeva calls "the limits of the unthinkable" ("Place Names 276). Hero is born in what Kristeva calls the 'semiotic *chora*,' "this 'space' prior to the sign, this archaic disposition of primary narcissism that a poet brings to light in order to challenge the closure of meaning" ("Place Names" 281). Griggs is the poet challenging the closure of meaning as it relates to infancy. A consciousness that Kristeva and others already believe to be present in the infant is inscribed by Griggs who gives it language so that it may be ascertained. While Hero acknowledges that "the river of sound" exploding from her tongue is the result of it being "a flailing, undisciplined instrument," and that all she can offer to the world is "raw underspeech," this will not always be the case. Griggs moves into that rawness and fills it up with words.

Griggs's unfolding of infant consciousness traverses into the realm of magic realism. Some of the elements seem grounded in biological fact. The baby's vision would be impaired from the vernix that covers its body. And if it was slapped on the buttocks, they might likely be stinging. However, the connection to the real evaporates in the baby's command of perception and an interior, if not spoken, language. I find this to be a fascinating depiction of infant consciousness because it transgresses much of what has come before in the way of representations. The baby acts, comes prepared to exert herself on her cousin Nile who is "pelting away like a hunted man" (188). She tells him in "raw underspeech," in that semiotic, presymbolic functioning that resists closure, to get his *balls in order, boy, your Hero's come to town*" (189).

While Griggs's inscription of infancy is a departure from others discussed in this chapter, it is compelling from an ideological perspective because she writes against the tendency to see the baby either as silent or as the object of a dichotomous relationship with its mother. Griggs's babies are subjects in their own right. In the story, "Public Mischief," Griggs represents babies who act. As Miss Ritchie states, "Babies arrive when they want to…usually on trains late at night. They are resourceful creatures and have no trouble getting here" (*Quickening* 94). The walls of the uterus do not limit Griggs. We are told, for example, about Baby Harold, another baby yet to be born, who

> was after Tiger. As usual, there was the problem of Mary Stinchcombe, the thick layer of her that Baby had to sock his fist into to get the cat's attention. Baby, *in utero*, would punch and Tiger would bat at the sudden leaping knot of flesh, like a mouse trying to break through Mary's skin. But Tiger had grown tired of the game and had wandered off to caper on the wedding cake. Baby Harold blamed his mother. He whaled away at her, making the satin stretched tight across her belly pucker and buckle. (102)

The typical movement of the baby within the mother is invested by Griggs with intentionality. "Harold," she writes, "blamed his mother" for getting between him and the cat, for being an obstacle to his action in the world. Griggs builds on that sensation of either watching or seeing the undulations across a woman's stomach when the baby is moving, often with surprising force. This is the peculiar interior/exterior dichotomy that pregnant women experience. Griggs suggests that what is ascertained from the interior sensation and the exterior evidence is that the infant exerts itself, sometimes with apparent will.

In "Bird Story," Griggs extends the fairy story narratives about birth that children might once have been told about babies coming from the cabbage patch or being left on doorsteps by storks. Griggs's stories build magic around familial narratives adopted to explain certain traits or characteristics. She opens the story by quoting Henry's father who used to say, *"You weren't born, you were hatched"* (114).

> Henry's brother Arnie they found behind the couch, a ball of dust and dog hair and thread loosely hanging together the way Arnie does when he shuffles into town on a Saturday night. Muriel came in a basket of apples, a fresh red-cheeked child with a swirl of golden delicious hair. Phyllis scooped her up out of the basket and shouted down to Dayland who was making whirligigs in the basement, *It's a girl!* Arnie, too, had been a surprise. *My goodness,* Phyllis said as she slid the couch aside during spring cleaning and Arnie rolled out, *a big one.* But Henry was another story—a long difficult birth. He sat on the kitchen counter for two years in a homemade eggcup, one of Dayland's old bowling trophies, picking up coffee stains and specks of grease from the fry pan. He annoyed Phyllis. He cluttered up the counter, he got in her way. *He was useless.* (114)

Eventually Henry's shell cracks and he emerges into the world, comforted by "the sound of his mother breaking dishes and smashing pots" (115). This is a story that makes fun out of family narratives, but its configuration of the infant, although playful, invites inquiry. Again, Griggs incorporates magical realism, juxtaposing details of everyday life, such as coffee stains and bowling trophies, with magical elements such as Phyllis's incubation of her son on the kitchen counter. The children's strange origins also draw Phyllis and Dayland closer together, helping Phyllis so that she "lightened up and nibbled with more amusement at her life. She lost weight and dyed her hair.... She bustled blithe and unburdened" (122). As for Dayland, he comes up from the basement, where he spends most of his time, to wander "outside and gaze up at the sky.... He hummed, he whistled" (122). The children's, particularly Henry's, proclivities affect even the cat "who had lately become a vegetarian" (122).

Critical to Griggs's representations is the word "amusement." She blurs the boundaries between the real world and the imaginary world in order to do the primary work of the text. It's not that Griggs tests the limits of reality so much as she ignores them completely. This is not to say that her writing does not acknowledge the difficult role of mothers in raising babies, but along with the difficulties, Griggs insists on joy. As such, she seems engaged in a textual free play that allows the baby to have a voice. Primarily, the text configures babies as amusing and strange, empowered with visionary gifts of perception, as well as agency. This is an ideologically loaded construction because it endows the baby with power, personality, charm, and hilarity. Griggs offers a narrative that writes against the absent baby, that proposes the infant as a forceful presence to which attention must be paid and which, in fact, seems to bless those who do pay attention. Her writing is fortified by optimism; the babies she creates enjoy what Sara Ruddick calls "the world's welcome" (217). Griggs's babies are enjoyable, interesting, and valuable in and of themselves, and not simply because they invest adult lives, male or female, with meaning and value.

This is a position that seems to acknowledge the inherent complexity and significance of human life at whatever age it exists. It is also a position that moves closer to the male writers' valuation of the baby without abnegating the women writers' understanding that having babies is difficult. The knowledge that women have of babies compels a re-evaluation of what has been considered a passive phase of human development. There is evidence that the women are both acting, that is, agents in the baby's life, and quite certainly acted upon in ways that go beyond the merely instinctual. Many Canadian women writers of the 1980s and 1990s have written about the baby in a voice that is doubled, laden with desire for the infant and the joy and love it can bring, and rejection of the constraint, isolation, and pain involved in being a mother. They write about the baby in a way that acknowledges women's heterogeneous experience and that acknowledges the complexity, as Kristeva writes, of women's knowledge of their bodies and their babies. These are significant considerations and ones that Griggs shares. In her writing there emerges the sense that in their connection to babies, the women she writes about "fulfil their own experience to a maximum" ("Women's Time" 198). Griggs's women do share women's history of birthing difficulties. There are suggestions of parental abuse and illegitimacy, but these are peripheral, finally, to the figure of the baby, which claims a place in Griggs's texts, as "the hope of the world" (Arendt 247). This "hope," this sense of value, seems in the last decades of the twentieth century to be something that male writers are only just becoming aware of. Griggs then, proposes a compelling and exuberant marriage of these gendered views of the infant.

CHAPTER 6

The Subject of the Dream
Is the Dreamer

> Outside the viewing window, a black woman in her fifties is waving, and
> with her a white woman in her twenties is jumping up and down. They
> are trying to attract the attention of what looks to be a baked potato, but
> is in fact a baby wrapped in aluminum foil..."to keep the heat in."
> — Annie Dillard, *For the Time Being*

Annie Dillard writes about the nature of perception, how a pre-
mature baby wrapped in foil for warmth resembles nothing so
much as a baked potato. It is small but significant to the people
dancing to get its attention. The image is analogous to infant representation in Canadian fiction. Over the twentieth century it has often
seemed that the baby in literature is of minimal significance, but the
century has seen a transformation in perception where infants are
concerned.

Historically, this is the century when government begins to formulate policy protecting infants, where physicians act in congress to
encourage mothers in pre- and postnatal care, and when experts of all
kinds and degrees write extensively about the best way to encourage
different kinds of "proper" infant development. It is also the century
that sees a tremendous change in the way psychoanalysis views
infancy from being a state of passivity to the more current view that
regards the infant as a subject in the making, both before and after it
enters into language. The ambivalence in perceptions of the infant also
becomes more evident and more polarized as writers inscribe the con-

tradictions inherent in a creature that embodies such paradoxical forces as hope and redemption, as well as constraint and chaos.

If, as Terry Eagleton writes, literary works are "forms of perception, particular ways of seeing the world" ("Marxism and Literary Criticism" 551), then these fictions provide particular insight into the baby. As a figure whose construction is ideologically charged, the infant as it is represented has changed, particularly over the last century; this change describes a movement from the margins into the centre of literary texts. This movement has been shaped not only by social and historical trends but also by the effects of such trends on gendered writing. Canadian men write differently about babies than women writers do and they have taken longer to realize the infant as an object of value. If one examines writing by men up until about 1980, one observes that the infant clearly occupies a peripheral position in stories. Writing by Frederick Philip Grove, Ernest Buckler, Charles Tory Bruce, Juan Butler, George Bowering, and Matt Cohen, among others, clearly situates the infant as an object of minimal importance. An exclusive analysis of these writers would lead to the conclusion that there are barely any babies in Canadian literature. When they occur they do so as imaginary, idealized sounds (Grove's "pitter-patter"), impediments to survival, objects of sexual constraint compelling men into unwanted marriage; babies are distant and disembodied. Concomitantly, women writers engage more frequently with the baby. But their representations are consistently informed by a tension between desire for infants, a desire that idealizes the infant in books by L.M. Montgomery and Gabrielle Roy, and a rejection of them as constraints for women, either because there are too many babies or because they are illegitimate. An ideological shift occurs near mid-century and after World War II when issues of illegitimacy, while still occupying texts about babies, begin to be treated with sympathy.

In the 1960s and '70s writing by Canadian women that engages with babies changes everything. While protagonists in books by men remain detached from the infant, some women are concerned with writing the experience of pregnancy, childbirth, and child rearing. Attached to explorations of the maternal, the infant moves with its mother toward centre stage. The work of Margaret Laurence, Margaret Atwood, Audrey Thomas, and Marion Engel is declarative: *This is our experience*, the work seems to say. *This is what we know.* By giving utterance to the loss of control that pregnancy brings about, the strictures inherent in the medicalization of childbirth, and the socially unrewarding work of caring for babies, these women draw attention to their world and concurrently, to the world of babies. The writing is socially oriented, artistic, political, and vibrant. Women's writing in the 1960s and '70s inaugurates the story of the baby's importance to women's identity and power in the most interesting way. These writers take what has been an oral culture of pregnancy and birth stories shared between women and put it in writing. Furthermore, Canadian women writers who write about women's connection to babies delineate many of the ways that babies infringe on identity and make women feel powerless. Most significantly, the figure of the infant is identified as a force to be reckoned with, a subject requiring attention.

This attention begins to be paid by writers in the last two decades of the twentieth century. There is a distinct intensification of the baby's importance in writing by both men and women. I find the change in men's writing about the baby, a change that demonstrates a sustained engagement with the infant, to be compelling. It is satisfying to consider that the feminist movement has made such a profound difference in the former conventions that insisted on men's distance from infants. However, I wonder about the impact of what some theorists (Sara Ruddick and Adrienne Rich, for example) have referred to as male envy of woman's capacity to give birth. There is no question that Leon Rooke's Raymond Toker will retain custody of the good baby. Rooke has developed this character in order to make such a conclusion inevitable. Thomas King's Will remains warmly involved with South Wing in whatever capacity Louise, her mother, will invite. But in David Arnason's story "My Baby and Me," the question of custody becomes more disturbing. The mother goes back to work, starts drinking, leaves more and more care to the baby's father, and then leaves the marriage. This father's answer to the question of custody is to steal the infant, which seems justified in the text. The mother-infant connection is undermined to a degree in writing by men about babies, superceded in the writing of Leon Rooke and David Arnason by a father figure or father-infant connection. Peter Cumming wonders if "men may be appropriating women's roles as a ploy to expand patriarchy's power base" (96). He agrees that "men's tentative steps towards feminization and 'male motherhood' have prompted understandable skepticism about 'new men' and 'present fathers'" (96), but he concludes in his study of Rooke's A Good Baby that Toker's "simple goodness" and his connection to "a baby who flies" offers "a humane path through the 'stinkpot and garden' of our gendered world" (106). Cumming's hope seems to be that kindness and babies combined will mitigate the animosities inherent in the assigning of "roles" to infant care. His view of "our gendered world" speaks to a larger question of ownership and brings into the feminist debate (that solicits men's involvement with their babies) the question of appropriation, of whether men are appropriating a role traditionally seen as the mother's, and if so, is this threatening to women? Desirable? This is a possible direction for future inquiry. At one level the infant in several literary texts takes up more space, does more, enlists in writing more attention from men, but at another level, the infant remains, and perhaps always will, as valuable, but powerless.

Many women writers in the last two decades of the twentieth century continue to explore the complexities of women's experience of babies. The baby is notable most often for its absence, an absence that haunts the pages of writing by Barbara Gowdy and Nancy Huston. Elyse Gasco's compelling narratives explore some mothers' lack of love toward their babies, yet even that lack is tinged with a sense of longing, a sense that infants mark the female protagonists in ways they will not escape. Terry Griggs is exceptional for her imaginative entry into infant consciousness. Apart, but not independent, from their relationships with their mothers or fathers or aunts, babies act in the world, have thoughts and intentions and fetishes. The babies are ebullient and their value exists because they do. Griggs's babies transcend the duality of longing and rejection. For Griggs, babies *are*.

In much of women's writing about babies throughout the twentieth century, the infant is a site of both desire and rejection. The reasons for this duality are myriad. Women grow babies within their bodies and have for centuries dealt with the strangeness and uniqueness of their biological ability. Canadian fictional representations of the infant manifest women's struggle to be set free from the constraint imposed by their connection to the baby, the difficulties of pregnancy, childbirth, and child rearing. But women have also found that the infant propels them into a relationship of love, the like of which they have never before experienced. Kristeva attempts to navigate this tension in "Stabat Mater," configuring the essay as a visually separate unfolding, part analysis, part inquiry into the unfathomable. She writes about the paradox of motherhood, the "deprivation and benefit of childbirth" (168) that sees the newly born baby as he "wends his way while [she] remain[s] henceforth like a framework.... There is him, however, his own flesh, which was [hers] yesterday" (169). The infant presents her with "nights of wakefulness, scattered sleep, sweetness of the child, warm mercury in [her] arms, cajolery, affection, defenceless body, his or mine, sheltered, protected" (171-72). The intimate connection between mother and baby is evident in Kristeva's writing, as is the pain mothers feel as the "framework" for the infant. This is a relationship that will never be unproblematic, but it can empower women. Feminists have written, demonstrated, and argued against being marginalized or constituted as "the second sex." As Jeffner Allen and Iris Marion Young write in *The Thinking Muse*, women have been engaged in an "encounter with such oppression" (5). Women, they state, have been constituted by men "as the inessential, the other. Much of women's experience can be understood as an encounter with such oppression, whether in resistance to it, in complicity with it, or both" (5). What the infant does for women is enable them to constitute men as "other." It is men who lack the capacity to nurture life inside their bodies. Far from being constituted as "other" by virtue of lacking a penis, women who write about babies find amplitude in the figure of the baby growing inside the uterus. The infant permits a discourse of resistance to women's marginalization. In their capacity to give birth to babies, women situate themselves as subjects in an arena where they are unequalled.

And yet, as Kristeva writes, one cannot use the infant for the "repudiation of the other sex (the masculine)" ("Stabat Mater" 184). She urges rather that the baby "as go-between: 'neither me, nor you, but him, the child, the third person" invites the possibility of "strong *equivalents of power*.... Rather to lead to an acknowledgement of what is irreducible, of the irreconcilable interest of both sexes in asserting their differences, in the quest of each one—and of women, after all—for an appropriate fulfilment" (184). The desire for "an appropriate fulfilment" whatever that is, will most likely never be satisfied, but it is clear that the infant, both for men and for women, becomes significant to some aspects of that fulfillment. This sense of fulfillment is accompanied in writing about the baby by a parallel sense of happiness. What engages me most as a reader, writer, and critic is the manner in which writers invest the infant with joy. Sara Ruddick writes that to "respond to the promise of birth is to respect a birthing woman's hope in her infant and infant's hope in the world" (218). It seems to me that if infants have hope in the world, it is through artistic envisioning that respects such hope. The recent writing by Rooke, Arnason, and Griggs in the late twentieth century shows a movement toward such equivalence of power as male protagonists begin to value the babies in the texts and form strong relationships with them, and as the babies assert themselves as subjects.

This study has been conducted within particular cultural parameters as a starting point for discussion. The next logical step would be to trace representations of infants across cultures, across national literatures, and across genres. In Native writing, for example, by Thomas King, Beatrice Culleton, Joan Crate, and others, the infant is represented in ways that are informed by another culture. What's compelling is that the infant is valuable as a marker of family heritage and cultural survival, but mostly, in the late twentieth century, the infant is valuable as an object of love.

What, then, is there to say about babies? According to Mary O'Brien, "childbirth is hard and often painful labour, a strenuous task peculiarly unsuited to being performed under a halo, but, equally clearly, it is a social and cultural affair" (9). Only in the last thirty years have infants begun to be studied as agents, as individuals with motivations and desires distinct from adult presumptions and perceptions. And even considering the new knowledge available about infant behaviour, the fact remains that not only is childbirth a social and cultural affair, but infants themselves are "social and cultural" in their constitution, neither straightforward nor universal, but rather shaped by adult voices and adult desires. As Catherine Belsey claims, "the object of the critic…is to seek not the unity of the work, but the multiplicity and diversity of its possible meanings, its incompleteness, the omissions which it displays but cannot describe, and above all, its contradictions" (604). Writing about the baby is multiplicitous and diverse, inflected by gender, by history, and always by perception. As Elizabeth Goodenough reminds us, the Latin cognate for "infant" is *infans*, literally "unspeaking." Therefore, "attempts at articulation must be translated by adults into a world of discourse" even though "the experience of being a child may be irrecoverable" (3). The construction of babies in Canadian fiction has been shaped by a contradiction between desire and rejection and by artists' own archaic memories of infancy and the manner in which these find their way into stories. Most surprising is the lack of critical attention paid to the way writers write about babies, considering the number and variety of babies created by Canadian writers.

In *For the Time Being*, Dillard quotes the *Memoirs of a Cape Breton Doctor*, who describes the delivery of a transverse-presenting baby:

"I looked after the baby.... I think I had the most worry because I had to use artifical respiration for a long time. I didn't time how long I was using mouth-to-mouth breathing, but I remember thinking during the last several minutes that it was hopeless. But I persisted, and was finally rewarded when Anna MacRae of Middle River, Victoria County, came to life." She came to life. There was a blue baby-shaped bunch of cells between the two hands of Dr. C. Lamont MacMillan, and then there was a person who had a name and a birthday, like the rest of us. Genetically she bore precisely one of the 8.4 million possible mixes of her mother's and father's genes, like the rest of us. On December 1, 1931, Anna MacRae came to life. How many centuries would you have to live before this, and thousands of incidents like it every day, ceased to astound you? (35-36)

I have not ceased to be astounded. Infant consciousness might be considered to be a sort of last frontier of voice appropriation since babies will likely never argue the point. Perhaps because of this lack of voice, because of their helplessness, their softness, their fragrance, their potential, the impossibility of access to their thoughts, writers keep on writing about them, filling up with words the mystery of that consciousness. Of course, the words reveal more about us than they do about the baby. If "the subject of the dream is the dreamer," then analysis of infant representations seems indispensable for a deeper understanding of how we imagine ourselves.

NOTES

INTRODUCTION

1 Similarly, many studies of British and American origin that purport to be about infants on the contrary employ a generous definition of infancy, extending it up to and including puberty. See Elizabeth Goodenough's *Infant Tongues: The Voice of the Child in Literature*; Adam Potkay's "A Satire on Myself: Wordsworth and the Infant Prodigy"; Robert McLean's "How 'the Infant Phenomenon' Began the World: The Managing of Jean Margaret Davenport (1822-1903)"; and Sharmila Sreekumar's "The Portrait of the Alien/the Other in a Modern American Novel: Toni Morrison's *Tar Baby*," among others.

2 As Lorraine McMullen writes in her introduction to *Re(Dis)covering Our Foremothers*, "Nathaniel Hawthorne was not referring to Canadians when he complained of 'that damnd mob of scribbling women,' but he could have been. There was certainly a mob of women writing in Canada in the nineteenth century, a much larger mob than is generally appreciated" (4). McMullen's "mob" includes writers like Catharine Parr Traill, Susanna Moodie, Anna Jameson, Frances Brooke, Sara Jeannette Duncan, Nellie McClung, and L.M. Montgomery, among others. See Carol Gerson's chapter, "Anthologies and the Canon of Early Canadian Women Writers" in McMullen (71-75), specifically her tables of anthologized women poets, journalists, and fiction writers.

3 The scope of my study requires that limits be set on genre for the present. Prose representations seemed a logical choice because of their wider popular dissemination in comparison with poetry or drama.

4 While this may seem to relate to the perceptions of the mother only, it is nevertheless true that the construction of the mother shapes the con-

struction of the infant. The fact that legitimacy or illegitimacy loses significance has a direct impact on representations of the infant. The
infant itself becomes important, rather than the circumstances of its
conception. As such, the infant becomes much more an agent and less
a marker of propriety. This is evident in both Terry Griggs's short stories and in Elyse Gasco's, for example.

5 Terry Eagleton claims that it is ideology that "persuades men and
women to mistake each other from time to time for gods or vermin"
(*Ideology: An Introduction* xiii). Eagleton further argues that the "most
efficient oppressor is the one who persuades his underlings to love,
desire and identify with his power" (xiii). By this definition the infant
is a kind of "efficient oppressor" since its capacity to create love and to
have its needs met seems to endow it with power in spite of its obvious
weakness. The sense of mystery, awe, and love inspired by the infant
has the potential to attenuate our tendency to demonize or valorize
each other according to gender, race, class, or religion. Having and caring for babies are, apart from medical or ethical considerations, acts
that disregard these discriminations.

6 The revisitation may also be a function of the decline in the birth rate
which, despite the baby boomers' echo, is causing a re-examination of
the treatment of infants in a society that seems to value them exceed-
ingly, if not excessively. Often conceiving infants is such an extremely
high priority for women who are unable to conceive that millions of
dollars are spent in the effort to produce a child through scientific
means, or to adopt one domestically or internationally. Current issues
concerning infertility are more salient, raising questions about the ease
of "getting" children for the 86 percent of women using fertility clinics
who don't succeed in getting pregnant (Chisolm 59).

For example, in a recent issue of *The New Yorker*, Susan Orlean
reports on women who travel to Bhutan, a nation adorned by huge
penis paintings and sculptures that holds annual fertility blessings to
help women get pregnant. Orlean travelled to Bhutan with "a group of
American women who were hoping to get pregnant by being blessed
at Bhutanese fertility ceremonies" (58). If this seems extreme, add to it
the millions of dollars paid by women throughout the world for new
reproductive technologies, and add the desperation, disappointment,
and terrible hope of these women. *Maclean's* magazine reported in 1999
that there were twenty-three fertility clinics operating in Canada with
each cycle of *in vitro* fertilization costing approximately $4,000 (Geddes
23-24). *Time* magazine Canada reported in 2002 that there has been a
"100% rise in past [*sic*] 20 years of childless women ages 40-44"
(Horowitz 42). The article's focus is on the increasing difficulty, in spite
of new reproductive technologies, for women older than thirty-five to
conceive a baby. From the *Saturday Night Live* sketch about the whiners

who gratingly complain, "*We wanna have a ba-by!*" to the more considerable heartache of couples who endure painful fertility procedures or equally painful and risky surrogacy arrangements, it's clear that the tremendous desire to produce a baby has permeated popular culture and compelled women and men to expensive and sometimes dangerous extremes to realize this goal. In the past, infertility was suffered more or less quietly and where possible, adoption filled the void. However, the drive to have a baby for a generation of people used to forging their own relatively opulent destinies has opened the door for science and religion to offer, sometimes with the slimmest chance of success, solutions to infertility.

7   Sheila Watson's *The Double Hook* (1959), written more than ten years later, provides an interesting opposition to other novels' concerns about legitimacy. Watson's novel is a powerful, poetic unfolding of a narrative whose rhythms echo those of a labouring woman, with repetitions of a building tension followed by relaxation which ultimately result in the birth of Lenchen's baby. This birth contradicts the standard unwed-mother narrative since Lenchen is not made to feel ashamed of herself and since the birth of her child follows the cataclysm of Greta's death and indicates a redeemed future of harmony for the inhabitants of the valley.

8   These titles are taken from an extensive sample of novels where babies play a more or less significant role. The task of compiling a comprehensive list of titles was complicated because of the often-marginalized location of the baby. Key-word computer searches were not helpful in directing me to primary sources. I began searching for Canadian books that figured babies to varying degrees, first of all by brainstorming, recording the titles of everything I could think of. I next relied on annotated bibliographies and readers' guides to Canadian literature, among these, Fee and Cawker's bibliography of Canadian literature, and John Moss's and William New's guides to Canadian literature. As one does in taking on a study of this nature, I talked about fictional babies everywhere, at dinner parties, in the classroom, and on planes and I asked people for recommendations. I also searched secondary sources in Canadian literary criticism, sifting through studies, particularly those on the maternal like Di Brandt's *Wild Mother Dancing*. Finally, I went online to the National Library's Canadian literature discussion group and sent a request for help. This group was most helpful in contributing to a comprehensive list of titles where infants are configured. The list in chronological order is appended (see Appendix).

9   Lacan focuses his analytical framework on the creation of subjectivity through language development. He writes that at about "the age of six months" (1) the infant is able to recognize its image in a mirror, even though it is still unable "to walk, or even to stand up" (1). Fascinated by

the infant's gaze into the mirror which occurs even though the infant is "still sunk in his motor incapacity and nursling dependence" (2), Lacan calls this recognition of the infant's self "*an identification*" (2), a primordial recognition of the "*I*...before language restores to it, in the universal, its function as a subject" (2). The crucial moment of the infant's entry into subjectivity is its entry into the "mirror stage," that is, "the formulation of the I as we experience it in psychoanalysis" (1).

10 But the question emerges, at what point is an infant capable of conscious signification? Experts like Israeli neurophysiologist, Dr. Jacob Steiner, are coming to the conclusion that infants only hours old have the capacity to make choices based on cognition (Jackson and Jackson 4). Daniel Stern states that infants who are four days old not only know their own mothers' smell but also prefer it and demonstrate their preference (2).

11 Bell, writing in 1975, asserts the pre-eminence of the mother as the primary caregiver and offers no data on the infant's connection to the father should he be in the position of primary caregiver. Thus, he does not establish that the infant knows its mother or its father from before birth, but rather focuses on post-partum infant behaviour.

12 The infant's capacity to "woo" is something new to researchers, not to mothers who have experienced it first-hand.

13 Also from the 1920s until 1945, East Chester Nova Scotia was home to William and Lila Young, proprietors of the Ideal Maternity Home. The Youngs specialized in maternity services, particularly for unwed mothers. They extracted exorbitant fees, both from the birth mothers and from the adoptive parents, and left many babies to starve to death. These infants became known as "the butterbox babies," so named for the butter boxes from the local grocer in which they were buried. By 1933 Dr. Frank Roy Davis, Minister of Public Health, began investigating the Youngs, but it took twelve years before the home was closed down. See Bette Cahill's "The Butterbox Babies: The Story of the Ideal Maternity Home" (http://www3.ns.sympatico.ca/bhartlen).

14 Katherine Arnup has found that by 1907, "196 of every thousand babies were reported to have died" and that "Montreal claimed the highest infant mortality rate in North America, as one in three babies died before reaching its first birthday" (15).

15 Comacchio cites Department of Health annual reports, the *Report of the Ontario Health Survey Committee*, and medical journals such as *The Canadian Medical Association Journal*, relying extensively on Dr. C.A. Hodgetts's article, "Infant Mortality in Canada" published in 1911 (vol. 1, no. 8). Sutherland cites the *Canadian Therapeutist*, 1 (August 1910) and the Saskatchewan Bureau of Health *Report* (1910), and argues that these publications influenced the public health movement to improve the quality of milk used in "artificial feeding" (59). This had an imme-

diate and widespread effect on infant mortality and was, Sutherland asserts, part of movements that were occurring at about the same time in both Europe and the United States. Zelizer's study focuses on American trends and while she mentions infant mortality, she quotes the popular press (the *New York Times* from November 1, 1908) only in connection to the high incidence of child death from external causes such as carriage or motor car accidents. These accidents were, as Zelizer states, "highly visible," engendering public reaction that was "immediate, indignant, and violent" (36).

16 Katherine Arnup says that the task of documenting "parental concern is a difficult matter, particularly in an era when the vast majority of the population could neither read nor write" (15). She supports Pollock's argument citing autobiographical evidence from the nineteenth century that "clearly indicates both a high rate of infant death and the deep sadness mothers experienced at the loss of their children" (16).

17 These programs included those aimed at encouraging women "not to wean their babies in July, August, or September in order to minimize the infant's contact with impure milk.... They forbad giving any sort of soother to infants" also because of the risk of germ contamination (Sutherland 59). Comacchio tells how, in 1900, the Imperial Order of Daughters of the Empire "established and maintained well-baby clinics" (21). Comacchio also cites the Council on Child Welfare's "immensely popular prenatal and postnatal 'letter series,' which were circulated by direct subscription" with names provided by doctors' patient lists. Furthermore, "Five magazines—*The Canadian Home Journal*, *The Farmer's Advocate*, *Le Droit*, *La Revue Moderne*, and *La Bonne Fermière*—also featured the council's educational services in every issue.... Other mass-circulation magazines, in particular *Chatelaine* and *Maclean's*...ran regular childrearing advice columns that frequently cited the council's literature" (97).

18 According to Sutherland, the public effort to improve the quality of milk given to newborns, among other developments, "aroused a worldwide interest in infant mortality. One consequence was that France called the first Congrès des Gouttes de Lait in Paris in 1905...[which] inspired British campaigners to call their National Conference on Infantile Mortality the following year. A larger Band assembled in Brussels in 1905 for the second Congrès des Gouttes de Lait and in 1911 in Berlin for the third Congress on Infantile Mortality" (59).

19 The Council on Child and Family Welfare's "prenatal informations series" strongly asserted that "our first and most important instruction to you is that you will at once place yourself under the care of your family physician for regular advice and supervision" (Letter no. 2). Furthermore, Dr. Alan Brown insisted in *The Normal Child* that "every

detail of the child's daily life should be under the oversight of the physician, and if he is to do his full duty he must give a certain amount of voluntary unsought advice" (qtd. in Comacchio 112).

20 Comacchio provides several examples of advertisements that incorporated infants in the early part of the century. These include products such as Castoria, an infant laxative, Horlick's Malted Milk (which urges mothers that in order to help "this little fellow" on the "threshold of life...with his battles all before him" to "do as family physicians have done for generations; give him Horlick's"), as well as an advertisement sponsored by the pharmaceutical company, Parke-Davis, "urging parents to keep up medical supervision for their children" (186-90). All four advertisements appear in *Maclean's* between 1928 and 1937.

21 The government's Dominion Council of Health requested that publication be made available "on maternal and child welfare." Furthermore, the "Canadian Government Films News Service in advertisements included in the newsreels that typically preceded feature films at theatres throughout the country" promoted the reading of these publications to its audiences (Comacchio 96). There can be no doubt that the government took action and made policy toward caring for pregnant women and babies.

22 Hardyment focuses here on the arbitrary "milestones" established by Mabel Liddiard, author of the *Mothercraft Manual* (1948). These milestones "mapped the *correct* points at which the baby smiled, kicked, sat and walked." The milestone chart "included little clocks indicating shifting sleeping patterns, weight increases, and when nappies could be dispensed with" (qtd. in Hardyment 161). For example, Liddiard asserts that at age four months, the normal baby will weigh thirteen and a half pounds, will sleep twenty-one hours, will experience the "dawn of will power" and will "know friends from strangers" (qtd. in Hardyment 162). Anyone with personal experience with babies knows first-hand the absurdity of such intransigent assertions. It is to such standards of normalcy that Hardyment directs her criticism and not to prudent and necessary medical care of infants and mothers.

CHAPTER ONE

1 In pioneer narratives, the dream of owning land, getting married, and having children is articulate. In light of infant mortality rates and in order to ensure family survival to the next generation on the land, women bore several babies. So survival becomes a two-edged sword. Too many babies sap a woman's energy and destroy her life. The children, then, who are a means of survival are also a threat to the women who bear them.

2 Robert Lecker writes in 1995 that of the sixty-five anthologies of Cana-

dian literature published between 1922 and 1992, Grove's work appears in 41 percent and Montgomery's in 11 percent. Lecker also attributes Montgomery with opening up the Canadian canon for women writers in much the same way that Catharine Parr Traill had done. See *Making It Real: The Canonization of English-Canadian Literature*, 136, 143.

3   Genevieve Wiggins says that by "1942 there had been 69 printings." The royalties indicate "the early sale of almost 2,000 copies" (36). Further, by 1912, *Anne of Green Gables* "had been translated into Swedish, Dutch, and Polish" (37).

4   Rubio's text does not give a date for Montgomery's induction into the Royal Society and indeed cites only Montgomery's own clipping book as a reference.

5   See Desmond Pacey's chapter, "Fiction: 1920-40" in *The Literary History of Canada*, Carl F. Klinck (Toronto: University of Toronto Press, 1965) and John Moss's *A Reader's Guide to the Canadian Novel* (Toronto: McClelland and Stewart, 1981).

6   Rubio's intent in *Harvesting Thistles* is to foreground current readings of Montgomery's writing, to "present new interpretations by critics who have had the advantage of reading Montgomery's journals and thus deepen[ed] their reading of her novels" (7). Some of these critics include Gabriella Åhmansson, Catherine Ross, Clara Thomas, and Elizabeth Waterston. Indeed, Åhmansson asserts that "the first serious critical evaluation of *Anne of Green Gables* was made by Elizabeth Waterston" (65) whose 1966 assessment "constitutes a major break from the critical attitudes displayed by Desmond Pacey, E.K. Brown, Arthur Phelps, et al. and is the first serious critical article which treats Montgomery with respect" (20).

7   Although Montgomery shows a trend toward sympathy in her portrayal of the upright Mrs. Lynde, it occurs only after her children are grown and gone, leaving her essentially free of them.

8   Much of the criticism of the later sequels to *Anne of Green Gables* discusses Anne's subscription to the dominant social order. For example, Gillian Thomas writes, "If the Anne of the first book is often considered a spirited individualist, then the Anne of the final book seems a rather dreary conformist" (37). The discrepancy in Anne's character has to do with her shift from transgressor of social norms to subscriber, and, finally, inscriber. While this is attributable to Anne's physical and emotional maturity, the central catalyst is the loss of her baby (Åhmansson 157). In the beginning, Anne challenges social restrictions, speaks her mind, has tantrums, wreaks hyperbolic apologies for them, and cuts a wide swath in the world of Avonlea. This, in large part, explains her persistent appeal to people who are, for whatever reason, disenfranchised. In her article, "Readers Reading L.M. Mont-

gomery," Catherine Sheldrick Ross states that in her interviews of readers "there is a common theme of shared experience," that they place Anne of Green Gables in a "category of books [where] a hostile, imprisoning world is transformed into a safe place" (29). More evocative for the purposes of this study is the change Anne undergoes. As the sequels unfold, Anne begins to conform to a socially accepted standard of behaviour. She reigns in her explosive tendencies to the point where, in *Anne of Ingleside*, she enforces a separation between her daughter, Di, and Di's new best friend, Jenny Penny, and endures in silence the relentless badgering of Gilbert's Aunt Mary Maria. This is self-restraint that she could not exercise when attacked by Rachel Lynde in the opening scenes of the first novel and it is discretion she learns when her baby dies.

9   Prentice and colleagues write that at the turn of the century, "childbirth still remained the single greatest cause of death among women of childbearing age, and puerperal infection continued to be common, despite the medical knowledge that it was preventable with the use of antiseptic techniques. In 1921 the Canadian maternal mortality rate was 4.7 per 1,000 live births, a rate higher than that experienced in most other western countries" (166).

10 While Grove's novel was written before a husband could legally be charged with raping his wife, the text is explicit about Mrs. Amundsen's pleas and the struggle, feeble as it is, that ensues: "Once she said, still defending herself, You know, John, it means a child again. You know how often I have been a murderess already. John, Please! Please!... And the struggle began again, to end with the defeat of the woman" (112). The implication of sexual assault could not, in 1925, be clearer.

CHAPTER TWO

1   Martha Ostenso's *Wild Geese*, first published in 1925, provides an exception. A brutal husband, Caleb Gare, whom John Moss calls "a fascinating misanthrope," dominates the mother in Ostenso's text (*Reader's Guide* 225). Gare repeatedly threatens to expose the fact that his wife gave birth more than twenty years previous to an illegitimate baby. The wife is liberated by her own daughter's illegitimate pregnancy. As Moss writes, "Jude's pregnancy is triumph. Through her, the whole family is set free" (*Reader's Guide* 225).

2   Among whom would be Mabel Liddiard, Dr. Benjamin Spock, and the Canadian Council on Child and Family Welfare.

3   See Kroetsch's "The Fear of Women in Prairie Fiction: An Erotics of Space" and Moss's "As for Me and My House" in *Patterns of Isolation in English-Canadian Fiction*.

4 I refer to Ross's homoerotic subtext as an "illegitimacy" only in the sense in which it would have been perceived in 1941 at the novel's publication. Furthermore, Ross himself took decades before he would acknowledge it and even then, was less than straightforward about the influence of his sexuality on the writing.

5 Most recently, Timothy R. Cramer has written that new information about Ross's own sexuality has influenced the way critics have perceived *House*. Cramer argues that the Bentley story is characterized by Mrs. Bentley's "desperate series of *if I justs*: *if I just* give Philip plenty of private time he will notice me; *if I just* get Philip another pipe he will apppreciate me; *if I just* give Philip a son of his own he will value me" (52). Cramer posits that Philip is perhaps unable to desire Mrs. Bentley "because he has other desires" (52).

6 Fraser had some doubts about whether Ross himself was aware of the homosexual references in the text. Ross vacillates on the point and, when he finally admits they exist, he maintains they are "unintentional" (Fraser 41). Yet on another occasion, Ross refers to Philip's hands on Steve's shoulders as a "very homosexual gesture. (I knew it was when I wrote it)." Ross also alludes to Philip's persistent staring at Steve, "his patent jealousy over Steve, his desire to shut his wife out and have the boy to himself" (59-60). Fraser believes that Ross here contradicts "a later claim" (59), specifically, that the references were unintentional.

7 The Bentleys both refuse to complete their thoughts in a sentence on several occasions. According to Mrs. Bentley's diary entry, Philip breaks off in mid-sentence about Judith's mistake since she is "the kind like that, who slip just once—" (193). Mrs. Bentley's use of that suggestive dash might suggest that Philip stopped himself because of the sudden realization that he ought to have no idea whether Judith "slipped" once or ten times. Also, when Mrs. Findley tries to talk her out of adopting Steve in favour of their "own kind—clean, decent people—" (81), Mrs. Bentley replies that they are meant to help "the sick…not the whole—" (81), suggesting that Steve, because of his Eastern European background, is among the "sick" and that adopting him is an act of Christian charity. Mrs. Findley does not complete her thought perhaps because she prefers suggestion rather than blunt declaration. Mrs. Bentley leaves the sentence dangling because she knows that using Christianity against Mrs. Findley is "the devil quoting scripture" (81). She also leaves her sentence incomplete when she insists to Philip that they must "make the break and get away from Horizon—" (204). This usage occurs directly after Philip dodges the issue of telling Judith immediately that they will adopt her baby so as not to affect her "mental condition" since, he says, "it's to be our child—" (204). The Bentleys' inability to communicate fully to one another is manifest at the level of punctuation.

8 In Ernest Buckler's *The Mountain and the Valley*, Effie dies after having
   a sexual relationship with David. Also, in David's view, his brother,
   Chris, is trapped, not by his own sexual misconduct, but by Charlotte's willingness to transgress. Ironically, after they have been married briefly, Charlotte miscarries. Chris is indeed trapped with a wife
   who has lost the "richness" and "ripeness" of her youth, who has
   suddenly, in the bliss of marriage, become the sort of person whose
   "small black hairs at the corners of her lips" (191) have become more
   evident. Although she does not die, because of her sexual transgression Charlotte is forced to sacrifice both her freedom and her appearance. In Bruce's *The Channel Shore*, Hazel, though she marries after
   she is pregnant, also dies shortly after her illegitimately conceived
   child is born. It's interesting that in these three novels—Ross's, Buckler's, and Bruce's—the women die, but in Gabrielle Roy's *The Tin
   Flute*, Florentine gets married and presumably lives after the baby's
   birth and in Sheila Watson's *The Double Hook*, the illegitimacy of
   Lenchen's baby is not at issue. Indeed, that baby brings the community together. This speaks to the difference in perception between
   men and women regarding the significance of a baby's (il)legitimacy,
   particularly since legitimacy is a paternity, not a maternity issue. As
   O'Brien claims, women do not experience the anxiety of origin
   regarding the infant (30).

9 While critics such as David Williams, E.J. Hinz, and J.J. Teunissen have
   argued about whether Philip is indeed the father of Judith's baby, the
   point is moot as far Mrs. Bentley is concerned. She wants the baby and
   the connection to Philip that it will help her forge, regardless of questions of de facto paternity. See Stouck's *Sinclair Ross's As for Me and My
   House: Five Decades of Criticism*.

10 Judith endures the pregnancy, the shame and difficulty of it, and stays
   sane. But when Philip tells her that he will take her baby away, the
   news wrecks her hold on sanity and on life itself. She gives up the baby,
   delivering it from her body a month early, and then she gives up her
   life. His revised vision of the ending (where Judith keeps the baby and
   lives) compelled Ross to conceive a different title for the book: *If Judith
   Were Different* (*As for Me and My Body* 53).

11 Prentice and colleagues say that "the infant death rate almost halved
   between 1946 and 1960.... Furthermore, fewer adult women died in
   childbirth as maternal mortality rates fell dramatically after 1940. The
   likelihood of a Canadian woman dying because of pregnancy fell from
   one in 150 in the 1930s to one in 3,000 by the 1960s" (323). Although
   sharply decreased, maternal mortality was still a factor in Canada in 1954
   when this book was written. Hazel suffered during her pregnancy from
   poverty, anxiety, and illness. It is not surprising that she barely survives
   the birth of her baby. Since all of these factors are engendered by the

shame of her situation, her death functions in the text both at the level of historical verisimilitude and also as a moral lesson. Kulyk Keefer believes that Hazel "is dying of tuberculosis in Toronto" (57); however, I can find no direct references to the disease in Bruce's text.

12 Rose-Anna's eldest son is already out of the house and not counted among the ten who live there.

13 Whitfield cites André Brochu's "Thèmes et structures de *Bonheur d'occasion*" in *Ecrits du Canada Francais* 20 (1966).

CHAPTER THREE

1 There are fine distinctions here, semantic hazards to be aware of when one refers to a fetus as an infant. My choice of such discourse reflects in all instances the discourse of the writers. Where the writers refer to the pregnant body as carrying a fetus, I do too. Where they refer to a baby growing inside, I echo such phrasing.

2 These novels are particularly suitable for study because they are emblematic of the gender difference in fictional approaches to the infant during this time. The titles emerge from a range of novels published in the 1960s and '70s that demonstrate the disparity between writing by men and women. Among such are H.G. Green's *A Time to Pass Over* (1962), Ernest Buckler's *The Cruelest Month* (1964), George Bowering's *The Mirror on the Floor* (1967), and David Adams Richards's *Blood Ties* (1976). Compared to Audrey Thomas's *Blown Figures* (1974), Marian Engel's *No Clouds of Glory* (1968), Adele Wiseman's *Crackpot* (1974), among others, the obvious differences in writing by men and women are apparent (see Appendix).

3 After the national centennial, a sense of cultural nationalism provoked "Canadians' desire…to regain control of the publication and book distribution industries from American companies" (New 221). Technology made publication easier and more economical; as well, "government arts support further encouraged developments in publication" (New 226).

4 Margaret Atwood also recognizes the situation. In her introduction to the 1986 edition of *Roughing It in the Bush*, Atwood insists that, in studying Canada's literary heritage it would be impossible to "ignore the women.… The percentage of prominent and admittedly accomplished women writers, in both prose and poetry, is higher in Canada than it is in any of the other English-speaking countries" (xiv).

5 This sociological evolution is reflected in the increase in apartment construction, "particularly rapid between 1961 and 1970," that contributed to the "92% percent increase in households with single, never-married heads" (Prentice and colleagues 319). The increase in women in the work force and the number of women leaving the parental home to live on their own also fostered "the unprecedented freedom—economic, social,

sexual—enjoyed by the generation of Canadians coming of age in the 1960s" (Prentice et al. 320), otherwise known as the sexual revolution.

6 This movement also had the result of privileging so-called natural childbirth over presumably "unnatural" birth, which included to varying degrees, medical intervention. See John Stackhouse's article in *Homemaker's Magazine*, June 2000. Stackhouse writes of the Caesarean birth of his daughter in "the comfort of Toronto's North York General Hospital" (45), comparing Canadian care for women during pregnancy and childbirth to that available to women in the developing world: "At the start of the twenty-first century, no measure of human progress divides the world more than the chances of a woman's survival during pregnancy and childbirth" (45). Stackhouse offers an important view of the medicalization of pregnancy—that medical aid profoundly benefits mothers and babies and ought not to be opposed. What's significant in the debate over intervention is the availability of choice for women, a choice based on need and desire. This choice in the 1940s and '50s was denied women who were routinely anaesthetized and whose babies were sometimes damaged by forceps delivery that was not always necessary. Now women have birthing options to the extent that most contemporary pregnancy and baby books include a section on formulating a "birth plan" (see *The Canadian Medical Association Complete Book of Mother and Baby Care* by E. Fenwick or Penelope Leach's *Your Baby and Child*, among many others).

7 In writing by men in the 1960s and '70s, there is a fundamental lack of connection to the infant as a figure of meaning, except in the most conventional way. Erik is able to perceive the importance of the infant in only the most minimal fashion. Brian wants a baby to "colonize" the farm. In H. Gordon Green's, *A Time to Pass Over*, subtitled "the candid, courageous (and uncensored) reminiscences of a pioneer grandmother," Mary Ann pursues and marries Bill Green and promptly becomes pregnant with the first of many babies. When Bill is in the kitchen with friends who have come to toast his good fortune and to tease him about the baby's paternity, he insists that the child is his son if only by virtue of the fact that he was "caught in my trap" (61). This is the extent of Bill's involvement with the babies, apart from working to provide their needs. Juan Butler's Michael loathes babies for the noise and mess and responsibility they might impose on his life. Each of these characters enforces a perception of masculinity that is removed from imminent engagement with babies and is focused on achieving some measure of success in terms of a personal gratification that excludes the infant as a figure of importance. This is characteristic of texts like George Bowering's *The Mirror on the Floor*, which explores the relationship between a young male student and a girl who has had an abortion. The baby in Ernest Buckler's *The Cruelest Month* is yet to be

born and upon it are placed the hopes of marriage reconciliation and all future happiness. The baby appears at the end of the text, in the form of what Margaret Atwood calls a "Baby ex Machina, since it is lowered at the end of the book to solve problems for the characters which they obviously can't solve for themselves" (*Survival* 207).

8 For example, John Skandl builds "a golden column of ice" (47) to woo Tiddy. Ebbe Else charges a bull (169). The men of Big Indian wage a war against the sky (151).

9 Furthermore, the men die strange deaths. Martin Lang freezes to death, John Skandl's plane crashes, Tiddy's baby, JG, who can walk only in figure eights, escapes from the house and having never seen a tree before, climbs it and tries to step into the sky. Anna Marie's husband, Nick Droniuk, falls into a threshing machine "while raging at the sky" (140); Mick O'Holleran drowns in ash; Joe Lightning falls from an eagle's talons to the earth; Jerry Lapanne, a prisoner to whom Rita had been writing, invents a flying machine without including landing gear and "was found hanged in the telephone wires that were strung along the side of the old CN bridge" (206); and Vera's boy drowns.

10 Feminist critics have not failed to note that, despite having gained so much ground in terms of women's control of their birth experience, if women are having difficulty getting pregnant, "solutions to infertility" will mean an "increase in medical control of women's bodies as researchers learn how to flush out human eggs, fertilize them outside the body…and implant them, sometimes in a different woman's womb" (Prentice and colleagues 394). The implications of such technology are grounded in the vigorously renewed treatment of women's bodies as baby-making machines, something feminists of the 1960s and '70s fought so hard against. Our distaste for reproduction or our inability to reproduce, and our consequent reliance on cybernetically produced infants, has already begun to constitute babies as, in fact, products or commodities to be sought after or terminated according to preference. All these elements come into play in women's writing about babies during the late 1960s, early '70s, and beyond.

11 While Laurence's Rachel Cameron is not married and therefore not necessarily past courtship, she is nevertheless constructed as someone whose options have narrowed, an older woman, though clearly not beyond the possibility of romantic dreams.

12 Although these works are all classified under the broad heading of novel, they are also differentiated within that genre. *Mrs. Blood* reads like an extended prose poem with imagery and symbolism that are dense and abstruse. *The Edible Woman* uses comedy as its primary vehicle for meaning. *A Jest of God* is a more realistic depiction of life and events, as is *The Honeyman Festival*.

13 Like Gabrielle Roy, Laurence also indicts male irresponsibility through
    the character of Nick who tells Rachel, after their first sexual encounter,
    to "fix herself" for the next time because "it's better that way" (99). Like
    Richard in *The Disinherited*, Nick does not take responsibility for using
    contraception and Rachel cannot physically force herself to go into the
    local pharmacy or visit her family doctor to get "fixed." In fact, apart
    from these vague instructions, he gives no thought to the possible out-
    come of his actions.

14 See Jonathan Kertzer's essay on Margaret Laurence in *Canadian Writers
    and Their Works*, 253-312; Nora Stovel's, *Rachel's Children: Margaret Lau-
    rence's* A Jest of God; and Helen Buss's *Mother and Daughter Relation-
    ships in the Manawaka Works of Margaret Laurence*, among others.

15 See George Woodcock's *Introduction to Canadian Fiction*; Anne Archer's
    "Real Mummies"; Barbara Godard's chapter, "Audrey Thomas" *Cana-
    dian Writers and Their Works*; George Bowering's "The Site of Blood."

16 Dorothy Warburton, Julianne Byrne, Nina Canki, *Chromosome Anom-
    alies and Prenatal Development: An Atlas*; Thomas Moe, *Pastoral Care in
    Pregnancy Loss: A Ministry Long Needed*. For a moving exploration of the
    loss of a pre-birth baby, see Beth Powning's, *Shadow Child*.

17 Both are expatriate doctors from India who work in Africa where
    Mrs. Blood's family has moved.

18 In spite of Clara's chaotic life and barnaclesque children, it is, strangely,
    her visit to Clara's house that makes Ainsley decide to have a baby. She
    believes that Joe's appropriation of the traditional female role (cooking,
    bottle-feeding the baby, doing the laundry) is what has undermined
    order in Clara's family. She intends to have a baby and exclude "the
    thing that ruins families these days," the husband (34). Ainsley believes
    that "every woman should have at least one baby" in order to fulfil her
    "deepest femininity" (35). Ainsley's aim is "wholeness" which for her
    means single motherhood. To Marian's protest that she will be bringing
    "an illegitimate child" into the world "in cold blood," Ainsley replies,
    "Birth is legitimate, isn't it?" (36). Here Atwood negates, though satiri-
    cally, centuries of emphasis on propriety and legitimacy, declaring
    through Ainsley the intrinsic legitimacy of the infant itself, regardless
    of the circumstances of its conception. Ainsley accuses Marian and soci-
    ety of prudishness and establishes herself as the voice and womb of
    protest against bourgeois morality. When Ainsley marks time on the
    calendar, calculating the most opportune days for impregnation, Mar-
    ian compares her to "a general plotting a major campaign" (81). Her
    calculated fertility is as heavily satirized as Clara's helpless fertility.
    Once she has succeeded in becoming pregnant, she starts assessing
    whether she is having cravings; she examines the "profile of her belly"
    in a mirror; and, finally, she retches "into the kitchen sink, to her
    immense satisfaction" (157). However, even though Ainsley breaks

with the traditional requirement of motherhood—marriage to the father—by the novel's end, Marian states that Ainsley has become as "morally earnest as the lady down below" (286). Interestingly, until Ainsley begins to plan to have a baby, she has led a relatively irresponsible existence, arriving late for work and insulting the landlady and Marian's friends. She is never so calculating as when she organizes her strategy for seducing Leonard Slank to get a baby. This is an exertion of control that Marian might admire. However, Ainsley's life choices place her firmly in the realm of a different sort of womanhood than Clara's, but it is a construction of the female that is equally rejected by Marian.

19 In order to understand clearly what Kristeva means by the "apparatus" that women might "call into question," Kristeva's full paragraph follows: "The analytic situation indeed shows that it is the penis which, becoming the major referent in this operation of separation ["*separation from a presumed state of nature, of pleasure fused with nature*"], gives full meaning to the *lack* or to the *desire* which constitutes the subject during his or her insertion into the order of language. I should only like to indicate here that, in order for this operation constitutive of the symbolic and social to appear in its full truth and for it to be understood by both sexes, it would be just to emphasize its extension to all that is privation of fulfilment and of totality; exclusion of a pleasing, natural and sound state: in short, the break indispensable to the advent of the symbolic" ("Women's Time" 198).

20 Julia Kristeva believes that Hannah Arendt "calls attention to the miracle of birth and life, to that human specificity that makes each life a tale of individually experienced events" (qtd. in Kuprel 26). Arendt claims that the "most general condition of human existence" is the fact of "birth and death, natality and mortality" (8). Arendt's book, *The Human Condition*, explores "the human condition of natality; the new beginning inherent in birth" that "can make itself felt in the world only because the newcomer possesses the capacity of beginning something anew" (9). The "newcomer" possessed of the capacity to begin something new is precisely the baby's function at the end of *Surfacing*.

21 The concept of staying home to raise children rather than participating in the work force was becoming in the 1970s a choice that "diminishes women's future economic and social options" (McDaniel 108). By 1971, 37 percent of married women worked outside the home, a 26 percent increase over 1951 rates (McDaniel 109).

22 This term is not meant to be totalizing or reductive of the birthing experience of other cultures and it is used within the parameters of the study to relate to protagonists configured by this specific group of white women writers.

Chapter Four

1   Other novels by men where babies play more or less significant roles include Timothy Findley's *Not Wanted on the Voyage*, David Adams Richards's *Nights below Station Street*, Douglas Coupland's *Life after God*, and Keath Fraser's *Popular Anatomy*, among others.

2   In his book, *The Role of the Father in Child Development*, Dr. Michael Lamb writes that in 1953 he "was present at the birth of [his] firstborn," that, as far as he knew, this was "the first known instance of the father's being present at a birth in the modern history of [New York] city" (70). Lamb states further that as late as 1975, studies were beginning to assert that "presence at the delivery is likely to increase fathers' involvement with the infant" (80). Lamb's book, published in 1976, adopts the view that fathers should be permitted in the delivery room. By 1984, Alan Fogel documents a similar shift in attitude in his book, *Infancy*. He says that, "during the last ten or fifteen years, a number of centers have been developed to offer women an alternative to the usual hospital procedures. Birthing rooms; the presence of the husband; and rooming-in" (75).

3   See Chodorow on "cathexis" as "love" (115).

4   If there is equivocation at all, it is only at the level of "individual's constant oscillation between separation from and reconciliation with the world" (Gorjup 272).

5   By "traditional maternal narrative," I mean one that probes the intricacies and contradictions of the relationship between mother and fetus and mother and baby. The term is not intended to essentialize the multiplicitous representations of these relationships in writing by women, but rather is intended to establish the startling nature of the paternal narrative itself as a development of the '80s and '90s. A maternal narrative that depicts the caregiver's sustained engagement with the baby is found in Engel's *The Honeyman Festival* or more recently in Miriam Toews's *The Summer of My Amazing Luck*, among others.

6   Herb Wyile says that as "a non-Native and non-expert writing on the work of (Native) writer Thomas King" he aims for "a critical practice grounded in a historicized, pluralistic and nuanced cultural literacy" (106). As a non-Native writing about this book, I want to avoid using the image of a totalized "Native" baby to suit my own purposes without considering that "nuanced cultural literacy."

7   See Kimberley Blaeser's "Native Literature: Seeking a Critical Center," in *Looking at the Words of Our People*, ed. Jeanette Armstrong (Penticton: Theytus, 1995), 51-62; and Percy Walton's "'Tell Our Own Stories': Politics and the Fiction of Thomas King," in *World Fictions of the Canadian West* (Durham: Duke UP, 1994), among others.

8   King offers the term "associational" to describe Native writing. As well

as "associational" literature, King also suggests using the terms tribal, interfusional, and polemical, ("Godzilla" 13) as critical tools for discussing Native writing. He explains how "associational literature leans toward the group rather than the single, isolated character, creating a fiction that de-values heroes and villains in favour of the members of a community, a fiction which eschews judgements and conclusions" ("Godzilla versus the Postcolonial" 14). Clearly, *Medicine River* is written in conformity with this vision since King privileges the familial/community connection and the role of baby South Wing in accomplishing this connection in Will's life.

9 Fogel says that "infants [are] innately attuned to social signals from the environment and that infants [are] born with a ready-made set of expressions that served to attract adults to them" (27).

CHAPTER FIVE

1 There are at least twenty-five fictional texts about babies written by women between 1980 and 1999. Please see Appendix for a more complete list.

2 As Simone Weil claims, "at the bottom of the heart of every human being, from earliest infancy until the tomb, there is something that goes on indomitably expecting, in the teeth of all experience of crimes committed, suffered, and witnessed, that good and not evil will be done to him. It is this above all that is sacred in every human being" (315).

3 Kristeva argues that biological strangeness involves an awareness of the ramifications of one's own birth as well as the babies to come. Diana Kuprel's question to Kristeva is itself framed in a way that indicates the inherent contradiction at the heart of infant representation. She states that "through birth the world is constantly being invaded by foreigners and newcomers" (23). The usage of "foreigners" is compelling alongside the term "newcomers." One term seems more alienating than the other.

4 For a similarly violent and macabre birth scene, see Ann-Marie MacDonald's *Fall on Your Knees*.

5 See Alan Fogel, *Infancy: Infant, Family, and Society*; Michael Lewis and Leonard Rosenblum, eds., *The Effect of the Infant on Its Caregiver*; Jackson and Jackson, *Infant Culture*; and Michael Lamb, "The Changing Roles of Fathers" in *Becoming a Father*, among many others.

6 This is to some degree an instinctual response to stimuli, but current studies on bi-directionality and on the mother-child dyad are unambiguous in the conclusion that infants act in their own behalf.

APPENDIX

Twentieth-Century Canadian
Fiction Featuring Babies

1900-39

Montgomery, L.M. *Anne of Green Gables*. 1908. New York: Scholastic, 1989.
———. *Anne's House of Dreams*. 1922. Toronto: McClelland and Stewart, 1972.
———. *Anne of Ingleside*. 1939. Toronto: McClelland and Stewart, 1972.
Grove, Frederick Philip. *Settlers of the Marsh*. 1925. Toronto: McClelland and
    Stewart, 1965.
McClung, Nellie. *All We Like Sheep*. Toronto: Thomas Allen, 1926.
———. *Painted Fires*. Toronto: Ryerson, 1925.
Ostenso, Martha. *Wild Geese*. 1925. Toronto: McClelland and Stewart, 1971.

1940-59

Bruce, Charles Tory. *The Channel Shore*. Toronto: McClelland and Stewart,
    1954.
Buckler, Ernest. *The Mountain and the Valley*. 1952. Toronto: McClelland and
    Stewart, 1970.
Coburn, Kathleen. *The Grandmothers*. Toronto: U of Toronto P, 1949.
Mitchell, W.O. *Who Has Seen the Wind*. 1947. Toronto: Macmillan, 1976.
Ross, Sinclair. *As for Me and My House*. 1941. Toronto: McClelland and Stew-
    art, 1991.
Roy, Gabrielle. *The Tin Flute*. 1947. Trans. Hannah Josephson. Toronto:
    McClelland and Stewart, 1969.
———. *Where Nests the Water Hen*. 1951. Trans. Harry L. Binesse. Toronto:
    McClelland and Stewart, 1970.
Watson, Sheila. *The Double Hook*. 1959. Toronto: McClelland and Stewart, 1991.
Wilson, Ethel. *Swamp Angel*. 1954. Toronto: McClelland and Stewart, 1990.

1960-79

Atwood, Margaret. *The Edible Woman*. 1969. Toronto: McClelland and Stewart, 1989.

————. *Surfacing*. Toronto: McClelland and Stewart, 1972.

Bessette, Gerard. *Incubation*. Trans. Glen Shortliffe. Toronto: Macmillan, 1967.

Blais, Marie-Claire. *A Season in the Life of Emmanuel*. 1965. Trans. Derek Coltman. New York: Grosset and Dunlap, 1966.

Bowering, George. *The Mirror on the Floor*. Toronto: McClelland and Stewart, 1967.

Buckler, Ernest. *The Cruelest Month*. 1963. Toronto: McClelland and Stewart, 1977.

Butler, Juan. *Cabbagetown Diary: A Documentary*. 1970. Toronto: Peter Martin, 1971.

Cohen, Matt. *The Disinherited*. Toronto: McClelland and Stewart, 1974.

Davies, Robertson. *Fifth Business*. 1970. Markham: Penguin, 1984.

Engel, Marian. *No Clouds of Glory*. Toronto: Longman, 1968.

————. *The Glassy Sea*. 1978. Toronto: Seal Books, 1979.

————. *The Honeyman Festival*. Toronto: Anansi, 1970.

Gibson, Margaret. "Considering Her Condition." *The Butterfly Ward*. 1976. Toronto: HarperCollins, 1994. 61-96.

Green, Henry Gordon. *A Time to Pass Over: Life with a Pioneer Grandmother*. Toronto:

McClelland and Stewart, 1962.

Harvor, Beth. *Women and Children*. Ottawa: Oberon, 1973.

Hébert, Anne. *Kamouraska*. 1970. Trans. Clarence Gagnon. Toronto: General, 1982.

Kroetsch, Robert. *What the Crow Said*. 1978. Toronto: General, 1983.

Laurence, Margaret. *A Jest of God*. 1966. Toronto: McClelland and Stewart, 1974.

————. *The Stone Angel*. 1968. Toronto: McClelland and Stewart, 1985.

————. *The Fire-Dwellers*. New York: Knopf, 1969.

————. *The Diviners*. Toronto: McClelland and Stewart, 1978.

O'Hagan, Howard. *Tay John*. 1960. Toronto: McClelland and Stewart, 1989.

Ross, Sinclair. *The Lamp at Noon and Other Stories*. 1968. Toronto: McClelland and Stewart, 1988.

Thomas, Audrey. *Mrs. Blood*. Vancouver: Talonbooks, 1970.

————. *Blown Figures*. Vancouver: Talonbooks, 1974.

Truss, Jan. *Bird at the Window*. Toronto: Macmillan, 1974.

Wiseman, Adele. *Crackpot*. Toronto: McClelland and Stewart, 1974.

1980-99

Arnason, David. *The Circus Performer's Bar*. Vancouver: Talon, 1984.

————. *The Dragon and the Dry Goods Princess*. Winnipeg: Turnstone, 1994.

————. *The Happiest Man in the World*. Vancouver: Talon, 1989.

Atwood, Margaret. *The Handmaid's Tale*. Toronto: McClelland and Stewart, 1985.

Blaise, Clark. *If I Were Me*. Erin: Porcupine's Quill, 1997.

Coady, Lynn. *Strange Heaven*. Fredericton: Goose Lane, 1998.

Coupland, Douglas. *Life after God*. New York: Simon and Schuster, 1994.

Crate, Joan. *Breathing Water*. Edmonton: NeWest, 1989.

Culleton, Beatrice. *In Search of April Raintree*. 1983. Winnipeg: Pemmican, 1987.

Davies, Robertson. *The Lyre of Orpheus*. 1988. Markham: Penguin, 1989.

Engel, Marian. *Lunatic Villas*. Toronto: McClelland and Stewart, 1981.

Findley, Timothy. *Not Wanted on the Voyage*. Toronto: Penguin, 1984.

Fraser, Keath. *Popular Anatomy*. Erin: Porcupine's Quill, 1995.

Gasco, Elyse. *Can You Wave Bye Bye, Baby?* Toronto: McClelland and Stewart, 1999.

Gowdy, Barbara. *Falling Angels*. Toronto: Somerville, 1989.

————. *Mister Sandman*. Toronto: Somerville, 1996.

Griggs, Terry. *Quickening*. Erin: Porcupine's Quill, 1990.

————. *The Lusty Man*. Erin: Porcupine's Quill, 1995.

————. "Momma Had a Baby." *New Quarterly* 16.3 (1996): 182-89.

Huston, Nancy. *Instruments of Darkness*. Toronto: Little, Brown, 1997.

————.*Slow Emergencies*. Toronto: Little, Brown, 1996.

King, Thomas. *Green Grass, Running Water*. Toronto: HarperCollins, 1993.

————. *Medicine River*. New York: Penguin, 1989.

Lee, Sky. *Disappearing Moon Café*. Vancouver: Douglas and McIntyre, 1990.

MacDonald, Ann-Marie. *Fall on Your Knees*. Toronto: Knopf, 1996.

Marlatt, Daphne. *Ana Historic*. Toronto: Coach House, 1988.

Miller, K.D. *Give Me Your Answer*. Erin: Porcupine's Quill, 1999.

Ricci, Nino. *Lives of the Saints*. 1990. Dunvegan: Cormorant, 1991.

Richards, David Adams. *Nights below Station Street*. Toronto: McClelland and Stewart, 1988.

Rooke, Leon. *A Good Baby*. Toronto: McClelland and Stewart, 1989.

Rule, Jane. *Memory Board*. Toronto: Macmillan, 1987.

Schoemperlen, Diane. *In the Language of Love*. Toronto: HarperCollins, 1994.

————. *Forms of Devotion*. Toronto: HarperCollins, 1998.

Shields, Carol. *The Stone Diaries*. Toronto: Vintage, 1993.

Toews, Miriam. *The Summer of My Amazing Luck*. Winnipeg: Turnstone, 1996.

————. *A Boy of Good Breeding*. Toronto: Stoddart, 1998.

BIBLIOGRAPHY

Achilles, Rona. "Desperately Seeking Babies: New Technologies of Hope and Despair." *Delivering Motherhood*. Ed. Katherine Arnup, Andrée Levesque, and Ruth Roach Pierson. London: Routledge, 1990. 284-312.

Abrams, M.H. *A Glossary of Literary Terms*. 6th ed. Fort Worth, TX: Harcourt Brace Jovanovich, 1993.

Åhmansson, Gabriella. *A Life and Its Mirrors: A Feminist Reading of L.M. Montgomery's Fiction*. Vol. 1. Stockholm: Almqvist and Wiksell, 1991.

Allen, Jeffner, and Iris Marion Young, eds. *The Thinking Muse*. Bloomington: Indiana UP, 1989.

Archer, Anne. "Real Mummies." *Studies in Canadian Literature* 9.2 (1985): 214-23.

Arendt, Hannah. *The Human Condition*. 1958. Chicago: U of Chicago P, 1971.

Ariès, Philippe. *Centuries of Childhood*. Trans. Robert Baldick. Vintage: New York, 1962.

Arnason, David. *The Circus Performer's Bar*. Vancouver: Talon, 1984.

———. *The Dragon and the Dry Goods Princess*. Winnipeg: Turnstone, 1994.

———. *The Happiest Man in the World*. Vancouver: Talon, 1989.

Arnup, Katherine. *Education for Motherhood: Advice for Mothers in Twentieth-Century Canada*. Toronto: U of Toronto P, 1994.

Arnup, Katherine, André Lévesque, and Ruth Roach Pierson, eds. *Delivering Motherhood*. London: Routledge, 1990.

Atwood, Margaret. *The Edible Woman*. 1969. Toronto: McClelland and Stewart, 1989.

———. "Great Unexpectations: An Autobiographical Foreword." *Margaret Atwood: Vision and Forms*. Ed. Kathryn VanSpanckeren and Jan Garden Castro. Carbondale: Southern Illinois UP, 1988. xiii-xvi.

———. *The Handmaid's Tale*. Toronto: McClelland and Stewart, 1985.

————. Introduction. *Roughing It in the Bush*. By Susannah Moodie. London: Virago, 1986. x-xvii.

————. *Surfacing*. Toronto: McClelland and Stewart, 1972.

————. *Survival*. Toronto: Anansi, 1972.

Augier, Valerie. "An Analysis of *Surfacing* by Margaret Atwood." *Commonwealth Essays and Studies* 11.2 (1989): 11-17.

Babby, Ellen Reisman. *The Play of Language and Spectacle*. Toronto: ECW, 1985.

Bakhtin, Mikhail. *The Dialogic Imagination*. Trans. Caryl Emerson and Michael Holquist. Austin: U of Texas P, 1982.

Bell, Richard Q. "Contributions of Human Infants to Caregiving and Social Interaction." *The Effect of the Infant on Its Caregiver*. Ed. Michael Lewis and Leonard A. Rosenblum. New York: John Wiley and Sons, 1974. 1-19.

Belsey, Catherine. "Constructing the Subject: Deconstructing the Text." *Feminisms*. Ed. Robyn Warhol and Diane Price Herndl. New Brunswick, NJ: Rutgers UP, 1993. 593-609.

Benoit, Cecilia. "Mothering in a Newfoundland Community." *Education for Motherhood: Advice for Mothers in Twentieth-Century Canada*. Ed. Katherine Arnup et al. London: Routledge, 1990. 173-89.

Bessette, Gerard. *Incubation*. Trans. Glen Shortliffe. Toronto: Macmillan, 1967.

Blais, Marie-Claire. *A Season in the Life of Emmanuel*. 1965. Trans. Derek Coltman. New York: Grosset and Dunlap, 1966.

Blaise, Clark. *If I Were Me*. Erin, ON: Porcupine's Quill, 1997.

Bowering, George. *The Mirror on the Floor*. Toronto: McClelland and Stewart, 1967.

————. "The Site of Blood." *Canadian Literature* 65 (1975): 86-91.

Brady, Elizabeth. "Marian Engel and Her Works." *Canadian Writers and Their Works*. Ed. Robert Lecker, Jack David, and Ellen Quigley. Vol. 9. Toronto: ECW Press, 1987. 179-249.

Brandt, Di. *Wild Mother Dancing*. Winnipeg: U of Manitoba P, 1993.

Bruce, Charles Tory. *The Channel Shore*. Toronto: McClelland and Stewart, 1954.

Brydon, Diana. "Silence, Voice and the Mirror: Margaret Laurence and Women." *Crossing the River: Essays in Honour of Margaret Laurence*. Ed. Kristjana Gunnars. Winnipeg: Turnstone Press, 1988. 183-205.

Buckler, Ernest. *The Cruelest Month*. 1963. Toronto: McClelland and Stewart, 1977.

————. *The Mountain and The Valley*. 1952. Toronto: McClelland and Stewart, 1991.

Burt, Sandra, Lorraine Code, and Lindsay Dorney, eds. *Changing Patterns: Women in Canada*. Toronto: McClelland and Stewart, 1988.

Buss, Helen. *Mother and Daughter Relationships in the Manawaka Works of Margaret Laurence*. Victoria: U Victoria, 1985.

Butler, Juan. *Cabbagetown Diary: A Documentary*. 1970. Toronto: Peter Martin, 1971.

Butler, Judith. *Gender Trouble*. New York: Routledge, 1990.

Cahill, Bette. "The Butterbox Babies: The Story of the Ideal Maternity Home." Dec. 2000. <http://www3.ns.sympatico.ca/bhartlen/htm>.

Canadian Association for Adult Education and the Royal Commission on the Status of Women in Canada. *What's in It?* Ottawa: National Council of Women in Canada, 1970.

Chisolm, Patricia. "For Infertile Couples, Heartache and Hope." *Maclean's* 6 Dec. 1999: 58-60.

Cixous, Hélène. "The Laugh of the Medusa." *Feminisms*. Ed. Robyn Warhol and Diane Price Herndl. New Brunswick, NJ: Rutgers UP, 1993. 334-49.

Coady, Lynn. *Strange Heaven*. Fredericton, NB: Goose Lane Editions, 1998.

Chodorow, Nancy. *The Reproduction of Mothering*. Berkeley: U of California P, 1978.

Clemente, Linda. *Gabrielle Roy: Creation and Memory*. Toronto: ECW, 1997.

Coburn, Kathleen. *The Grandmothers*. Toronto: U of Toronto P, 1949.

Cohen, Matt. *The Disinherited*. Toronto: McClelland and Stewart, 1974.

———. "The Rise and Fall of Serious CanLit." *Canadian Novelists and the Novel*. Ed. Douglas Daymond and Leslie Monkman. Ottawa: Borealis, 1981. 278-82.

Coleman, Patrick. *The Limits of Sympathy: Gabrielle Roy's The Tin Flute*. Canadian Fiction Studies 26. Toronto: ECW Press, 1993.

Comacchio, Cynthia R. *Nations Are Built of Babies: Saving Ontario's Mothers and Children, 1900-1914*. Montreal and Kingston: McGill-Queen's UP, 1993.

Coupland, Douglas. *Life after God*. New York: Simon and Schuster, 1994.

Cramer, Timothy R. "Sinclair Ross's *As for Me and My House*." *Ariel* 30.2 (1999): 49-60.

Crate, Joan. *Breathing Water*. Edmonton: NeWest, 1989.

Culleton, Beatrice. *In Search of April Raintree*. 1983. Winnipeg: Pemmican, 1987.

Cumming, Peter. "When Men Have Babies: The Good Father in Leon Rooke's *A Good Baby*." *Textual Studies in Canada* 8 (1996): 96-108.

Cuzzort, R.P. *Humanity and Modern Sociological Thought*. New York: Holt, Rinehart, and Winston, 1969.

Davidson, Arnold E. *Coyote Country: Fictions of the Canadian West*. Durham, NC: Duke UP, 1994.

Davies, Robertson. *Fifth Business*. 1970. Markham, ON: Penguin, 1984.

———. *The Lyre of Orpheus*. 1988. Markham, ON: Penguin, 1989.

Davey, Frank. *Margaret Atwood: A Feminist Poetics*. Vancouver: Talonbooks, 1984.

Dean, Misao. *Practising Femininity: Domestic Realism and the Performance of Gender in Early Canadian Fiction*. Toronto: U of Toronto P, 1998.

Delbaere-Garant, Jeanne. "*Surfacing*: Retracing the Boundaries." *Common-wealth Essays and Studies* 11.2 (1989): 1-10.

Dick-Read, Grantly. *Childbirth without Fear*. 1944. New York: Harper and Row, 1972.

Dillard, Annie. *For the Time Being*. Middlesex: Viking, 1999.

Eagleton, Terry. *Ideology: An Introduction*. London: Verso, 1991.

———. "Marxism and Literary Criticism." *Criticism: Major Statements*. Ed. Charles Kaplan and William Anderson. New York: St. Martin's Press, 1991. 551-73.

Ehrensaft, Diane. "Bringing in Fathers." *Becoming a Father: Contemporary Social, Developmental, and Clinical Perspectives*. Ed. Jerold Lee Shapiro, Michael J. Diamond, and Martin Greenberg. New York: Springer, 1995. 43-59.

Engel, Marian. *No Clouds of Glory*. Toronto: Longman, 1968.

———. *The Glassy Sea*. 1978. Toronto: Seal Books, 1979.

———. *The Honeyman Festival*. Toronto: Anansi, 1970.

———. *Lunatic Villas*. Toronto: McClelland and Stewart, 1981.

Fee, Margery, and Ruth Cawker. *Canadian Fiction: An Annotated Bibliography*. Toronto: Peter Martin, 1976.

Fenwick, Elizabeth. *The Canadian Medical Association Complete Book of Mother and Baby Care*. New York: Reader's Digest Association, 1997.

Findley, Timothy. *Not Wanted on the Voyage*. 1984. Toronto: Penguin, 1984.

Florby, Gunilla. *The Margin Speaks: A Study of Margaret Laurence and Robert Kroetsch from a Post-Colonial Point of View*. Lund, Sweden: Lund UP, 1997.

Fogel, Alan. *Infancy: Infant, Family, and Society*. St. Paul MN: West Publishing, 1984.

Frailberg, Selma. "Blind Infants and Their Mothers." *The Effect of the Infant on Its Caregiver*. Ed. Michael Lewis and Leonard A. Rosenblum. New York: John Wiley and Sons. 215-32.

Fraser, Keath. *As for Me and My Body*. Toronto: ECW, 1997.

———. *Popular Anatomy*. Erin: Porcupine's Quill, 1995.

Freud, Sigmund. *The Three Essays on the Theory of Sexuality*. London: Hogarth, 1966. Vol. 7 of *The Standard Edition of the Complete Psychological Works of Sigmund Freud*. Ed. and trans. James Strachey. 23 vols.

Friedman, Bonnie. "Writing about the Living." *The Best Writing on Writing*. Ed. Jack Heffron. Cincinnati: Story Press, 1994. 37-57.

Frye, Northrop, *The Great Code*. 1981. New York: Harcourt, Brace, Jovanovich, 1982.

Gallop, Jane. *The Daughter's Seduction: Feminism and Psychoanalysis*. Ithaca, NY: Cornell UP, 1982.

———. *Reading Lacan*. Ithaca, NY: Cornell UP, 1985.

Gammel, Irene. *Sexualizing Power in Naturalism: Theodore Dreiser and Frederick Philip Grove*. Calgary: U of Calgary P, 1994.

Garebian, Keith. "Leon Rooke." *Canadian Writers and Their Works*. Ed. Robert Lecker, Jack David, and Ellen Quigley. Vol. 8. Toronto: ECW Press, 1989. 129-91.

Gasco, Elyse. *Can You Wave Bye Bye, Baby?* Toronto: McClelland and Stewart, 1999.

Geddes, John. "Making Babies." *Maclean's* 6 Dec. 1999. 52-56.

Gibson, Margaret. "Considering Her Condition." *The Butterfly Ward*. 1976. Toronto: HarperCollins, 1994. 61-96.

Godard, Barbara. "Audrey Thomas." *Canadian Writers and Their Works*. Volume 8. Ed. Robert Lecker, Jack David, and Ellen Quigley. Toronto: ECW, 1989. 193-275.

———. *Gynocritics*. Toronto: ECW Press, 1987.

———. "Mapmaking: A Survey of Feminist Criticism." *Gynocritics*. Toronto: ECW, 1987. 1-30.

———. "Structuralism/Post-Structuralism: Language, Reality and Canadian Culture." *Future Indicative: Literary Theory and Canadian Literature*. Ed. John Moss. Reappraisals: Canadian Writers Series, 13. Ottawa: U of Ottawa P, 1987. 25-52.

Goodenough, Elizabeth, ed. *Infant Tongues: The Voice of the Child in Literature*. Detroit: Wayne State UP, 1994.

Gorjup, Branko. "Perseus and the Mirror: Leon Rooke's Imaginary Worlds." *World Literature Today* 73 (1999): 269-74.

Gowdy, Barbara. *Falling Angels*. Toronto: Somerville, 1989.

———. *Mister Sandman*. Toronto: Somerville, 1996.

Green, Henry Gordon. *A Time to Pass Over: Life with a Pioneer Grandmother*. Toronto: McClelland and Stewart, 1962.

Griggs, Terry. *Quickening*. Erin, ON: Porcupine's Quill, 1990.

———. *The Lusty Man*. Erin, ON: Porcupine's Quill, 1995.

———. "Momma Had a Baby." *New Quarterly* 16.3 (1996): 182-89.

Grove, Frederick Philip. *Settlers of the Marsh*. 1925. Toronto: McClelland and Stewart, 1965.

Grosz, Elisabeth. *Jacques Lacan: A Feminist Introduction*. London: Routledge, 1990.

Hancock, Geoff. "Interview with Leon Rooke." *Canadian Fiction Magazine* 38 (1981): 107-33.

Hansen, Elaine Tuttle. *Mother without Child: Contemporary Fiction and the Crisis of Motherhood*. Berkeley: U of California P, 1997.

Hardyment, Christina. *Dream Babies: Childcare from Locke to Spock*. London: Jonathan Cape, 1983.

Harvor, Beth. *Women and Children*. Ottawa: Oberon, 1973.

Hébert, Anne. *Kamouraska*. 1970. Trans. Clarence Gagnon. Toronto: General, 1982.

Holy Bible. New American Standard Version. Philadelphia: A.J. Holman, 1975.

Horowitz, Janice M., Julie Raw, and Sora Song. "Making Time for a Baby."
    Time (Canadian Edition) 15 April 2002. 36-42.

Howells, Coral Ann. *Private and Fictional Worlds*. London: Methuen, 1987.

Husserl, Edmund. "Phenomenology." *Deconstruction in Context: Literature
    and Philosophy*. Ed. Mark C. Taylor. Chicago: U of Chicago P, 1986. 121-
    40.

Huston, Nancy. *Instruments of Darkness*. Toronto: Little, Brown, 1997.

———. *Slow Emergencies*. Toronto: Little, Brown, 1996.

Hutcheon, Linda. *The Canadian Postmodern*. Toronto: Oxford UP, 1988.

———. "'Shape Shifters': Canadian Women Novelists and the Challenge to
    Tradition." *A Mazing Space: Writing Canadian Women Writing*. Ed. Shirley
    Neuman and Smaro Kamboureli. Edmonton: Longspoon/NeWest,
    1986. 219-27.

"Hysteria." *Webster's Dictionary*. 2nd Edition, 1956.

Irvine, Lorna. *Sub/Version*. Toronto: ECW, 1986.

Jackson, Jane Flannery and Joseph H. Jackson. *Infant Culture*. New York:
    Thomas Y. Crowell, 1978.

James, William Closson. *Locations of the Sacred*. Waterloo, ON: Wilfrid Lau-
    rier UP, 1998.

Johnson, Barbara. "Apostrophe, Animation, and Abortion." *Feminisms*. Ed.
    Robyn Warhol and Diane Price Herndl. New Brunswick, NJ: Rutgers
    UP, 1993. 630-43.

Kaltemback, Michele. "Leon Rooke's Distinctive Mode of Writing in *A Good
    Baby*." *Commonwealth Essays and Studies* 14.1 (1991): 41-46.

Kelly, Darlene. "'Either Way, I Stand Condemned': A Woman's Place in
    Margaret Atwood's *The Edible Woman* and Margaret Drabble's *The
    Waterfall*." *English Studies in Canada* 21.3 (1995): 320-32.

Kertzer, Jon. "Margaret Laurence and Her Works." *Canadian Writers and
    Their Works*. Vol. 9. Ed. Robert Lecker, David Jack, Ellen Quigley.
    Toronto: ECW Press, 1987. 253-312.

———. "Time and Its Victims: The Writing of Matt Cohen." *Essays on Cana-
    dian Writing* 17 (1980): 93-101.

King, Thomas. "Godzilla vs. Post-Colonial." *World Literature Written in Eng-
    lish* 30.2 (1990): 10-16.

———. *Medicine River*. New York: Penguin, 1989.

Klinck, Carl F., ed. *The Literary History of Canada*. Toronto: U of Toronto P, 1965.

Kockelmans, Joseph J. *A First Introduction to Husserl's Phenomenology*. Pitts-
    burgh: Duquesne UP, 1967.

Korner, Annelise F. "The Effect of the Infant's State, Level of Arousal, Sex,
    and Ontogenetic Stage on the Caregiver." *The Effect of the Infant on Its
    Caregiver*. Ed. Michael Lewis and Leonard A. Rosenblum. New York:
    John Wiley and Sons, 1974. 105-122.

Kristeva, Julia. *Desire in Language*. Ed. Leon S. Roudiez. Trans. Thomas Gora,
    Alice Jardine, and Leon S. Roudiez. New York: Columbia UP, 1980.

———. "Place Names." *Desire in Language*. Roudiez 271-94.

———. "Revolution in Poetic Language." *The Kristeva Reader*. Ed. Toril Moi. Trans. Leon S. Roudiez. London: Basil Blackwell, 1986. 89-136.

———. "Stabat Mater." *The Kristeva Reader*. 160-86.

———. "Women's Time." *The Kristeva Reader*. 187-213.

———. "Word, Dialogue, and Novel." *Desire in Language*. 64-91.

———. "From One Identity to Another." *Desire in Language*. 124-47.

Kroetsch, Robert. "The Fear of Women in Prairie Fiction: An Erotics of Space." *Sinclair Ross's As for Me and My House: Five Decades of Criticism*. Ed. David Stouck. Toronto: U of Toronto P, 1991. 111-20.

———. *Labyrinths of Voice: Conversations with Robert Kroetsch*. Edmonton: NeWest P, 1982.

———. *What the Crow Said*. 1978. Toronto: General, 1983.

Kulyk Keefer, Janice. *Under Eastern Eyes: A Critical Reading of Maritime Fiction*. Toronto: U of Toronto P, 1987.

Kuprel, Diana. "In Defence of Human Singularity: Diana Kuprel Speaks with Julia Kristeva." *Books in Canada* 28 (2000). 23-25.

Lacan, Jacques. *Écrits: A Selection*. Trans. Alan Sheridan. New York: Norton, 1977.

Lamb, Michael. "The Changing Roles of Fathers." *Becoming a Father: Contemporary Social, Developmental, and Clinical Perspectives*. Ed. Jerold Lee Shapiro, Michael J. Diamond, and Martin Greenberg. New York: Springer. 18-35.

———. ed. *The Role of the Father in Child Development*. New York: John Wiley and Sons, 1976.

Landsberg, Michele. *Women and Children First*. Toronto: MacMillan, 1982.

Laurence, Margaret. *A Jest of God*. 1966. Toronto: McClelland and Stewart, 1974.

———. *The Stone Angel*. 1968. Toronto: McClelland and Stewart, 1985.

———. *The Fire-Dwellers*. New York: Knopf, 1969.

———. *The Diviners*. Toronto: McClelland and Stewart, 1978.

Leach, Penelope. *Your Baby and Child*. 1977. New York: Knopf, 1998.

Lecker, Robert. *Making It Real: The Canonization of English-Canadian Literature*. Concord, ON: Anansi, 1995.

———. "Past the Grinning Masks: Temporal Form and Structure in *The Disinherited*." *Journal of Canadian Studies* 77.2 (1981): 46-52.

LeClaire, Jacques. "Enclosure and Disclosure in *Surfacing* by Margaret Atwood." *Commonwealth Essays and Studies* 11.2 (1989): 18-24.

Lee, Sky. *Disappearing Moon Café*. Vancouver: Douglas and McIntyre, 1990.

Lewis, Jane. "'Motherhood Issues' in the Late Nineteenth and Twentieth Centuries." *Delivering Motherhood*. Ed. Katherine Arnup, André Lévesque, and Ruth Roach. London: Routledge, 1990. 1-19.

Lewis, Michael, and Leonard A. Rosenblum, eds. *The Effect of the Infant on Its Caregiver*. New York: John Wiley and Sons, 1974.

Lewis, Paula Gilbert. *The Literary Vision of Gabrielle Roy.* Birmingham: Summa, 1984.

MacDaniel, Susan A. "The Changing Canadian Family: Women's Roles and the Impact of Feminism." *Changing Patterns: Women in Canada.* Ed. Sandra Burt, Lorraine Code, and Lindsay Dorney. Toronto: McClelland and Stewart, 1988. 103-28.

MacDonald, Ann-Marie. *Fall on Your Knees.* Toronto: Knopf, 1996.

Marlatt, Daphne. *Ana Historic.* Toronto: Coach House, 1988.

———. "Musing with Mothertongue." *Gynocritics.* 223-26.

Mathews, Lawrence. "Snakes and Tongues: Power and Spirituality in *The Disinherited.*" *World Literature Written in English* 28.1 (1988): 82-91.

McClung, Nellie. *All We Like Sheep.* Toronto: Thomas Allen, 1926.

———. *Painted Fires.* Toronto: Ryerson Press, 1925.

McLean, Robert. "How 'the Infant Phenomenon' Began the World: The Managing of Jean Margaret Davenport (182?-1903)." *The Dickensian* 88.3 (1992): 133-53.

McMullen, Lorraine. *Re(dis)covering Our Foremothers: Nineteenth Century Canadian Women Writers.* Ottawa: U of Ottawa P, 1990.

McMullen, Stanley. "Grove and the Promised Land." *The Canadian Novel in the Twentieth Century.* Ed. George Woodcock. Toronto: McClelland and Stewart, 1975. 28-37

Miller, K.D. *Give Me Your Answer.* Erin, ON: Porcupine's Quill, 1999.

Mitchell, Ken. *Sinclair Ross: A Reader's Guide.* Regina: Coteau Books, 1981.

Mitchell, W.O. *Who Has Seen the Wind.* 1947. Toronto: Macmillan, 1976.

Mitchinson, Wendy. "The Medical Treatment of Women." *Changing Patterns: Women in Canada.* Ed. Sandra Burt, Lorraine Code, and Lindsay Dorney. Toronto: McClelland and Stewart, 1988. 237-63.

Moe, Thomas. *Pastoral Care in Pregnancy Loss: A Ministry Long Needed.* New York: Haworth Pastoral Press, 1997.

Moi, Toril, ed. *The Kristeva Reader.* Trans. Leon S. Roudiez. London: Basil Blackwell, 1986.

Montgomery, L.M. *Anne of Green Gables.* 1908. New York: Scholastic, 1989.

———. *Anne's House of Dreams.* 1922. McClelland and Stewart, 1972.

———. *Anne of Ingleside.* 1939. Toronto: McClelland and Stewart, 1972.

Morrison, Toni. *Playing in the Dark: Whiteness and the Literary Imagination.* 1992. New York: Vintage, 1993.

Moss, John. *Patterns of Isolation in English Canadian Fiction.* Toronto: McClelland and Stewart, 1974.

———. *A Reader's Guide to the Canadian Novel.* Toronto: McClelland and Stewart, 1981.

———. *Sex and Violence in the Canadian Novel: The Ancestral Present.* Toronto: McClelland and Stewart, 1977.

Munsch, Robert. *Murmel, Murmel.* Toronto: Annick, 1982.

Murphy, Sarah. "Putting the Great Mother Together Again or How the Cunt Lost Its Tongue." *A Mazing Space: Writing Canadian Women Writing*. Ed. Shirley Neuman and Smaro Kamboureli. Edmonton: Longspoon/NeWest, 1986.

Neuman, Shirley, and Smaro Kamboureli, eds. *A Mazing Space: Writing Canadian Women Writing*. Edmonton: Longspoon/NeWest, 1986.

———. "Importing the Difference: Feminist Theory and Canadian Women Writers." *Future Indicative: Literary Theory and Canadian Literature*. Ed. John Moss. Reappraisals: Canadian Writers Series, 13. Ottawa: U of Ottawa P, 1987. 95-116.

——— and Robert Wilson, eds. *Labyrinths of Voice: Conversations with Robert Kroetsch*. Vol. 3. Western Canadian Literary Documents Series. Edmonton: NeWest Press, 1982.

New, W.H. *A History of Canadian Literature*. London: Macmillan Education, 1989.

Nims, John Frederick. *Western Wind: An Introduction to Poetry*. New York: Random House, 1974.

O'Brien, Mary. *The Politics of Reproduction*. 1981. London: Routledge, 1983.

O'Hagan, Howard. *Tay John*. 1960. Toronto: McClelland and Stewart, 1989.

Orlean, Susan. "Fertile Ground." *The New Yorker* 7 June 1999: 58-65.

Ostenso, Martha. *Wild Geese*. 1925. Toronto: McClelland and Stewart, 1971.

Perelman, Chaim, and Lucie Olbrechts-Tyteca. *The New Rhetoric: A Treatise on Argumentation*. Trans. John Wilkinson and Purcell Weaver. Notre Dame, IN: U of Notre Dame P, 1971.

Pollock, Linda. *Forgotten Children: Parent-Child Relations from 1500 to 1900*. Cambridge, UK: Cambridge UP, 1983.

Potkay, Adam. "'A Satire on Myself': Wordsworth and the Infant Prodigy." *Nineteenth Century Literature* 49.2 (1994): 149-66.

Powning, Beth. *Shadow Child*. Toronto: Viking, 1999.

Prentice, Allison, Paula Bourne, Gail Cuthbert Brandt, Beth Light, Wendy Mitchinson, and Naomi Black. *Canadian Women: A History*. Toronto: Harcourt, Brace, Jovanovich, 1988.

Quigley, Theresa. *The Child Hero in the Canadian Novel*. Toronto: NC Press, 1991.

Raoul, Valerie. "Straight or Bent: Textual/Sexual T(ri)angles in *As for Me and My House*." *Canadian Literature* 156 (1998): 13-28.

Ragland-Sullivan, Ellie. "Seeking the Third Term." *Feminism and Psychoanalysis*. Ed. Richard Feldstein and Judith Roof. Ithaca, NY: Cornell UP, 1989. 40-64.

Rich, Adrienne. "When We Dead Awaken: Writing as Re-Vision." *Reading Our World: The Guelph Anthology*. Ed. Constance Rooke, Renée Hulan, and Linda Warley, Needham Heights, MA: Ginn Press, 1993. 148-58.

———. *Of Woman Born*. New York: Bantam, 1977.

Ricci, Nino. *Lives of the Saints*. 1990. Dunvegan, ON: Cormorant, 1991.

Richards, David Adams. *Blood Ties*. Ottawa: Oberon Press, 1976.

———. *Nights Below Station Street*. Toronto: McClelland and Stewart, 1988.

Ricou, Laurence. *Everyday Magic: Child Languages in Canadian Literature*. Vancouver: UBC Press, 1987.

———. "Phyllis Webb, Daphne Marlatt and Similitude." *A Mazing Space: Writing Canadian Women Writing*. Edmonton: Longspoon/NeWest, 1986. 205-18.

Rooke, Constance. "Interview with Thomas King." *World Literature Written in English* 30.2 (1990): 62-76.

———. *The Writer's Path*. Toronto: ITP Nelson, 1998.

Rooke, Leon. *A Good Baby*. Toronto: McClelland and Stewart, 1989.

Ross, Catherine Sheldrick. "Readers Reading L.M. Montgomery." *Harvesting Thistles: The Textual Garden of L.M. Montgomery*. Ed. Mary Henley Rubio. Guelph, ON: Canadian Children's Press, 1994. 23-35.

Ross, Sinclair. *As for Me and My House*. 1941. Toronto: McClelland and Stewart, 1991.

———. *The Lamp at Noon and Other Stories*. 1968. Toronto: McClelland and Stewart, 1988.

Roy, Gabrielle. *The Tin Flute*. 1947. Trans. Hannah Josephson. Toronto: McClelland and Stewart, 1969.

———. *Where Nests the Water Hen*. 1951. Trans. Harry L. Binesse. Toronto: McClelland and Stewart, 1970.

Rubio, Mary Henley, ed. *Harvesting Thistles: The Textual Garden of L.M. Montgomery*. Guelph, ON: Canadian Children's Press, 1994.

Ruddick, Sara. *Maternal Thinking: Toward a Politics of Peace*. Boston: Beacon Press, 1989.

Rudy Dorscht, Susan. *Women, Reading, Kroetsch: Telling the Difference*. Waterloo, ON: Wilfrid Laurier UP, 1991.

Rule, Jane. *Memory Board*. Toronto: Macmillan, 1987.

Schoemperlen, Diane. *Forms of Devotion*. Toronto: HarperCollins, 1998.

———. *In the Language of Love*. Toronto: HarperCollins, 1994.

Seaman. A.T. "Visions of Fulfilment in Ernest Buckler and Charles Bruce." *Essays on Canadian Writing* 31 (1985): 158-74.

Shapiro, Jerrold Lee, Michael J. Diamond, and Martin Greenberg, eds. *Becoming a Father: Contemporary Social, Developmental, and Clinical Perspectives*. New York: Springer, 1995.

Shields, Carol. *The Stone Diaries*. Toronto: Vintage, 1993.

Smith, Barbara Hernstein. *Contingencies of Value*. Cambridge, MA: Harvard UP, 1988.

Spock, Benjamin. *The Common Sense Book of Baby and Child Care*. 1945. New York: Simon and Schuster, 1998.

Sprengnether, Madelon. "(M)other Eve." *Feminism and Psychoanalysis*. Ed. Richard Feldstien and Judith Roof. Ithaca, NY: Cornell UP, 1989. 298-322.

———. ed. *The Spectral Mother*. Ithaca, NY: Cornell UP, 1990.

Sreekumar, Sharmila. "The Portrait of the Alien/The Other in a Modern American Novel: Toni Morrison's *Tar Baby*." *The Indian Journal of American Studies* 26.2 (1996): 105-108.

Stackhouse, Robert. "The Great Divide." *Homemaker* June 2000: 45-52.

Stanton, Donna. "Difference on Trial." *The Thinking Muse*. Ed. Jennifer Allen and Iris Marion Young. Bloomington: Indiana UP, 1989. 156-79.

Stephenson, Marylee. *Women in Canada*. Toronto: New Press, 1973.

Stern, Daniel. *Diary of a Baby*. 1990. New York: Basic Books, 1998.

Stouck, David. *Sinclair Ross's* As for Me and My House*: Five Decades of Criticism*. Toronto: U of Toronto P, 1991.

Stovel, Nora. *Rachel's Children: Margaret Laurence's* A Jest of God. *Canadian Fiction Studies* 12. Toronto: ECW Press, 1992.

Strong-Boag, Veronica. "Intruders in the Nursery: Childcare Professionals Reshape the Years One to Five, 1920-1940." *Childhood and Family in Canadian History*. Ed. Joy Parr. Toronto: McClelland and Stewart, 1982.

Sutherland, Neil. *Children in English-Canadian Society*: Framing the Twentieth-Century Consensus. Waterloo: Wilfrid Laurier UP, 2000.

Thomas, Audrey. *Blown Figures*. Vancouver: Talonbooks, 1974.

———. *Mrs. Blood*. Vancouver: Talonbooks, 1970.

Thomas, Gillian. "The Decline of Anne: Matron vs. Child." *L.M. Montgomery: An Assessment*. Ed. John Robert Sorfleet. Guelph, ON: Canadian Children's Press, 1976. 37-64.

Toews, Miriam. *A Boy of Good Breeding*. Toronto: Stoddart, 1998.

———. *The Summer of My Amazing Luck*. Winnipeg: Turnstone, 1996.

Truss, Jan. *Bird at the Window*. Toronto: Macmillan, 1974.

Verduyn, Christl. *Lifelines: Marian Engel's Writings*. Montreal and Kingston: McGill-Queen's UP, 1998.

Wainwright, J.A. "Days of Future Past: Time in the Fiction of Charles Bruce." *Studies in Canadian Literature* 8.2 (1983): 238-47.

Walton, Percy. "'Tell Our Own Stories': Politics and the Fiction of Thomas King." *World Literature Written in English* 30.2 (1990): 77-84.

Warburton, Dorothy, Julianne Byrne, and Nina Canki. *Chromosome Anomalies and Prenatal Development: An Atlas*. New York: Oxford UP, 1991.

Warhol, Robyn, and Diane Price Herndl, eds. *Feminisms*. New Brunswick, NJ: Rutgers UP, 1993.

Watson, Sheila. *The Double Hook*. 1959. Toronto: McClelland and Stewart, 1991.

Weil, Simone. "Human Personality." *The Simone Weil Reader*. Ed. George A. Panichas. New York: Moyer Bell, 1977. 327-48.

Whitfield, Agnes. "Gabrielle Roy as Feminist: Re-reading the Critical Myths." *Canadian Literature* 126 (1990): 20-31.

Wiggins, Genevieve. *L.M. Montgomery*. Toronto: Maxwell MacMillan Canada, 1992.

Wilkinson, Shelagh. "By and about Women." *Changing Patterns: Women in Canada*. Ed. Sandra Burt, Lorraine Code, and Lindsay Dorney. Toronto: McClelland and Stewart, 1988. 204-36.

Wilson, Ethel. *Swamp Angel*. 1954. Toronto: McClelland and Stewart, 1990.

Wiseman, Adele. *Crackpot*. Toronto: McClelland and Stewart, 1974.

Woodcock, George. "Matt Cohen." *Canadian Writers and Their Works*. Vol. 9. Ed. Robert Lecker, David Jack, Ellen Quigley. Toronto: ECW Press, 1987. 119-80.

—————. *Introduction to Canadian Fiction*. Toronto. ECW, 1993

Woolf, Virginia. *A Room of One's Own*. 1929. Oxford: Oxford UP, 1992.

Wyile, Herb. "'Trust Tonto': Thomas King's Subversive Fictions and the Politics of Cultural Literacy. *Canadian Literature* 165 (2000): 105-29.

Young, Iris Marion. "Pregnant Embodiment: Subjectivity and Alienation." *Feminism and Philosophy*. Ed. Nancy Tuana and Rosemarie Tong. Boulder, CO: Westview, 1995. 407-19.

Zelizer, Viviana. *Pricing the Priceless Child: The Changing Social Value of Children*. New York: Basic Books, 1985.

INDEX

abandonment, 80, 120, 187, 188, 189-90
abduction, 158, 161
abortion, 9, 80, 101, 106, 220n7; effects of, 119, 123-24, 179, 182-86; legalized, 85, 103, 116, 123, 181; as reaction, 171, 173, 177, 178; redemption for, 124-25; self-induced, 46, 104
absence, 49, 55, 123; of babies, 170, 171, 175, 200, 204; of mother, 162, 190-91
adoption, 22, 150, 186, 211n6, 212n13; and legitimacy, 58-60, 217n7, 218n10; as loss, 11, 170, 190-91
adultery, 54, 57, 87, 90, 197
advertising, 25-26, 214n20-21
agency, 5-6, 125; of babies, 10, 12, 13-16, 18-19, 27-29, 67, 145, 154, 169, 192, 193-94, 200, 206; mother's, 172, 188, 200; mutual, 190; negation of, 122, 124
Åhmansson, Gabriella, 36-37, 39, 215n6
Allen, Jeffner, 139, 205
All We Like Sheep (McClung), 32

"Angel, Baby" (Arnason), 145, 158, 164-66
Anne of Green Gables (Montgomery), 5, 33-34, 36, 215n8
Anne of Ingleside (Montgomery), 33-34, 39, 216n8
Anne's House of Dreams (Montgomery), 7, 33, 36-45
apostrophe, 171, 184
Archer, Anne, 107
Arendt, Hannah, 1, 2, 3-4, 13, 44, 92, 128, 163, 223n20
Ariès, Philippe, 31
Arnason, David, 10, 138, 140, 141, 187, 206; "Angel, Baby," 145, 158, 164-66; "Mary Yvette," 158, 162-63; "My Baby and Me," 145, 158-62, 203
Arnup, Katherine, 23, 212n14, 213n16
As for Me and My Body (Fraser), 54-55
As for Me and My House (Ross), 8, 52, 54-61, 76, 144, 217n4, 218nn8-9
Atwood, Margaret, 129, 155, 219n4; on babies as *deus ex machina*, 3, 56, 221n7; *The Edible Woman*, 10,